ISBN 9798378240050

Shouty Husband!

By

Anne Feenan

For David Whitehouse

My friend who gave me the strength to say NO!

You are loved, you are missed x

Acknowledgements

To my mum, who named me the purple haired warrior and has been there for my journey with tea and good advice.

The ladies from We Aten't Dead, all over the world, who kept me writing as they wanted the next instalment.

Rebecca Parsley, who took my ramblings and knocked them into shape. For believing that my book had legs. Thank you!

My wonderful daughter in law who gave my ramblings the final polish.

Thank you all for your support! I would never have been able to do it without you all.

Annie, the purple haired warrior with knobs on x

Cast List

The cast of my little book, the ones who pop up throughout.

Mother and Joe - Shouty Husband's mother and Stepdad

Vincent - Shouty Husband's best friend in his late teens

Karen - Vincent's wife and Shouty Husbands long time on off girlfriend

Sarah and Paula - Shouty Husband's sisters

Bill - Paula's husband

Charlie, Tommy, and Billy - Shouty Husband's cousins

Jinx - The first Mrs Shouty husband

Graham - Another one of Shouty Husband's best friends and mentor

Max and Sharon - The friends who pop in and out over a lot of years

Trev and Karen - The friends and Shouty Husband's best man

Little John - A friend

Tracey - A good friend to us both

Steve fish face Craddock the haddock - A friend

Lottie - Steve's wife

Mick aka the Sav - A great friend

The boy's dad

My boys, Jordan, and Luke

Spanish Train Chris de Burgh

'The real purpose of a coven was to meet friends, even if they were friends simply because they were really the only people you could talk to freely as they had the same problems and would understand what you were moaning about.'
Wintersmith, Terry Pratchett

Prologue

Let me take you back in time to Easter 1986. I had just turned 20, and I had also just gotten engaged to the man who would become my boy's dad and my first husband. My second husband was Shouty Husband, who you will find out about soon!

All the boy's dad's family had gathered to spend time together. You know what I mean – high days and holidays, Christmas, Easter, Whitsun – the occasions when everybody makes the effort to be civil to each other for a couple of days.

That particular Good Friday, we were in the pub. And, for the first time, I met the man who would be the catalyst for me later becoming the purple-haired warrior with knobs on.

My best friend – the one, the only, David Whitehouse. David was the boy's dad's uncle, which was strange as there were only six years between them.

David was 28 years old, and his family thought he was gay. He was overweight, shy, quiet and introverted. He never talked about any girlfriends, and he'd never taken a girl home to meet his mum. Their logical conclusion, then, was that he must be gay.

I had no filter back then, so I decided to ask him about it. I mean, why pussyfoot around a subject? If you want to know, just ask.

Maybe I shouldn't have done it while David was drinking his Coke, though. He sputtered into the glass and then laughed out loud. Generally, he was a quietly spoken man, but he did have a great boomy laugh.

David told me talking to women involved a set of social skills he did not possess. But I didn't count as a woman, apparently – I was his nephew's fiancée, which was different.

Sometimes in life, you're lucky enough to meet someone with whom you just click, and that's what happened on that April afternoon. Between our initial meeting and the moment he died, David and I became best friends.

David was the keeper of secrets; he knew where all the bodies were buried. We could talk about anything and everything, and we were there for each other no matter what, during the best and worst times of our lives. It was a true friendship, and anyone who says a man and woman can't ever be 'just friends' is wrong. They never met David and me. We were the exception to the rule.

Settle back. Get comfy. Grab a glass of something. Get ready for life, death, David, some great music and, of course...

Even though we lived 200 miles apart, we made the effort to stay in touch. David would come and stay with me at least once a year, usually at Christmas, and he'd call me every week to put the world to rights.

That's what we did every week for 33 years. David and I put the world to rights, shared our thoughts and did silly. We were a coven of two.

David was a cornerstone of my world, and he's one reason I am the person I am today. These ramblings are a tribute to him, and I hope you enjoy them – and the soundtrack that goes with them.

SHOUTY HUSBAND!!!!!

Patricia the Stripper - Chris de Burgh

The beginning of the end.

It was just a normal Tuesday in March. The weather was gloomy, and the wind was blowy. There was nothing odd. My day at work had been unremarkable, and the only thing on my mind was that I hadn't heard from David for two weeks. That was unusual.

I'd texted, emailed, and left three messages threatening to get in the car and drive the 200 miles to make sure he was okay if he didn't reply soon. I'd still heard nothing, and now I was getting worried.

He hadn't even rung me on his birthday. He never wanted a fuss and hated remembering it, but of course, I always did. This year had been no different – I'd sent him a funny, silly card, but he hadn't gotten in touch.

I planned to ring him again when I got home. I hoped Shouty Husband – who you will get to know in all his glory – wasn't there when I got back. In those days, he did job and knock in his big lorry. If there was nothing more for him to do, his day would end early, and he'd come home. It was unpaid, but it was better than him hanging around getting bored. Boredom and Shouty Husband didn't make a good combination!

I pulled onto the drive and breathed a sigh of relief. No car, so no Shouty Husband. I had time to do some housework, run the vacuum round, empty the dishwasher, and make as much noise as I liked.

When I get home, if I know I'm not going anywhere else and I'm not expecting anybody, the first thing I do is change into what Shouty Husband called my scruffs. You know – comfy clothes. PJ bottoms, a t-shirt, and a sweatshirt. The next thing I do, when I remember, is to check the phone for messages. On that Tuesday in March, I wished I had forgotten.

The disembodied voice announced I had four messages. The first two were from my youngest son, Luke, telling me he still felt rotten and had finally made a doctor's appointment. Then one of my favourite voices, that of the lovely lady at the library telling me that she had four books for me to collect.

The last one was a warm, posh voice that introduced herself as Vanessa. She was ringing from Hampshire Environmental Health Services in connection to the passing of David Whitehouse, she said, and could I call her back?

Wait – what? 'The passing of David Whitehouse?' My first thought was, 'Passed what?' And then it hit me like a bullet between the eyes.

David was dead.

I sat on the bed and listened to the message four more times. Finally, it sank in enough to make me realise I had better ring this lady back. I had to listen again to write down the phone number.

Vanessa wasn't available, but a nice man – his name never registered with me - told me they'd been trying to get hold of the first number on David's emergency contact list without any luck.

Well, that was hardly surprising – the number belonged to David's sister, my ex-mother-in-law. She died 15 years ago, I explained to the nice man. 'Are you sure?' he asked. That made me laugh aloud. 'I hope so,' I said. 'We cremated her.' The things you say when you're in shock!

My number was next on the list, which is why they rang me. The nice man said he was sorry to tell me that David had died in hospital on his birthday. He didn't know the cause, but, as he so nicely put it, David was now taking up space, and someone needed to make the necessary arrangements. That job now fell to me, it seemed. I agreed to take care of it, though I think I'd have gone along with anything the nice man said at that stage. I felt numb and wanted him to get off the phone, so I could process what had happened.

I don't fall apart when things happen. I'm not the type. I'm always the one who gets stuff sorted. So, I told the nice man to leave it with me and I'd be back in touch in the morning.

First on my new 'to-do' list was to pour myself a very large glass of wine, take a deep breath, and work out who to call first.

David had family, so I should ring his nephew – my first husband. We rarely spoke, but I did have his phone number in case of emergencies. The problem was that he'd had a heart attack a month before, so I really did not want to stress him out.

The boy's dad, my first husband, asked all the questions I had no answers to, but he did say he would try to contact David's brother, Ted. I passed on the number for the environmental health department and told the boy's dad that if Ted needed to talk to me, it was okay to pass on my number.

Then I just sat there for a while, played music that I felt fit with David's passing, and waited for my second husband, Shouty Husband, to come home.

I knew what David's wishes were for when his time came because we'd discussed it. 'Just burn me or donate me to medical science,' he'd said. 'And if you dare have a funeral for me, I will come back to haunt you! I will move your bookmark in your book, so you are never on the right page.' The thought of dying never bothered him, and he knew I'd carry out his wishes – so I was the right choice to manage things when he died.

Shouty Husband and David were sort of friends. The only thing they had in common was me, but they made the effort to get on for my sake.

I knew that springing the news on Shouty Husband when he walked in from work was not the way to go; it would end badly. My world had collapsed, but I had to stay strong for a bit longer. I managed an hour, and then I blurted out the news and broke down in tears.

When I said I had agreed to sort everything out, Shouty Husband refused. 'No, you are not. He wasn't blood, and I am not paying for his funeral. He has family, and that's the end of it,' he said. Then he got up, patted me on the shoulder, and went into his chill room. We did not speak of David again that evening.

I sat there alone, numb and in pain, while the one person I needed, the one who could have made it easier to bear, had walked away and left me.

That was the catalyst. It sparked the chain of events that led to me being reborn and to Shouty Husband no longer being in my life.

When My Mind's Gone – Mott the Hoople

Shouty Husband was friends with the boy's dad, so he knew his family. When Ted rang me to try to make sense of his brother's death, Shouty Husband was not happy.

There was no way I could drive to Hampshire to sort out the death certificate and organise David's flat, but Ted was great. He told me he'd arrange the funeral, sort probate, and clear the flat.

I was really grateful and offered to help by finding a funeral director. Fifteen phone calls later, I found a lovely lady who could take care of everything.

After a flurry of phone calls, Ted and his partner, Jane, announced they'd be coming up on Sunday to see the boy's dad and me and sort out the last few bits. I hadn't seen either of them for fourteen years, so, in spite of the circumstances, in a funny way, I was looking forward to it.

When I told Shouty Husband what was going on, he went off on one. 'No, he is not coming in my house!' When Shouty Husband put his foot down, he would never change his mind. I knew that. I tried to argue that it was my house too, but it didn't work.

In the end, I went to the boy's dad's home. He, his then-wife, and I didn't get along, so you can imagine how much fun that was.

Still, we sorted out David's funeral in line with his wishes, and the family kindly agreed that when it was all over, his ashes would come to me. They also offered me a keepsake from David's belongings. I chose his watch, which always reminded me of his visits – it needed sunshine to work, so he'd always put it on the dining room table.

The next month was a blur of phone calls back and forth with Ted, Shouty Husband being constantly annoyed with me, finalising David's funeral wishes, and applying for probate.

I was fragile, to say the least, and then it was my birthday and my 13th wedding anniversary on the same day. Shouty Husband did what he always did – he left it to the last minute to get me a cheap birthday card and didn't bother with one for our anniversary. Now it made me question why I had spent the last twenty- three years with a man who treated me so badly.

Death May Be Your Santa Claus – Mott the Hoople

The straw that broke the camel's back happened at 5.30 pm on April 2nd, 2019. When Shouty Husband came home, I left him in peace to destress after his terribly busy day driving his big truck.

This had become my habit, as getting my head bitten off was now an everyday occurrence. I could hear him ranting in the kitchen, but I left him to it – it was normal, and I wasn't in the mood to be bawled at yet again. Whatever was wrong would be my fault – it always was. In fact, according to Shouty Husband, the world could spontaneously combust, and that would be my fault, too.

On this occasion, the problem was the gas hob. A piece had previously chipped off the corner, and although Shouty Husband had glued it, it had come off again. Obviously, this was my fault. He shouted at me, but this time I saw red and shouted back.

I told him that if he didn't like being with me, he knew where the door was!

He glared and stomped off to his chill room in a strop. Again, this was the usual way of things. Usually, I'd give him a couple of hours to calm down, then I'd go and make a grovelling apology, and then things would be back to normal with him using me as his doormat.

This time, though, I decided I wasn't going to back down. Why should I? I wasn't in the wrong. Hmm – what was that twinge I could feel – could it be my backbone stiffening at long last? Apparently, it was. I went to bed without saying anything, he came up later, and we both blanked each other.

Things were still frosty the next day, and I was still determined not to back down. A bit of me honestly believed he would understand I was grieving and realise I needed comfort, not to be shouted at for something as stupid as a chip out of the cooker top.

Shouty Husband continued to ignore me, but he still came up to bed every night. At least, he did, until 'The Night of the Telly.'

He came up one night, and I was watching telly in bed. When I didn't immediately turn it off, he huffed and puffed and stomped off to the spare room. I know he'll have had a lousy night's sleep, as that bed is uncomfortable, but after that, he slept there every night for five weeks. The rest of the time, when he was home, he stayed in his chill room.

I carried on with my own life and stopped doing anything for him. The main problem with Shouty Husband ignoring me was that he was an amazing cook, and I hadn't had to make a meal for about fifteen years. He used to joke that I only knew how to reheat food, not cook it.

Every time I tried, he'd tell me I was doing it wrong and make me feel very small, so I stopped.

For those five weeks, I lived on salads for lunch at work and bacon sandwiches, toast, and tinned baked beans. Food had no appeal for me at all at that time. Shouty Husband didn't eat at home – I stayed in the dining room, so he'd have to see me if he wanted to cook. It was just a little bit of revenge – my two-fingered salute to him.

Once Upon a Time in the West – Dire Straits

Food was Shouty Husband's big love. I will give the man something - he could cook. I used to cook before he came along, but over the years I got out of the habit – Shouty Husband didn't let me do it.

Shouty Husband used food as a carrot, as he did so many things. If he thought I'd behaved well, he would feed me. If he was in a bad mood or had done something he thought was bad or wrong, he wouldn't cook.

The kitchen was his domain and his alone. I was only allowed in under sufferance. So, on the nights he didn't cook, my go-to food was toast. He'd watch me make beans on toast and pass judgement on how I did it. Is it really possible to make beans on toast wrongly? Well, according to Shouty Husband, I managed it!

My strength in the kitchen was being able to reheat. Shouty Husband told everyone that was the extent of my ability in the kitchen. And, when you hear something often enough, you believe it.

I believed it for years, so when Shouty Husband stopped talking to me, my options were limited. Then, one day, I decided microwave rice and fish fingers were getting rather boring.

When things between us had been better, Shouty Husband always told me I cooked a great chicken dinner, I remembered. So there was no reason why I couldn't do so again.

Right. Decision made. I pulled up my big girl pants, tackled the hated electric oven, and cooked myself a roast dinner for the first time in 15 years: lamb chops, potatoes, veg and gravy. No tin openers, no cold cuts, no microwave rice.

My, it was good. And, what's more, I enjoyed cooking it.

This was a massive step for me. I proved to myself that I wasn't worthless and useless, as Shouty Husband always said. He'd told me that for so long, I accepted it as the truth. It might sound funny, but that lamb dinner was the first step on the road to recovering my sanity.

Whole Lotta Rosie – AC/DC

Shouty Husband loved loud music but hated noise. I do understand that – he drove a big truck all day, and that was noisy.

He liked having a clean and tidy home but hated being around while I did what needed doing to keep the house up to his exacting standards – because I made noise.

Shouty Husband didn't do housework; that was my job. If the bin in the kitchen was smelly and needed to be emptied, he'd put it in the back garden rather than take it to the dustbin out the front and leave it for me to deal with. It's impossible to run a house and keep it clean without making noise but, good wife I was, I planned it like a military operation. Noisy chores, like running the washing machine and tumble dryer, I did either when he was in bed or before I went to work in the mornings. (Shouty Husband went to bed early as he always had early starts.) It was tiring, having to plan everything around him, but better to have a quiet life than have him shouting at me or pointedly ignoring me.

Every day I prayed he'd still be at work when I got home so I would have some time for housework. My time management skills when it comes to planning household chores are second to none – they had to be, with Shouty Husband ready to blast me for every misdemeanour!

Every now and again he'd have a night away in his big truck. Well, okay – not literally. He did get to sleep in a hotel. But he hated working away and didn't like being sent to Dundee – or 'cake land', as he called it.

He had to go to cake land while he wasn't talking to me, but of course, he didn't tell me. So, when he didn't come home that night, and there was no phone call, I panicked. I kept my resolve, though – even though I didn't sleep, I went to bed without phoning him. I wasn't in the wrong and I knew it, so I was blowed if I was going to chase him.

Not long after he had to go again, but this time he told me first. So, when I got home from work, I put the washing machine on, put some great rock music on the radio and turned the volume up, and got out the vacuum. It was so liberating to be able to do anything I wanted without having to walk on eggshells.

In the grand scheme of things it might sound minor, but knowing I will never have to plan cleaning again is, to me, a sign of my freedom.

Mr Blue Sky – ELO

Shouty Husband and I are grandparents to Everly and Carina, the daughters of my eldest son, Jordan, and his wife Laura. Shouty Husband is known as Super Grumps, and I am Grannie Annie.

The Easter holiday, during the great freeze, we were looking forward to a visit. I was determined not to let Shouty Husband ruin it and made plans to take Everly to the local Zoo for the afternoon.

The sun was shining, and I was looking forward to spending time with family.

Everly adores Grumps, so she went running into Shouty Husband's chill room to see him when she arrived. He was great with her and spent time with Jordan too, but he still blanked me.

After a few hours of family time, I started clearing up – honestly, it's unbelievable how much mess two small children can make.

Shouty Husband came into the dining room to talk to me as I was cleaning. It had been a month now since he had spoken to me, but I still hadn't yet given up on my marriage.

I tried to tell him that I was in pain and how much he was hurting me, but he refused to see my side. He thought I was just 'being funny with him'. Then I did the worst thing you could do with Shouty Husband - I burst into tears.

I tried to reason with him, asking if he was really prepared to throw away all the years, we'd had together. But it turned out he was – so, at that moment, I gave up on having any kind of life with him.

He was going. It was just a matter of time now until he left.

Baby, Stop Crying – Bob Dylan

I'm very lucky to have a great friend in Stella. She's the person who knew about the problems I was having with Shouty Husband.

I decided I needed a wine and chat session with Stella. I didn't want to talk to family – I needed someone objective who had no prior connection with Shouty Husband.

Stella was brilliant, and talking to her was just what the doctor ordered. After five hours on the phone – and the bottle of wine – I felt better. Admittedly, I was shocked when my phone bill came – the call had cost £35 – but it was worth every penny.

With Shouty Husband at work, my days were my own, so I was delighted when Stella invited me over for coffee and another chat. After five hours of me sobbing down the phone, she was still prepared to listen to more.

At that time, because of all the stress, most food tasted like cardboard. But when Stella offered me some home-made chilli con carne, I decided a small portion would be nice. She's a great cook. Two platefuls later, I was feeling better in my bones.

Good food and great company makes the world a more bearable place. Stella was a wonderful friend to me then, and remains so today.

Sometimes, when you're at your lowest, having someone who is prepared to listen to you is the best possible medicine.

On the Road Again – Canned Heat

I was so lucky as David's family allowed me to have his ashes. I couldn't bear to think of him being scattered just anywhere or, worse, dumped in a bin.

So I paid the £100 to have David sent from Hampshire to me. I didn't know when he'd arrive, so I arranged for him to be dropped off at my parents' house – they're rarely out together, so the chances were someone would be home.

Of course, David came home on the one day when I'd taken both my parents shopping. Their neighbour ended up taking him in; a card was left saying so, and I went to collect him from Mrs Moscrop, who I'd known forever.

David was in a big box covered with brown paper and was surprisingly heavy. He'd been a large man in life, but I hadn't expected him to weigh so much in death. Mrs Moscrop was surprised when I told her what was in the box and said she'd have taken him inside if she'd known rather than leave him out on the porch.

David stayed wrapped up on my dining room table for a couple of hours while I got drunk, played some music, and cried.

Shouty Husband came in; he saw the box, of course, but he didn't ask what it was, and I wasn't about to tell him.

When I finally got round to opening the parcel, I found a certificate telling me I now had David's remains; for some reason, it made me laugh out loud to think he'd earned a certificate for being dead.

I steeled myself to be brave and opened the box. Inside was what looked like a vacuum cleaner bag, and – oh! Yes, David's ashes were grey, as expected, but he also sparked with bits of pink and black in the light.

I had plans for David's ashes. It had to be something different – he wasn't just anybody.

Some of David lives on in refillable hourglasses, displayed on my bookcases – one in the dining room and another in the living room. He would have approved.

It's My Party – Lesley Gore

Yesterday was Shouty Husband's 61st birthday. We all gave him cards, and Luke bought him a Hobgoblin glass – one of his favourite beers – and a bottle of the brew.

Today I discovered he'd moved all his clothes out of his wardrobe. When Luke, my son moved out, he took my wardrobe with him. Shouty Husband, who had all of three pairs of jeans, six shirts and a suit in his, wouldn't share the space with me. So, until we could afford a new wardrobe for me, I bought a clothes rail from Argos, and my stuff had to live on and in various boxes in the spare room.

It lasted three years before it fell to bits, and then I bought a new, small wardrobe. Now, though, I could have the big wardrobe for my clothes! I can spread them out, so they're not creased or crushed. It's another milestone. While the idea of being without him is scary – it's been 23 years, after all – I want my life back. That means he has to go. Shouty Husband shares his birthday with JM Barrie, the author of Peter Pan. It's one of my favourite books. The quote, 'What if I fall?' 'Oh, but my darling, what if you fly?' is one of my all-time favourites and perfectly sums up how I feel right now.

I will fly. It might take a while as my wings have been clipped for so long, but feathers grow back. I may fall as I try, but one day I will soar again. The fledgling Annie will grow into a strong and beautiful bird, spread her wings wide and discover the world.

Down by the River – Neil Young

Shouty Husband is moving out. I don't know where he's going – all I've learned is that it's to a flat somewhere. We are being very polite to each other. Twenty-three years and it comes down to, 'Can I take a set of saucepans?' Well, why not? We have two sets after all. Just the small stuff to sort out later, and we're done. I did give him the four boxes of Earl Grey tea. (I make a perfect cup of Earl Grey, by the way – I had lots of practice getting it right for him.)

He ate the corned beef and the luncheon meat. The tin of tomato soup and a tin of stewed steak, so he took them with him. I gave him his towel from the tumble dryer – easy to work out as his are green and mine are blue. I pointed out the whiskey glass I'd given him – surely, he'd want that? (Something else I did – I always bought him great whiskey.)

He had to talk to break the silence and talk to me today as his car tax and insurance was due, and I always sort that out online. I tried to use it as an olive branch for us to start speaking, but no joy. Oh well, his loss. He's the one cutting off his nose to spite his face.

Let it be noted that I was a dutiful wife to the end. I renewed his car insurance and the car tax. I made sure to use his debit card, though, and not my credit card – which he'd spent on already, knowing he was leaving!

He stood over me while I did it and offered advice, even though he didn't have a clue how to do it. I told him to shut up and just watch, otherwise he could do it himself. It made me feel better, standing up to him.

The problem is that it's big bill month. The council tax, water rates and house insurance were all due, coming in at £1,600 and sitting on my credit card. Usually, I could afford to pay it off with the housekeeping money from Shouty Husband, which he handed over at the end of the month.

But of course, I won't be getting that now, so financially, I'm stuffed. I told him he wouldn't be getting a penny from the house, as I'd have to pay all the bills myself now.

It makes me sad to think it's come to this. Twenty-three years down the drain because I shouted back at him over a stupid broken cooker top after my best friend died. You'd think I meant more than that to him. Clearly not.

Well, he hasn't won. I'm not broken, just a bit battered. As Mick, one of my oldest friends, says: 'Don't mess with Annie. She is small but fierce. You won't win — she's determined.' I'm not sure he knew he was paraphrasing Shakespeare.

I Don't Love You Anymore - London Quireboys

It's the first day of 'it's all mine now'. Got the windows open, Planet Rock on the radio, and joss sticks burning.

I've organised the freezer, and I'm not going to starve.

I can sort out the pantry freely now, too. There's a bag of assorted sauces that have been in there forever, half used – they're going in the bin. Another bag, packet mixes this time, but they're in date – they can go to the food bank. Pasta and noodles – well, I reckon they'll feature heavily in my future food choices, so they stay. Tins of red salmon – it had to be red salmon, Shouty Husband insisted on it. I'm not fussed. I prefer tuna. So, they can go to my mum.

I'm meal planning. I've bought jars of sauces so I can make spag bol, chilli and curries. Shouty Husband always did them from scratch, but he would use a sauce as a base sometimes. I know they're good, so I've got the same ones. Once my head gets more into cooking, I will learn to love the food I make. Shouty Husband cooked very well, and I picked up some tips. This is MY kitchen now – it's time to try them out.

Shouty Husband is no longer in my house, though there's a toad salt and pepper set that's a reminder of him. I don't remember where they came from, but they've been around forever. We probably picked them up at a car boot sale or from a charity shop. They've been part of every family Sunday lunch. They belong in my home, so they are staying.

Oh, there's the frog with the broken leg candle holder. I bought it for Shouty Husband 23 years ago, but it holds so many memories. It is mine.

Most of the food that was his has gone to my mum's — salmon, jam, jelly, and some expensive cheese. (I know people love cheese, but I'm only in the mood for it about three times a year. It'd go mouldy before I ate it.) Tubs of parsley sauce — yuck. I hate the stuff. Some of the stuff went in the bin, like the two bottles of gravy browning that went out of date in 2010. There were unopened and barely used bags of sultanas, too — I put those out for the birds.

I'm making a start. This is the first day of the rest of my life, and I have time to get it right.

Free Bird – Lynyrd Skynyrd

Luke, my son is a star. He came and emptied the loft for me, filled his car with stuff for the tip, and sorted out the insulation. I need to get more of that, but at least now, everything I need to get to – cat boxes, my granddaughter's toy box for when she visits and so on – are near the hatch and in easy reach. There's a loft ladder and a light. Sorted.

As I already had bags and boxes handy, I then packed up all Shouty Husband's bits. I was careful and used newspaper. His chill room is full of stuff, just waiting for him to pick it up, but he won't come back. Once he cuts you off, that's it.

His chill room used to be the garage – we converted it. So Shouty Husbands' chill room, has bin bags and bags of books and teddies all neatly placed, waiting for Luke to take them to him. Who knows what I'll do with it now? I've already replaced the photo of us that was in the dining room – now it's one of me as a baby with my parents. It's a start – small steps, and I'll get there in the end.

My Visa bill has come in and I'm cheered to see I'm not as broke as I thought I was. All the big yearly bills were paid while Shouty Husband was giving me the silent treatment, and I thought I'd get the housekeeping money at the end of the month to cover them. But then he left...

I knew my parents had given me £1,000. (They gave my brother and my sons gifts too.) I didn't tell Shouty Husband about it; originally, I'd planned to put it towards a new car for him. I won't be now! He can sort himself out — and his current car will cost him a lot of money soon.

Anyway, thanks to Mum and Dad my council tax is paid for 12 months and there's enough to cover the water, gas, and electric bills. It gives me some breathing space and, if I'm careful, I'll be ok while I put my plan together. I do have one, but I need to do some research. 'Always cover your backside' — one of Shouty Husband's sayings. I intend to!

Gimme! Gimme! Gimme! (A Man After Midnight) - Abba

One of the joys of working in a school is exam season. The pupils might not be so keen, but I get to sit in the library and have quiet time.

I like plans and lists; I am by nature an organised person. With Shouty Husband's departure, I know I now need to find out if I can get any financial support; I earn 2p and a biscuit, and it's not even a cream one – more bargain-bucket ginger nut!

So, with the Whitsun holidays coming up, it's time to put the plan into action.

I'm an overthinker, I know it, and although talking to myself has been helpful, I need more than just the inside of my own head. Much as I hate to admit it, I need some counselling.

I know it's not an instant fix. It will take a while. But I am determined. I find the phone number for the local Wellbeing service and call them. Answering service. Ok, I leave a message to say I need someone to talk to.

It takes four messages in all before someone rings me back, but at least I'm on the list now for a telephone consultation. Even though that will be another two weeks, I already feel better in my head.

Next up – making an appointment with the Citizens' Advice Bureau for when I'm on holiday. I'm on a roll! I am so doing this.

Some tax forms for Shouty Husband came in the post today. I finally have his address, thanks to Luke, so I'll post them on. Previously, we got a decent tax break after Shouty Husband learned that, as I didn't earn enough to pay tax, he could get a refund. (He's a fan of Radio 4 and heard it on their financial slot.) I was always the one who sorted out this kind of thing, so I dutifully did so, and it worked out. Hurrah. All was well with the world.

When the tax letter arrived for him, I decided that he wasn't getting my tax allowance anymore. It wouldn't make any difference to my wages, but it would mean he'd lose about £40 a month. What a shame.

So, after a call to the tax office and an explanation of my status, Shouty Husband's tax code was changed. I felt much better afterwards. I hit him where it hurts the most, right in the bank balance!

Telephone Line – ELO

As I've explained, I was the one to sort out all the household 'stuff'. Shouty Husband was not one to play, 'Press '1' to do this, press '2' to do that, press '109' to speak to a real, live person.' Yes, automated menus are annoying, but they're a fact of life. Shouty Husband would end up throwing the phone at the wall, so I dealt with everything.

Banking, tax, car insurance, house insurance – the lot. So when I got home from work today, it was a nice surprise to find a letter from one of the comparison sites thanking me for using them to arrange Shouty Husband's insurance. Even nicer was the cheque for £20 that came with it in my name. I certainly hadn't been expecting it.

Well, I earned it, even though it was his insurance. So, I'll enjoy spending it!

Bomber – Motorhead

Shouty Husband has made me 'spit feathers,' to use one of my mum's phrases. Luke came to pick up the hedge trimmers as the bushes in front of Shouty Husband's French doors are overgrown. He can have them – they're his, after all.

Luke told me Shouty Husband has lost a lot of weight. He really needed to, in all honesty – he was clinically obese. Apparently, he's all but ended his chemical romance, cut down on his beer, and is eating better.

While Luke was telling me all this, I could hear Shouty Husband in my head, telling me it was all my fault. I'd made him the way he was. I made him drink, smoke, and toke.

Shouty Husband had also told Luke to collect the bedside cabinet from the shed. Really? Even cleaned up, it's truly manky. He could have had his from our bedroom if he'd asked. Oh well, his choice.

Apparently, all the tools and other stuff in his shed has to stay where it is. He's not taking it, and I'm not allowed to get rid of it. My first thought was to dump it all out the front for the scrap man, but I'm a nice person, really. It can just sit in the shed until it rots.

Apart from that, though, the last of his stuff has gone now. I even sent his Old Bike Mart magazine, which is a monthly publication. I've changed the address once, but Luke gave me the wrong one, so I'm trying to sort it out again. I could just pass it on, I suppose, but Jordan bought the subscription as a birthday present for Shouty Husband.

Both Shouty Husband and my oldest friend, Mick, always said I had a big heart. I took five minutes out of my life to make Shouty Husband happy, not because I'm soft but just because that's how I am. If I did nothing, the little voice in my head that sounds like my mum would tell me off.

Shouty Husband planted a cotoneaster bush at the top of our drive. About twice a year, it needs a haircut. Our next-door neighbours have a big privet hedge. It gets messy because they're not gardeners.

Our road is a waiting room for the gods, so there are unwritten rules about messy hedges. I was told oh-so-nicely that the bush needed a trim (don't snigger!), so, I planned to get the shears out today; I'm going to have to do it by hand as Shouty Husband has got the electric hedge trimmers.

So, I get home from shopping to see my lovely neighbour cutting his privet. Then, ten minutes later, I find that the cotoneaster is tidy again, too. Turns out they'd worked out Shouty Husband had left, so decided to do me a favour. They didn't ask for the details – just wanted to know that I was ok and if there was anything I needed.

How lovely. My front is tidy, I'm back in the good books with the rest of the street, and I have brilliant neighbours. I love where I live.

Broadway Hotel – Al Stewart

Today, at 8am, I had my first telephone counselling session. I was told I was now on a three-month waiting list for in-person counselling and was asked how I was dealing with everything.

Have you heard the saying, 'How do you eat a dinosaur? In bite-size pieces?' That's how I'm doing. My plate was too full this week, and I found it so overwhelming that it was hard to eat anything. I made a decent dent in it, though, and I've frozen the leftovers for later.

After talking about Shouty Husband for an hour, I decided some physical exercise might help me sleep. Shouty Husband hath murdered sleep, to misquote Shakespeare.

So, the back of both sheds is now clear. The rusty barbecues have been taken by the scrap man. My green bin is full, and I have swept everywhere. My back aches, and I have broken every fingernail, but my garden looks tidy. I even managed to do it before the rain came. My garden is now full of birds enjoying full bird boxes, suet pellets, and sunflower seeds.

I told the counsellor I was sharing everything with my lovely We Aten't Dead community online and about how much support and love I was getting back. And she said that if it helped me to talk about Shouty Husband, I should keep up the good work. On the back of that, I decided to ring an old friend who didn't know Shouty Husband had left. I knew it was something I had to tell my friends, and I've known Sue for a long time. She's been around forever and knows what he's like. I finally managed to catch her, rather than her answering machine. Sue is retired and has a caravan in Wales, where she spends quite a bit of time. She told me she was about to go back there but would be in touch when she was home.

She was as good as her word. She came back, dumped her husband and her laundry – I mean, dropped them at home, nothing more sinister! – and turned up at my door.

We put the world to rights, and it felt good to know someone else recognised Shouty Husband's need to be the centre of attention and gaslighting tendencies.

We drank a bottle of wine, and I was trying to only drink at weekends. The road to hell is paved with good intentions.

Only Women Bleed – Alice Cooper

A lot of the posts I shared with the We Aten't Dead group were about the emotional and physical abuse I received from Shouty Husband. At the time, I didn't realise his behaviour was abusive; it was only when I started to post that I realised the way he treated me was not normal in an equal, loving relationship. Of course, it seems so obvious now, but it took a long time before I took off my rose-tinted glasses and let the scales slip from my eyes. Shouty Husband had an extremely low boredom threshold, so he liked to torment me for entertainment. He'd undo my bra through my clothes, which really annoyed me. Or stick his cold hands down the front of my top, commenting, 'Name that telly programme, cold tits.' He'd poke me in the belly button while we were in bed. All these things were irritating, but the worst ones were him poking me in the ribs with a finger or grabbing my kneecap and squeezing really hard. It hurt. I would complain, and he'd tell me 'I never felt a thing' and 'It won't hurt when the pain's gone.' Yes, I understand now that this was abuse, but at the time, I didn't.

It is cold and miserable right now in my little corner of the world. At work, the other women were saying how they'd need a bath to get warm tonight. I told them Shouty Husband made me put his towel in the tumble dryer when he had a bath, so it was warm for when he got out, and they were gobsmacked. I also wasn't allowed to wash his towels with fabric softener; it made them soft, and he preferred a hard towel. Why did I put up with it? I must have been mad!

Anyway, tonight I had a bath and dried myself with a soft, untumbled towel. I'm warm, I have a hot water bottle, and I'm going to watch The Great British Bake Off and eat lots and lots of chocolate!

Rivers (Of the Hidden Funk) – Joe Walsh

Shouty Husband was a sleeping dog whose kennel never should be kicked. I knew this, so I left him alone, but I knew I needed to sort out the house and what would happen to it in the future.

After a phone call with Jordan one Saturday night, I did some thinking and overthinking and then worked out what to do. The issue, essentially, was this. What would happen if I got hit by the Number 13a bus as it came down my road and I met Death? Shouty Husband would get half the house. If he dies first, I get half. The other half would go to the boys, and they'd get all of it when Shouty Husband and I had both met Death. (That doesn't scare me, by the way. If you know Terry Pratchett's Death, you'll understand.)

Shouty Husband has major health issues. He's 61 years old to my 53. 'He smokes and drinks and don't come home at all (thank you, Alice Cooper, I do love a good lyric), and has a chemical romance. So, the chances are he will go first, but it's not guaranteed.

Then my mum popped into my head with the solution. I love it when that happens. She's always the voice of reason. Book a free, half-hour appointment with a solicitor, take a list of questions, and find out how to ring-fence my half for my boys. Then go with Mum to the solicitor we always use, who are brilliant.

I dug out our wills; it was time to change mine. I knew Shouty Husband would never think of changing his.

I felt better knowing I was making plans to keep my home and ensuring it would always be there for the boys. My worry was that if anything happened to me first, it would end up being sold to pay for Shouty Husband's care needs in later years, and they'd get nothing.

Jordan rang Shouty Husband and explained about me changing the deeds. As under the law, as we have the house as joint tenants, I cannot leave my half of the house to anybody else. As I have a will and Shouty Husband is named as joint owner it automatically goes to him. I wanted to change the deeds to the house to tenants in common, which means I could leave my half of the house to the boys, and there would be nothing he could do about it!

A small nuclear reaction later, and Shouty Husband rang me, very cold and polite. That's when he's at his most dangerous.

But I poured oil on troubled waters, put all the blame on my son and breathed a sigh of relief that, as long as I kept my head down, I could get away without having to do anything that involved solicitors. I will be a widow before I divorce him. He will never get my house!

No More Tears (Enough is Enough) – Barbra Streisand & Donna Summer

One Thursday in my little school, the last lesson was biology with my Year 10 class. They can be hard work at the best of times, but today was especially tough.

One of the boys washed his hands and then proceeded to wipe them down the back of the neck of the boy next to whom I was sitting. Shouty Husband used to do this to me, usually with cold water, and I HATED IT!!

So, I had a full-blown meltdown. The teacher had never seen me lose my temper and asked me if I needed a minute. The boy was sent out, and the rest of the class, which I'd worked with for two years, cheered me on. 'That's what happens when you piss Miss off!' shouted one. I glared at him for the comment and for swearing in class, but I was smiling inside. The teacher agreed it was abuse, and the boy got detention.

The following day I had a two-hour chemistry lesson with the same class – what fun for a Friday afternoon!

To make it easier, I take in a bag of boiled sweets each week as a treat.

Everyone knows life is better when you have a boiled sweet. The teacher doesn't mind; the kids aren't supposed to eat in class, but as long as it's not actually in a science lab, then he turns a blind eye.

I handed out the sweets and apologised to all the students for losing it the day before. Every single one of them told me it was ok and not to worry, and even the boy I'd screamed at – and it was proper screaming – said sorry to me in turn.

The class had spoken; 'Miss is OK,' they said, and they told him to apologise.

And the pear drops were a big hit. Must see what else I can buy for £1.

Original Mixed-Up Kids - Mott the Hoople

Happy Thursday to all you wonderful readers. It's a school night, but I'm enjoying a glass of wine and listening to the greatest hits of the 1970s. I thought that was apt as this is about my oldest friend Mick, aka The Sav.

We've been friends for 35 years. A lifetime ago, we were a couple for a while, but once we got the sex out of the way, we stayed friends. We've done it all – as well as the sex, there's been the drugs and rock 'n' roll, not to mention other great music, death, kids, and divorce.

My stock phrase with him has always been, 'I'm too young!' As Mick is ten years older than I am, and Shouty Husband is eight years older, I was still playing with my Tiny Tears doll while they were living it up in the 1970s clubs.

I should mention, Mick is also Shouty Husband's best friend and has been for 20 years. He has a sort of mental fence, so anything I say about Shouty Husband – and vice versa – goes in one ear and out of the other. He doesn't take sides, and it works.

Mick lived with Shouty Husband for three years, which I thought was brilliant at the time – the two most important men in my life under the same roof.

Mick called me two weeks ago to tell me he has early-stage dementia. While sad, it wasn't too much of a shock; Mick likes his drink and always has. After spending the best part of 50 years living in shared houses, he now has his own bedsit in an old folks' residential home. It's all his – he doesn't have to share, and he's happy.

So today, I drove the 12 miles over there to take my best friend out to lunch, paid for by the cash back I got from Shouty Husband's insurance company.

We walked by the river, and I poured two small jars of David into the water; he'll go all over the world now. As David never made it out of the UK, I thought he would like that.

Mick told me he still had hopes for me and Shouty Husband. So, to set him straight on that, I pointed out all the things he saw Shouty Husband do and reminded him of how things had been over the past 20 years. The one thing that made him go, 'That's not right,' was when I told him I had to ask Shouty Husband for a hug. Mick isn't especially tactile, but I know I can just hug him if I want to. With Shouty Husband, I always had to ask first – and usually wouldn't get. Withholding affection and sex was one of his 'punishments' if he thought I'd done something wrong.

Anyway, thank you, my Mickey, aka The Sav. Thank you for a lovely couple of hours, for a good roast beef dinner, for the conversation, and the hugs. I needed that.

I Know Him So Well – Elaine Paige & Barbara Dickson

Shouty Husband was highly competitive, whereas I really am not. I hated playing games like gin rummy or chess with him. He did try to teach me, but, in his words, I was too slow on the uptake.

He played Scrabble at every table in every house he lived in. His mum bought him a set when he was little; he loved the game, so it carried on. So, it's fair to say the sound of Shouty Husband rattling his Scrabble bag has been a big part of my life for the past 26 years. At least, until he discovered spider solitaire on his computer. From then on, hid behind a computer screen and stopped talking to me. Strangely, I missed the sound of rattling Scrabble tiles. And at least we'd always had a conversation we played. Shouty Husband rarely played Scrabble with other people as he was so quick. I tried my best, but he'd put my tiles on the board for me even while I was still trying to work out what words I could play, so I gave up. I used to buy every Scrabble set I saw in charity shops and at car boot sales because he wore the boards out so quickly.

When Luke took Shouty Husband's stuff, I sent all the Scrabble boards, tiles, and books, but for some reason, Shouty Husband sent one board back. He didn't send the tiles, though, so I ordered a cheap set from Amazon. Now I have my own Scrabble set.

We always joked that when Shouty Husband died, I would put his Scrabble board out at his spot at the table and play badly while I talked at him about life, the universe and everything. Well, why abandon a good plan? I just adapted it a bit. I set out the board with the Brontolo mug I bought for him in Rome – it has a picture of Grumpy from Snow White and the Seven Dwarfs on it – and I'm talking to the photo of him on the bookshelf behind his chair. I'm not playing quickly, and most of my words might only be three letters, but I'm taking the opportunity to tell him just why he's no longer here.

I'll improve the more I practise. And at least I won't be told off if the cats knock the board and the tiles go all over the floor. It's a win-win as far as I'm concerned!

(I posted this story on We Aten't Dead, and a lovely lady in California sent me a purple Crown Royal bag. Sadly, I only got the bag – not the bottle of 90% proof whiskey that was originally in it -damn! Never mind – the bag is brilliant, and I use it to shake my Scrabble tiles with enthusiasm!)

It's My Life – Bon Jovi

I never go to the hairdresser for anything fancier than a basic haircut. My hairdresser, Tara, is brilliant - she just scalps me, and that's it until next time. I've had short hair for more years than I care to remember. My hair is an independent entity with a mind of its own, and it goes a bit mad about three weeks after a cut.

My dear friend Mick describes me as "Annie, with come-to-bed eyes and just-got-out-of-bed hair!" You know the saying "pulled through a hedge backwards? That's me and my hair.

Anyway, my mum splashed out £25 to treat me to a cut, colour and blow dry.

As I'd been posting to my, We Aten't Dead online family about Shouty Husband. Some people asked if I'd post a photo of myself afterwards. My profile picture had always been my granddaughters, but it was time to be brave.

To tell the truth, I HATE having my photo taken. So did Shouty Husband, but he'd allow it sometimes as long as I asked; if I took his picture without permission, I'd be punished.

As it was summer holidays, I decided I could go a bit mad and had my hair dyed purple. I'm naturally dark-haired, so it wasn't as bright as I'd hoped, but it did suit me.

And it was a step into the light. Shouty Husband always told me if I'd gone the wrong shade of brown – I'd been dying my hair since I was 22 years old when I first started going grey at the temples. He liked me to go darker than I wanted to – it made my skin look sallow.

But no more. My 81-year-old mum picked purple, and I love it, and it's another four-fingered salute of 'Up yours' to Shouty Husband.

Mum took some photos afterwards. She's no David Bailey, bless her, but when she saw them, she told me I looked happy. Oh, and I needed a better-fitting bra! I do love my mum.

So, this is me. My friends call me Annie, my granddaughters call me Grannie Annie, my mum calls me Annie Panny. I'm 53 years old, and for the first time in what seems like forever, I'm happy and at peace with myself, and I love my hair.

As I think I've said, my mum has a quote for every occasion but never knows who said them. So, today's words of wisdom, which she dispensed after the, 'uplift for the downtrodden talk,' when she told me to go to Marks & Spencer's where they'd measure me properly for a bra, was this:

Polonius: 'This above all: to thine own self be true, and it must follow, as the night the day, thou canst not then be false to any man.'

Mum thought Charles Dickens had written this. She was quite surprised when I told her it was from Hamlet.

My hair colour lasted until I went back to work, and all my students loved it, so I decided to carry on with the purple dye. They now call me Grannie Plum!

Next summer, I'm planning to go a brighter purple.

I posted the photos to We Aten't Dead and got over 1000 likes and comments. That did my confidence a power of good. My counsellor was amazed when I mentioned it during my phone consultation and said that it was a great boost for my mental health.

The Boys Are Back in Town – Thin Lizzy

If you've made it this far, well done, and thank you. Now I think it's time for a bit about the supporting players in my own Greek tragedy.

I am mum to two sons, Jordan and Luke – or Lordan and Duke, as Shouty Husband called them. Laura, my daughter-in-law, is Jordan's wife, and they have two daughters, Everly and Carina. My daughter-in-law-to-be is Amber, who has been with Luke since forever. They're getting married soon, so I'll be needing a new hat.

Yesterday was my eldest son Jordan and my amazing daughter-in-law Laura's 6th wedding anniversary.

Shouty Husband's photo popped up on my memories on Facebook and has been in my head ever since.

From September 2012 to January 2014 was the beginning of the end of Shouty Husband and me, but there is a huge backstory to how we got there.

So, something that Shouty Husband always admired and told people about me. I can find obscure things. Mostly books and music but also training courses, little men to come and quote for the house.

My oldest friend Mick told Shouty Husband 20 years ago, 'Annie will sort it!' I have, and I still do!

So, the one that Shouty Husband never thought I could do was find a really obscure album on CD. I found a copy of another album on vinyl, but the one he wanted was too obscure, and I could do nothing to find it.

The CD he wanted was 'Another John Golding,' who was a very obscure folk singer from the 1970s. Shouty Husband had it on tape, but when he moved out from living with a friend of mine (31 years, it's complicated, really complicated!!), the tape stayed.

So, for 20 years, I used, as my Mum calls it, 'the Google.' The best I could do was one album of eBay. He only made 3 albums! I was not going to be beaten!

Every now and then, Shouty Husband would ask if I could have a hunt. I enjoy a challenge, so I always tried. Then, after 20 years and a lot of googling and emailing loads of obscure record sites, I hit gold! I found that 2 albums had been released on cd by the original record company! The one album that Shouty Husband loved and wanted I found on cd. It only took me 21 years, but I was not going to be beaten.

Shouty Husband played it to death and loved it. I enjoyed the hunt. I love to find things that are obscure. It keeps my brain working. Annie will sort it. Mick is right!

So, for 26 years of listening to this album and good memories with Shouty Husband, John Golding, 'Another John Golding' is still a favourite of mine. I also hunted down 'Tell me on a Sunday,' an Andrew Lloyd Webber musical with Marti Webb singing, that was not as hard to find. He loved that as well. Rick Wakeman 'White Rock' was not too bad, as they rereleased the back catalogue, I am good.

The only one that escaped me was 'Fill your head with Rock ', a sample album of well-known tracks and obscure ones. This one went when we moved to a new house, carrot time. We found the vinyl in a charity shop, and it was in mint condition. Luke's oldest friend Michael transferred it onto a disk so Shouty Husband could play it again. It has never been released on cd; I have tried over the years but with no joy!

After John Golding, I worked my magic and found a book that Shouty Husband had as a teenager. 'The Devil and All His Works' by Dennis Wheatley.

I used my local library and did an inter-county search, and the book came from Hampshire for Shouty Husband. It cost me £3.50 for the request, but he was in seventh heaven. As it had to go back, I started hunting for a copy to buy. eBay had one, and since Jordan has an eBay account, I asked him to get it for me, and I would give him the money.

Shouty Husband did not do Christmas but loved presents. He always felt them and tried to guess what they were. He worked out it was a book, and I did not buy him many books. The look on his face when he opened it was priceless. He loved it, and I earned great wife points. The only difference from the original copy he had was the front cover, but you cannot have everything.

It was a great Christmas, and we did not have many of them!

White Room - Cream

I've decided to write when things pop into my head rather than sitting down and trying to write at certain times. I think it will work better that way because Shouty Husband pops into my head at all kinds of weird times. I just hope I can read my scrawl afterwards.

This time, I'm going to tell you all about The Rules.
Think Fifty Shades of Grey, but without the ropes. Shouty Husband believed in the 'carrot and stick' method. Except he tended to keep the carrot for the boys, and with me, it was mostly the stick.

He made all the decisions. If we went out for the weekend or not, and where to; whether he cooked or not, and what it would be; whether he was in the mood to talk to me or if he was to be left alone.

He used affection as his main weapon of control. Shouty Husband wasn't tactile; he was an exclusion zone with razor wire and machine gun posts. He was hyper-vigilant and dangerous if you caught him unawares, so you never came up behind him by surprise. I always had to make my presence known first.

When Shouty Husband was fifteen, he broke the nose of his then-girlfriend's mum. It wasn't deliberate, but it's a great warning story – never startle him.

The mum came up behind him, bent down to offer him a cup of tea, and dropped a hand on his shoulder. Up and back went his fist, smack into her nose, and that was the end of that relationship.

So:

Golden rule number one

Never creep up, and always make yourself heard first.

Golden rule number two

Any affection is on his terms. This applies to everything, even a hug. He would hug me but poke his finger in my ribs when he'd had enough. Pain was always given alongside any pleasure. If I wanted a cuddle, I always had to ask and hope he was in the mood to say yes. At the time, I felt it was worth the pain just to be able to get close to him.

I would have crawled over broken glass to get him to show me the slightest signs of affection. The only time he was tactile was in bed, but that was on his terms too. He told everybody he would only sleep with me if we'd both had a hot bath with Dettol in it. At the time, this seemed normal; he was driving a bin wagon and always had a Dettol bath each night when he came home. Now, though, I realise that insisting I was disinfected before he would touch me was strange. It's not normal behaviour. I also now detest the smell of Dettol.

Golden rule number three

 If you make a big deal about Christmas or your birthday, it will be ignored. There will be no presents or cards. You will receive the silent treatment. If he'd decided I'd been good enough and he'd had enough work, he'd give me some money to buy myself something.

In the later years, his default 'something-on-the-day' present was earrings. To be fair, he did have great taste. The most expensive earrings he ever got me were garnets; they were beautiful, they cost £120, and I was terrified to wear them in case I lost them. Actually, I did lose one, but I never told him. I found it after he'd gone when I moved the bedroom around. I was glad, though I don't wear them now – they are part of the 'carrot' treatment.

In all the twenty-three years I was with Shouty Husband, I never experienced the romance, affection or other normal behaviours that normal couples use to show their love. But I was addicted to him, and I believed I deserved to be treated that way.

He always described himself as a mighty oak that wouldn't bend even in the highest winds. He told people that I was a willow, bending easily in the slightest breeze.

I still bend sometimes, but I think twice now before I do so!

Golden rule number four

Red is banned. No red clothes, bags, or anything else.

Shouty Husband hated red, which is ironic when you think it can be seen as an aggressive colour because 'aggressive' was his default setting. And it did make him angry. In his view, only whores wore red.

I did break this rule once and bought a dark red t-shirt with white spots on it. He hated it. I would wear it to work and change as soon as I got home, so he didn't know – my little bit of defiance!

Shouty Husband used to call me Monochrome Annie as I had a palette of black, blue, and white. Everything was muted, as he hated bright colours. My work uniform has always been trousers and a top, and at weekends, it's jeans and a top. I love comfortable clothes. Shouty Husband always told me I should dress more like his first wife, who wore pencil skirts and stockings with high heels. With my short hair and comfortable shoes, he told me I looked like a dyke and asked why I wasn't more feminine. I bought some shoes with a small heel, but he hated them. I did wear dresses for special occasions, but I loved my comfy clothes.

Golden rule number five

Holidays. We didn't do them. Actually, the holiday saga is a chapter all on its own, and I will explain, but at the moment, we are doing The Rules. Is it weird that I'm enjoying writing them? I lived by them for so long I didn't realise that's what they were; they were just part of life, and I rarely questioned them.

Shouty Husband's star sign is Taurus. I don't believe in astrology, but Taureans are said to be homebodies, so the excuse Shouty Husband gave for not allowing holidays was that he liked his own bed and his own toilet.

In 23 years together, we went away on holiday six times. The longest was a week, and the shortest was overnight.

Golden rule number six

Everything must run on Shouty Husband time. Procrastination is the thief of time, and Shouty Husband was a stupendous thief.

Before me, he put any mail he didn't like the look of under the microwave to deal with later. He did get around to sorting stuff out eventually, but always in his own time. You could never rush Shouty Husband, and the fallout from trying to wasn't worth it. Sometimes he'd get his act together and surprise me, but then I was never ready, so he'd get cross. I couldn't win.

Golden rule number seven

If you were lucky enough to have Shouty Husband cook for you, then you'd better eat up. He was actually an incredibly good cook, and he loved feeding people. He'd make meals for friends who visited, which they'd enjoy, but woe betide you if you dared criticise anything he'd cooked. That would be the end of the friendship.

Some people stayed in our lives, like his sister and her husband. They once made a comment about a Sunday lunch they were invited to. He never fed them again, though.

Shouty Husband would always criticise his own food; that was allowed. He'd say the gravy should have been warmer, or the spuds could have done with another five minutes. That was the cue for everyone around the table to protest and tell him how wonderful it all tasted, and what a great cook he was. Such validation made him happy, and a happy Shouty Husband meant a happy me.

Golden rule number eight

All clothes had to be boil washed! Shouty Husband was most insistent that even the most delicate garments must be boil-washed; otherwise, they were not clean.

The problem was he would wear his work clothes for a week without changing them, so I had to boil-wash his jeans to get them clean. The rest I did on a normal wash. Grey whites were the sign of a bad wife, so any that showed signs of being less than brilliant white immediately went into the rag bag.

Golden rule number nine

Shouty Husband must be the centre of attention at all times. If you take attention away from him, you will be punished. If you are talking to someone at the table, so they are not paying attention to me, he will tell you that you are talking too loudly and make you feel small.

'What's yours is mine, and what's mine is my own; you belong to me. You are property, a possession!' He believed in these rules too.

Well, now the bedroom is mine, the house is mine, and the telly is mine. I'll watch what I like when I like it, even if I've seen it before.

I have watched Star Trek at least six times, all the way through.

Golden rule number ten

If the phone rang and it was for me, I had to go into the living room to have a conversation. It didn't matter who it was. I was allowed to talk to whoever it was as long as Shouty Husband wasn't bored. Then, he'd appear in the doorway and glare; this was his signal that I'd been on the phone long enough, and it was time to end the call. If I didn't, I'd be punished. He would ignore me and sulk.

Rules for others

Shouty Husband also had rules for everyone he deemed worthy enough to enter his home. If you broke any of them – or if he thought, you had – you would be expelled from his life. There were very few exceptions. Hardly anyone was allowed back after their misdemeanours.

- Never lie to Shouty Husband.

- Never steal from Shouty Husband.

- Never bring anything hookey into his house.

- Always pay your rent on time. It pays my mortgage. This didn't apply to many people, as we only had a few lodgers. But God help those who forgot this one – they always left very quickly afterwards.

Dirty Deeds Done Dirt Cheap – AC/DC

Shouty Husband loved his hi-fi, and music was a huge part of his life. I had a good stereo system in my old house – Shouty Husband got it for me - and loads of CDs. They weren't all his choice; it was music that was mine, that shaped my life.

When we got married, my CDs became his CDs, and he didn't like my music at all.

I rarely played my music; the hi-fi system was Shouty Husband's, and he didn't like anyone else touching it. Instead, I used the DVD player for my CDs.

Then, when he left, he took all the music! He left me a small selection – some of mine, and some of his that he was not fussed about. But it was an odd mix, and there wasn't much I wanted to keep. But my CDs! The music I'd collected over 25 years - gone.

The bastard!

Then, to add insult to injury, he sent Luke round with my sister-in-law's old hi-fi. It was a top-of-the-range Technics system with separate components – it would have been very expensive about eight years before, and it was barely used. It was the dog's doodahs, and I know he probably paid for it. Well, I didn't want it!

I get my music on YouTube now, so apart from a few special CDs that I can play on my laptop, I decided to donate the rest to an old friend who will love me forever for it and who will listen to them.

I've been bad now, though – I've given Shouty Husband a guilt trip.

Luke came to pick up the Technics hi-fi for my friend Mick. I love it, but I don't want it, and I'll never use it because I can't afford to replace all the music he took. And I'll be damned before I ask for it back.

Shouty Husband was supposed to be going to Luke's to do the garden, but he put it off as it was forecast rain. As my daughter-in-law-to-be was at work, it meant Luke was free to help me with some jobs – moving furniture, pruning the apple tree and the like. We had a great couple of hours together, mother and son.

Luke works extremely hard, but money is tight. He has a mortgage to pay, his car to get through its MOT, and this is the second month in a row he's into his overdraft. At the end of last month, I gave him a carrier bag of food and some loo roll!

Luke asked if I could lend him some petrol money, So I gave him my credit card and sent him off to the local petrol station and the supermarket. He went home with a bag of pork chops, some sausages, a chicken pie, mince and some rare breed mince Shouty Husband had bought two weeks before he left.

After he'd gone, I texted Shouty Husband to tell him Luke was broke. I said I'd been feeding him for two months, and he wouldn't ask his dad for help because he was embarrassed. Ex is useless, Shouty Husband knows this, so

Luke is stuck, and Shouty Husband has always told people that his niece Sophie is the nearest to a daughter he has, and Luke is the son. I know what buttons to push. So, I pushed them! I feel good!

Down the Dust Pipe – Status Quo

Jordan rings me every week while he's walking Maddie, a toy poodle that belonged to his wife's late grandmother. I do enjoy our conversations, which are frequently interspersed with 'Hang on, Mum, just had to pick up poo' comments.

Yesterday he told me he'd phoned Shouty Husband, something he does just to keep him sweet. He worked out the best way to deal with him while doing A-level psychology.

Shouty Husband needs a new car. I know this as it was his main topic of conversation for the last twelve months. While his current car was well maintained it was old – a well-loved, comfy banger. It would cost more than it was worth to get it through its MOT. So Shouty Husband has taken out a car loan for £2000.

Jordan pointed out that I was safe where I was for at least two years because Shouty Husband couldn't afford to divorce me. The conversation took me back six years to another loan he took out, but that's another story or three, to be told another time.

Shouty Husband chases money when he owes it. He'll work every hour he can, not eat properly, and burn out. So naturally, I was worried. Not about his health – about what it would mean if he worked too hard, fell over, and hurt himself or got sick, and then lost his flat!

I know overthinking doesn't solve anything. So, after a night of listening to the tawny owls hoot from 3am till 5am, and a day feeling like my head would explode as I went through all the possible scenarios if things went pear-shaped, I had a bottle of wine (yes, on a school night) and made a decision. This was NOT MY PROBLEM. If he couldn't manage his money at the age of 61, then he never would, but this was not my circus, not my monkeys, not my fight.

When Jordan rang me again, he told me Shouty Husband had enough money in his account to pay the loan off in full. What? I'm trying to run a three-bedroom house on £797.35 a month, and Shouty Husband has a spare £2000 in his account? In what world can that be right?

I also had a call from Luke, who told me Shouty Husband needs new glasses. I feel for whichever optician he went to, as he is a nightmare. Shouty Husband has a really horrible prescription – new glasses have to be perfect with his centres spot on. As another glass-wearer with a horrible script, I do get that. But it means Shouty Husband has spent about £400 on new glasses and now has only £100 to last him until payday! Oh dear, what a pity, never mind!

If Looks Could Kill – Heart

Shouty Husband has two sisters, both younger than him. Sarah is the middle child, and the baby of the family is Paula.

Sarah lived in Cambridgeshire, and we didn't see her often. Paula lived around 20 miles away, so we used to visit her regularly. Shouty Husband loved Paula, and they got on well. Sarah, not so much.

Well, I like a clean house! Saturday morning is when I polish everything and give the place a thorough going over. During the week, it 'gets a cat's wash,' as my mum calls it. Towards the end, Shouty Husband would say I had OCD because I'd go out with him and then come home and start cleaning. It had to be Saturday – on Sundays, I went shopping with my mum. Nothing has changed, so I still clean my house on a Saturday!

When I first met her, my sister-in-law Paula was a hundred times worse than me. I hardly dared sit down in her house because I was scared, I'd mess up the cushions. It was like a show home! Shouty Husband knew that if Paula found any dust or dirt in her house, she'd go into meltdown and clean it from top to bottom – the windows, the oven, even the loft and in the garden.

So, if he felt she had slighted him, he'd get his own back. He'd put dirt or dust on his finger and run it along the top of a door frame in front of her. He'd then show it to her and say she'd missed a bit. Oh, the look on her face – and his. He was immensely proud of himself.

I used to tell him every time he was being cruel, but he told me to leave it – it was between him and his sister. The sister who, according to him, he adored. Shouty Husband had a cruel streak. I was blind to it then; I'm not anymore.

You Ain't Seen Nothing Yet - Bachman Turner Overdrive

As I have said, Shouty Husband was something of a foodie.

He loved to cook and would buy top-quality rare-breed meat. We'd do a 60-mile round trip to his favourite butcher, where all the staff knew us, and would spend at least £100 each time.

He was definitely the chef in our house, and my parents would come for lunch on high days and holidays – Easter, birthdays, and so on.

Now me – well, that's a different story. Six months ago, my idea of cooking was something-from-a-tin on toast or a bacon butty. If Shouty Husband was working away for a night, I'd get creative and poach some smoked haddock, but that was as good as it got. Four months ago, when Shouty Husband stopped feeding me, I got through a lot of tins.

But I've learned a lot in the three months since he left, and today I cooked a roast dinner for my parents. It must be 14 years since the last time.

And not just any roast dinner; this was a rare breed brisket from Shouty Husband's favourite butcher. I put it on a slow cook, and we had potatoes I dug up this morning. (Shouty Husband planted them, but I watered them, so as far as I'm concerned, they're all mine.) Mum brought runner beans grown by my dad. I did use granules to make the gravy but added the meat juices and veg water. The Yorkshire puddings were frozen but tasted great.

Afterwards, Dad said the only difference between my roast dinner and Shouty Husband's was that his gravy tasted beefier. Fair enough, Shouty Husband did do good gravy. But the afternoon was lovely – good food, good company, and nobody shouted.

When Shouty Husband was here, if I was too slow getting the plates out or was trying to have some quality time with my parents rather than attend to him, he tended to live up to his name.

Anyway, I'm proud of myself. I've gone from reheating to making a full dinner in four months. Go me.

Five Years - David Bowie

Shouty Husband's male friends have finally found out he has gone. These are friends from years back who appear from time to time to drink tea and talk about motorbikes. They're harmless but rather grubby round the edges.

Really, they should have been in the garage, but as that became Shouty Husband's chill room, they ended up in the house. I mean – even I was rarely allowed in his space, so the grubby gang didn't stand a chance!

One of them, Sam, came round last night to make sure I was ok. I gave him a cup of tea and listened to what was going on in his world. As he left, he told me I should give him a call if I was lonely, and he'd come and keep me company. And then he winked at me! What? No way! To use one of Shouty Husband's phrases – 'Not if your acid blasted him and it was someone else's.'

I'm not worried; he has no reason to come here again, and if he does, I know a text to Shouty Husband will soon sort that problem out.

But I am flattered in a funny kind of way. A strange man I'd have nothing to do with if it wasn't for Shouty Husband thinks I'm hot. It's good to know I've still got it.

After being around each other for 26 years, Shouty Husband and I obviously knew a lot of the same people and shared many friends.

Steve, aka 'Fish Face Craddock the Haddock,' was my friend first. We met at a party 28 years ago and hit it off over a mutual love of the same music. It helped that I knew his wife and had babysat his girls.

Steve met Shouty Husband through – well, I'd call her his previous victim, but to be honest, she was as bad as he was, and they deserved each other. They'd been trying to live with each other for years. It didn't work.

Anyway, together we partied our way through noughties' Saturday nights – me and Shouty Husband, Steve and his second wife, Lottie. Then Steve was single again, but we stayed friends.

Four years ago, Shouty Husband passed on two carrier bags of videos after Steve asked if he could borrow some porn. Steve liked his dope, too – he was a toker rather than a drinker.

I'd pop in for coffee and a chat with Steve and Lottie and carried on doing so when it was just Steve. In turn, he'd come and spend weekends with us sometimes, and we'd have a great laugh together. One day, Steve texted to ask if I'd pop over; not an unusual request, so I went after work. There'd been a lot of porn and a lot of dope, and that day Steve made a pass at me.

I'm often oblivious when this happens, but not this time. It was as obvious as a wet fish in the face.

Later, I told Shouty Husband. He didn't do anything because he knew that would freak Steve out more than anything. Steve was paranoid. So, nothing happened, but Steve went into the wilderness, and he wasn't in our lives anymore.

Then last year, I bumped into Steve again while I was shopping, and we had coffee. He'd heard Shouty Husband had gone. Last weekend, I went to visit him, and he popped round to mine for a couple of hours in the week. On Saturday, he came round again, and I fed him. It's so nice to have my friend back! He knows I enjoy his company, and I've forgiven him for trying it on, but he knows if it happens again, I will cut him out of my life for good this time.

We understand each other, and it's nice to have someone to be silly with. I've missed it.

Feel a Whole Lot Better - Tom Petty

When we moved into our new home, Shouty Husband promised he would make me a secret garden.

He didn't make many promises and tended to keep them when he did.

The garden then was a sort of combination of patio and dirt, with 40 feet of dirt and a grassed mound of use to neither man nor beast.

Shouty Husband planned what he would do, and Donkey, as we lovingly call Luke, did all the heavy digging.

It took 12 years and a lot of blood, sweat, and tears, but I now have a secret garden to enjoy. It is full of plants from neighbours, friends, car boot sales, church plant sales, and my dad, who still grows from seeds.

It is a garden that bursts with colour from May till Christmas every year and needs only a small amount of maintenance. My wonderful Donkey, Luke, still does all the heavy pruning.

I know the garden is one thing Shouty Husband will miss.

Hopefully, that explanation means this bit makes sense. Sometimes the gods smile and give you a special moment in time, and one such moment happened yesterday. My car and Luke's car happened to be in the garage together –

servicing, getting ready for MOTs – so we had the day together.

Luke lived with us for nine years and took care of all the heavy work in the garden. I told him my apple trees need heavy, hard pruning as they have brown rot. They had it last year, and my lovely We Aten't Dead family told me how to treat it. Shouty Husband was going to deal with it when we saw the symptoms in spring, but he ended up leaving. So, it was down to Luke.

When I told him to cut both the eating and cooking apple trees back to their trunks, he asked, 'Are you sure, Mum?'

The eating apple tree was Shouty Husband's 50th birthday present from his sister, Paula, and the cooking apple tree was a 52nd birthday present. He always wanted fruit trees, even though he didn't eat apples, and he wouldn't want to lose them.

I love the trees too. I take care of them, feeding and watering them. I love passing the fruit on to my mum, who gives it to the little old ladies she knows to make pies. I want them to survive.

But it needed doing, so Luke did it. I must thank my neighbours, John and Val, who donated their garden bins to me. To put the cutting in. Shouty Husband would just have burnt everything in his dustbin behind the shed. Luke probably would, too – he used to love burning things with Shouty Husband. But I'm not a fire fan, so I said no.

Luke also cut back my damson tree that had got too big; he looked at me like I was mad, but they either will grow back, or they won't. That was Shouty Husband's motto for gardening – plants will live, or they'll die.

I do my best, but I don't have green fingers. I do, however, ask for advice and pray to the gods.

I do hope my trees survive! *

_____

*   Ooh, I get to do my first footnote. How exciting! Well, since writing this, both trees have new leaves shooting out – so they are not dead!

At Seventeen - Janis Ian

Luke came today to help me dig out my fuchsia bush. I don't think it will kill it – Shouty Husband must have moved it half a dozen times in 13 years.

 The problem is it's never pruned back in the autumn, so it grows very woody and is huge. At its peak, it was ten feet high and four feet wide. Shouty Husband had been talking about moving it again for the past three years.

Eventually, my poor postman caught me one day and asked very nicely if I could move it away from the letter box as it was full of bees and making it difficult for him to post my mail.

Well, I'd have to be careful – a bee sting could kill me, so I have to carry an EpiPen. In spite of that, my garden is very bee friendly. My lavender is still in flower, and my spearmint and Michaelmas daisies are getting there.

Anyway, I mowed the lawn and made a start on the fuchsia, cutting it back to woody tooth. Then I dug round the root ball, and also dug a new hole for it to go in. When Luke came, it took half an hour of him digging and pulling before the root ball came out. He said it was like pulling a tooth!

My fuchsia has now been replanted in compost and well-watered. It can grow as big as it wants in its new spot and will be a haven for bees in the summer without me having to worry about killing any visitors.

Luke said he was going to visit Shouty Husband when he left mine as it had been a while. Shouty Husband would text 'Are you dead?' if he didn't hear from him, so he thought it was about time.

Set the Controls for the Heart of the Sun - Pink Floyd

Shouty Husband wanted to be as private as possible at home, so he planted laurel up the fences. They grew to be enormous, really high, and very bushy.

You could see them from the road, so I decided to have them cut back. I rang mum, and she sent John over. He's a gardener and a fencer, and I've known him all my life, so I trust him. After an hour with his chainsaw, my laurel was decimated.

Mum and Dad came for lunch, and Mum helped me paint all the fences that had been covered by the laurel. The garden looks really tidy now.

The garden swing that Shouty Husband loved has been taken apart and is due to be collected by a lady who wanted it after I advertised it as free to a good home on the local free recycling site. I'll be glad to see it go.

It's a happy Sunday, and I've enjoyed my alcoholic grape juice and typing up some garden memories.

What's more, it's November now, and my fuchsia still has flowers on it – so it still aten't dead.

Rock You Like a Hurricane - Scorpions

Feeling a bit fragile right now. I partied like it was 1984 with my best friend, Mick, for his birthday. I'm realising now that I'm not 18 anymore.

So, I'm having a nice quiet Sunday, on the sofa with some dry toast. Then my phone goes off.

Shouty Husband has his own ringtone: 'Warning, warning, the husband is calling you NOW!'

I still panic a bit when I hear it. Last time he called, he was threatening to take the house off me, so I did think twice before answering.

It turns out there's a problem with his council tax. They've added £500 onto his bill for my house. Since I paid it in full – and can prove it – I don't really have to do anything. I have the bills, but I've been waiting for the 'we're sending the bailiffs' letter before I go down and do a calm, collected Granny Weatherwax* on them.

However, Shouty Husband can't sort this out without me, and if it's left, then he could lose his rented flat.

_____

*   Ooh, another footnote. I'm getting good at this. Granny Weatherwax is a character from the brilliant Discworld books, written by Terry Pratchett. He's the master of the footnote. If you haven't read him, do.

I have two options. He can give me his bills, and I can go and deal with it. Or I could send him his bills and let him do it himself. He's got a book of stamps for me, as I've been forwarding his mail, so no problem there.

Now, I know you'll all be thinking I should do nothing. And I'll admit I shouted a few rude words at the phone after he hung up. But I'm better than that, and life generally is easier if he's on side. Shouty Husband is a sleeping dog – best to let him lie and not kick his kennel.

Another of his saying is about not having anything that can come back and bite you on the bum, so I decided to be helpful Annie. I agreed to help him out and contented myself with a four-fingered salute afterwards.

Just because I'm being nice doesn't mean I'm letting him win.

Well, after going to the council offices with my mum, I learned you have to ring them first, and they'll decide if you need an appointment. At least it was now being dealt with.

It took Gareth and Tim four hours to sort out the mess, which actually was my fault. (Shouty Husband says everything is my fault. This time, he was right.)

When I paid the entire year, I didn't tell the council tax people Shouty Husband had left because getting the single occupancy discount and then having to give it back is a pain in the bum. Been there, done that.

So instead, they'd opened a new account in my name and transferred half the money owed onto Shouty Husband's bill, which is why he was getting payment demands.

I was given 30 days' grace to send in a photo of my credit card statement to prove I'd paid the lot. Nothing's ever simple, is it? I shred all my old paperwork and no longer had the credit card bill I needed. So, I called the bank to request a new copy, only to find their system was down. Cock Wombles!

Finally, finally, I got through, made it up the call queue, and spoke to a nice lady who said she'd send me a copy of the statement. I've emailed the council to let them know, and once I've got the bill and have sent it, I'll double-check to make sure they've got it.

Gareth asked if Shouty Husband would contact the council to tell them he hadn't paid the bill. That would never happen!

Then he asked why I was dealing with it. Easy. If I hadn't done anything and Shouty Husband hadn't been able to sort it out quickly, he'd have found a way to make me suffer. Especially if he'd had to lose work as a result. So, to keep the peace in my life, it was easier to do it myself. And as it turned out, it was my fault – so the fallout would have been even worse. You live and learn.

Shouty Husband does want his bill posted back asap, so I'll use one of his stamps and do that tomorrow. Yes, I could have done it today. The post box is only five minutes away. But I didn't. I sat on my sofa and did nothing instead.

Just my small 'up yours' retaliation.

By now, you'll know that according to Shouty Husband, my culinary skills were limited to reheating. He used to say my boys had grown up on a bad diet of reheated food, but he was wrong – I did use to cook for them, and they grew up strong and healthy.

Well, let's squash that accusation because I have just cooked a 21-day aged sirloin steak with twice-cooked hand-cut chips and fresh corn on the cob. Those posh restaurants have got nothing on me!

This is the biggest and best four-finger salute I've given to Shouty Husband so far. And you know what? It felt amazing and tasted great. It was my first-time cooking steak. Okay, it could have done with a moment or two longer, as I'm not a big fan of bloody meat, but it was pretty much there.

In the 1960s, '70s, and '80s, Shouty Husband spent a lot of time in friends' houses, where the pervading smell was stewed tea, fags, rancid fat, and that strange biscuity smell of clothes that have never dried properly. So, to him, chips were considered a poor kind of food.

I get it. In the '70s and '80s I did the same, and I had friends whose staple diet was egg and chips with stewed tea.

I like chips, actually. So once a month, I've had oven chips — they were what Shouty Husband cooked, and he left a bag and a half in the freezer.

Occasionally, if I'd behaved myself or Shouty Husband had a good week at work, the gods would smile, and he'd cook proper hand-cut chips. If there was full sunshine in his world, he'd even cook them in beef dripping. (Anyone else remember the joy of proper chips in newspaper?)

After Shouty Husband moved out, I bought a chip pan and some Mazola oil. I love beef dripping, but it's a waste just for me; the oil I can reuse.

Today I decided it was time. I bought steak and wine and made proper chips. Who knows — I might even do it again next month!

Shouty Husband loved to rant. Even when he was young, he was still a grumpy old man. He'd moan about anything and everything, but food was one of his favourite topics.

When he could no longer find his favourite Daddies sauce in glass bottles, you'd have thought the world had ended. The fact that he ate it so infrequently that a bottle had a half-life of five years was irrelevant.

 Then came the checking of the supermarket and all the corner shops in case they had a few final glass bottles hidden away. Eventually, he had to accept the switch to plastic bottles and complained that the sauce didn't taste the same. He still ate it infrequently, and I had to throw several bottles out after he left.

Another example was when Shouty Husband suddenly fancied a particular kind of canned soup after not eating it for years and then finding out it had been discontinued. How dare they stop making it when he liked it so much? The roof would be raised with his fury. Gods help me if they changed the recipe of his staple foods – only Heinz beans and Kellogg's cornflakes would do.

Then our local council brought in recycling bins. As well as our normal rubbish bin, we had a green one for garden waste and a box for recyclables that filled up quickly with cat food tins and beer cans. It was a standing joke that the collection guys thought we lived on beer and cat food.

Then the council decided to give us a big purple bin for the recycling. We had a lot of stuff that went in there, so it was brilliant, but Shouty Husband really got on his high horse about having yet another bin out the front. They were his bugbear, along with life, the universe, and everything. Now he's gone, the council has given me two new bins for food waste. One lives in the house with the box I put the recycling in before it goes out in the big bin, and the other one lives out the front of the house. I am so glad he is not here to moan about yet another box.

His daily tirade was always about work. Sometimes he'd have a good day, but mostly he complained about stacker truck drivers who were slow or didn't appreciate being told how to stack crates on his truck. I wish I had £1 for every time he complained about people pulling out in front of him. Didn't they realise big trucks couldn't stop quickly? Did they want to die? Couldn't they read the road and be aware of what was happening at least six cars ahead, as he was? He also complained about various bosses over the years. There was one in particular, but you'll have to wait a while to hear about that – there's a big carrot for you.

Going out for food was very hit-and-miss. If we were in Wolverhampton and it was coming up to lunch time, the KFC by Waitrose was a good bet - we never had bad food from there. We never ate in; Shouty Husband would stay in the car while I went in and ordered. If he had a fizzy drink, I had to make sure there was no ice in it.

Occasionally, we'd go to our local Indian restaurant on a Friday night, and sometimes, if he was cash-rich, we'd order in. That stopped abruptly when the food once arrived an hour after we'd ordered – he'd been told it would be half an hour. He shut the door in the poor delivery driver's face, along with a mouthful of expletives!

We did go out for Sunday lunch once; we must have done a round trip of 40 miles to find a good one. Shouty Husband was very particular about where he sat, so the first pub we tried was no good. He always liked to sit with his back to a wall so he could see all around him, but they didn't have a suitable table. (He always told me that they were out to get him, not that he was paranoid!)

The second pub we went to didn't smell right…

At the third one, he said the waitress was rude. (She wasn't, but by now, he was raging.)

Eventually, we ended up at the brand-new KFC just up the road from us. I went in to order as normal – a two-piece meal with coleslaw for Shouty Husband. I gave him the bags so he could have first choice of the chicken pieces as usual. He threw the bag at me, got out of the car, and stormed into the restaurant. I followed at a distance; I knew it wasn't going to be good. The problem, apparently, was that the chicken pieces were tiny. The manager argued with Shouty Husband, which was a mistake. As I saw him turn cold and polite, with body language to match, I backed towards the door. This was when Shouty Husband was at his most dangerous. Shouting and ranting was normal - I knew how to deal with that. Anyway, our money was refunded, and Sunday lunch ended up being a bacon and egg sandwich, which he cooked at home, along with an afternoon's ranting.

Supermarkets also bore the brunt of Shouty Husband's rage. The first time he shopped in Aldi, he filled the trolley to the top. We managed to get to the other side of the till, and the checkout assistant told him which way to put the trolley. Shouty Husband didn't like being told to do anything, so he argued he would put the trolley where he liked. She explained that was how it was done there, so Shouty Husband told her to clear the belt and put everything back – he wasn't shopping there if he couldn't do it his way. 'The customer is always right,' was his parting shot. I followed him out, mouthing 'sorry' to the assistant and the people in the queue behind us. I think Shouty Husband is still banned from the first Aldi store in my hometown.

After that, whenever we went into the new Aldi or Lidl, he'd put the stuff on the belt, walk through, and wait for me to pack and pay

I Put a Spell on You - Creedence Clearwater Revival

Now for the science bit. Attachment disorder is a broad term intended to describe disorders of mood, behaviour and social relationships arising from a failure to form normal attachments to primary caregiving figures in early childhood. (I know, it's a bit of a mouthful.)

I went back to work this week. Every year we have training sessions, and this time it was about attachment disorder and narcissistic personality disorder. If help is not given early on, it can manifest itself in later life.

The font of this knowledge was an educational psychologist, who I know from working with students. I caught her in the break and bombarded her with questions; she was very obliging and answered them.

I felt like my head was under a big ringing bell with cannons going off at the same time. The educational psychologist was describing Shouty Husband and his sisters to an absolute tee.

The rest of the week was a bit of a nightmare, with no timetables and lots of time with not much to do, so I have had the chance to process all the things Shouty Husband told me about his childhood and his mum.

I really want to go and knock on her door and tell her how she destroyed her children. I could do it; I know where she lives. Shouty Husband has the worst problems, but they are all screwed up.

I'm not defending his behaviour, but it explains so much. He always told me he did guilt, but actually, it was shame.

Half of me wants to go to Shouty Husband and fix him. I know, broken – I've been doing it for the past 26 years while I've been with him.

The other half of me is screaming that it's too late. He can't be fixed. He would never agree to get help, he wouldn't change, and I'd be back to having no life.

Now I have a life. Nobody puts me down or torments me. I do what I want when I want and never have to worry about upsetting anybody except the cats – and they're happy as long as I feed them.

I asked myself, seriously, would I take Shouty Husband back. And my answer was immediate. NO! I am happy in my own skin. I'm content with the life I have found since he left.

But we were together for a long time, and sometimes I miss him. I had some time with him on Friday, and a bit of me did feel it. This week's been hard, and it triggered my anxiety – I've seen 2am, 3am, 4am when I should be asleep.

But I'm back to being me now. I survived life with him, and I have my own path now. I still feel for him – he's damaged, but it's been too long, and it goes too deep to change it now. It's time to be true to myself and who I am.

I'm Free – The Who

I've worn rings on my ring finger for the last 35 years, and, for the last 20 years, they've been rings Shouty Husband bought me. I rarely take them off as I feel naked without them; they're part of me.

But I decided I wanted to be free of the hold my wedding, engagement, and eternity rings had over me. They made me feel as though I was still Shouty Husband's property.

He looked at the ring fingers of all the females he met. That's what he called them – never women, always females. He judged how far he could tease them by the amount of money represented on their fingers.

He was very good at working out the cost of jewellery. The way he saw it, the more money on her finger, the more loved a woman was. Cheap rings meant the 'female' was easy, and he could play. Then, if they played back and got too friendly, he'd tell them about me - the wife who he loved completely. He enjoyed the reaction he got from them. He was a predator and cruel.

But back to the rings. Wearing them makes me feel dressed, along with my glasses. I am strange, I know!

I'm a big fan of Amazon. That site and the customer reviews have been my go-to for years now. I must have looked at 20 pages of rings before I made my choice. Just a plain, gold-plated wedding band. Nothing in your face – neat and understated. The only problem was that it was coming from the USA, so it would take a while. Never mind – I can keep wearing Shouty Husband's rings until it arrives.

Shouty Husband has been gone four months now. The summer holidays are over, and it's my first week back at work. I haven't slept well, and I've been feeling blue all week. Then I got home from a particularly exhausting day to find my freedom ring waiting for me. It fitted perfectly.

Sometimes, the universe listens. It gave me what I needed and, as The Who sang, 'I'm free'!

As well as coping with my best friend dying and Shouty Husband leaving, I'm also going through the menopause. I have no plumbing – I had a hysterectomy at 28, started early perimenopause at 30, and went onto HRT, so I've been OK.

Last year I stopped taking HRT and crashed and burned, so my doctor put me back on it, and we agreed I'd come off it slowly and gently. Now, I'm down to the lowest dose of progesterone every three days.

When I had my HRT MOT with my doctor, who is a lovely lady around my age, I broke down and cried, told her everything, then gave her 'the glare' when she asked about Shouty Husband and whether I'd take him back. She got the point, and I apologised. She understood.

She suggested I go back on HRT for six months, but I declined. Instead, I asked for antidepressants. I need to get my head onto a level playing field.

My head is full, and I need some alone time to get myself into a good place. Most of the time, I do NOT miss Shouty Husband, but there's still four weeks left of term. I've got a new timetable, which is OK – I know the lessons and can cope, but I still feel like I'm being stretched very thin.

My doctor said she could sign me off sick for two weeks while the antidepressants kicked in, but I said no. Only 2 people at work know about Shouty Husband – he's a very small part of my life now, and I've got some counselling lined up for September. Bring on the side effects – I can do this. Then I'll take some time to sleep and do my garden and get my head in a good place.

As my friend Mick says, 'You have to kill your own snakes.' Well, my snakes need a good stomping!

Oh Well - Fleetwood Mac

You'll laugh at this, but today I had an opinion and wasn't told I was wrong. My friend Stella at work showed me a photo of a picture her daughter had done to relax after a hard day at uni. Just for fun, she asked, 'What did I see?'

I saw a mosaic floor and a beautiful, deep blue night sky with stars. I told Stella this and then said, 'I knew I was wrong; what did it really show?' She looked at me and said there was no 'wrong' – what I saw was right.

I told her Shouty Husband bought me tarot cards and borrowed a great book from his cousin so I could learn to read them. I did read the book and tried to work out the cards—just the Major Arcana. When I told Shouty Husband I was trying, he made me do a three-card spread and read them. He told me to say what I saw. So, I did, and then he said I'd got it totally wrong and told me what they really were, according to him. I ended up giving the cards to his niece, Sophie, but I kept the book.

There was the right way, the wrong way and Shouty Husband's way, which held sway overall. It still feels strange to know I can look at something now and give my own free opinion. I can be right, I can be wrong, but above all, I can be me! Why did I not see it?

Mr Soft - Steve Harley and Cockney Rebel

Finally, my appointment to see a counsellor came through – one session each week, lasting an hour, starting at 5pm. This meant driving in the dark, which I hate, and I also hate the local ring road. Having to do this journey during rush hour is my idea of hell, but I've managed it.

My counsellor, Neil, is lovely. He's very beige and has a nice voice, and, as a higher-level counsellor, he's been worth waiting six months for.

I was unsure about seeing a man, but talking has helped. I told him about my online We Aten't Dead 'family', and he said whatever helped me was amazing. Slowly but surely, although I'm still a bit fried, I've started feeling better.

I came out of the first lot of sessions feeling completely drained. But they – and Neil – worked their magic. What with talking everything out and the happy pills, my head is in a much better place now.

Today was my last session. I'd got Neil a card to say thank you, but I wasn't sure what I could give him as a gift. Then the gods smiled and put me in the right place at the right time. My local library was having a book sale, and I got a copy of The Wit and Wisdom of Terry Pratchett for 50p.

Of course, a book was the perfect way to say thank you! Neil was really pleased – I do hope he enjoys the quotes and the puns.

Die Young - Black Sabbath

I love breaking rules. To be exact, I love to break Shouty Husband's rules.

All the silly things that were banned or not allowed, I now have – an alarm clock that ticks, for example. No red in the house? I've replaced all the mugs with new ones – red, yellow, and blue—and they're hanging from a pillar-box-red mug tree. I've even bought a red washing-up bowl.

I've got new bedding, a new duvet, new pillows, and a heavy bedspread. I've moved the living room furniture around, so it's how I want it. I've bought clothes I love, which Shouty Husband would hate and would never have let me keep. (If I picked clothes for myself and he didn't approve, back they'd go to the shop.)

It's taken a while to get things my way, but I've got there.

My house, my rules!

Pour Some Sugar on Me - Def Leppard

I've always been on the plump-to-fat side.

Shouty Husband always told me it didn't matter what I weighed—he'd always love me anyway. Well, that was a big, fat lie!

If anyone offered me cake when we were out together, or if I so much as looked at it, I'd get a look that said, 'You're on a diet. Don't argue with me, you won't win, and I'll remember and hold it against you.'

Sometimes I stood up to him, but I always ended up backing down. It was easier.

Whenever I got chocolates from the kids at school at the end of term or Christmas, I always gave them to my mum. I was allowed treats sometimes; Sunday evenings were fruit cake and custard. I wasn't a huge fan, to be honest. I did love his bread pudding, but that was incredibly fattening.

I don't run. I walk fast and wobble a lot. Shouty Husband used to tell everyone that. It was cruel, but that was how he was.

Though since Shouty Husband has left, I have actually lost some weight. Not through dieting or trying, though – just loss of appetite through the stress. I'm eating well, but with smaller portions and fewer carbs. Shouty Husband's staple diet was bacon, eggs, potatoes, cheese, and bread; he especially did a lot with potatoes and bread.

Well, today I had a bit of Stella's chocolate brownie – so rich and wonderful, I loved it. And in the morning, my eldest son is bringing me some Belgian chocolates he got for me in Brussels.

I might take forever to eat them, but I'll enjoy every one and won't feel the least bit guilty for doing so.

Happy Xmas (War is Over) - John Lennon

This year I have a Christmas tree. It's a big deal – in the last 23 years with Shouty Husband, we only had a Christmas tree twice.

Steve and I went out and picked the tree, and then we spent a fun Sunday afternoon putting it all together with pretty lights.

There's tinsel everywhere in the living room and dining room, in all kinds of colours. Nothing matches, and he'd hate it, but I love it!

In fact, the only bit of Christmas he enjoyed was having the week off work.

He never took holidays during the year, even when he had a full-time job. But at Christmas, he'd finish on Christmas Eve and not go back until after New Year's Day.

So this year, together with Steve, I cooked a roast chicken dinner with all the trimmings. I put out the good china and even used the tureens for the veg and potatoes, sod the amount of extra washing up! We put out place settings for Shouty Husband, David, and Mick and had a really good time.

If you'd told me this time last year that I'd be on my own and cooking a Christmas lunch, I would have laughed.

Take that, Shouty Husband – I can do more than just reheat, after all!

Du Hast - Rammstein

My baby turns 30 this week. Where on earth has the time gone? He was only tiny last week – I remember it clearly. Anyway, a big happy 30th birthday to you, Luke.

I do have some good memories, so here's the tale of the Great Ape and the Little Chimp.

Shouty Husband tells everybody about his lads and how proud he is of both of them. Luke is the closest thing Shouty Husband has to a son of his own, and they do have a genuinely strong bond.

If you ever wanted to know what mood Shouty Husband was in, you could just ask Luke. He could read him like a book, which was no easy feat for anyone else. Luke is autistic. He won't mind me sharing that; he tells everyone. It's not a problem for him or for us.

Shouty Husband taught Luke how to deal with the big bad world. He helped him develop his sarcasm, his humour, and his moral compass. Luke has a wicked sense of humour; he and Shouty Husband used to gang up on me, and I must admit, I loved it. When he got older, if Luke got too cheeky, I'd wag my finger at him and gently pull his beard.

But it wasn't always plain sailing for their relationship; they bashed heads sometimes as the old met the new. Still, Luke tells everybody that Shouty Husband is more of a dad to him than his real father.

So, the Great Ape and the little Chimp. Shouty Husband had long hair for years, halfway down his back, until he felt he was too old for that and shaved it all off.

Luke has had a beard since he was 18, and it really suits him. Anyway, the two of them would get together to use the hair clippers.

They'd stand in the dining room, both stripped to the waist, making a great hairy mess on my carpet. Shouty Husband was overweight and looked like a silverback gorilla, so Luke nicknamed him the Great Ape. In reply, Shouty Husband called Luke the Little Chimp. Watching the two of them go through their mutual hair-shaving ritual was like watching a nature documentary.

Luke still visits Shouty Husband. He gets advice and a helping hand when he needs it, and Shouty Husband tells Luke how to do the garden while he stands and watches. They're good for each other, and I hope that carries on. I won't interfere in their relationship – as long as Shouty Husband behaves himself.

Weak - Skunk Anansie

Shouty Husband never let me forget it when I got things wrong – not just big things but all the silly stuff. He loved to tell people about me having my moments.

He'd pick me up on my grammar when I mispronounced words and on my singing. I'm not a great singer, I know, but I like to sing along to the radio. He'd also shout at me in public for being too slow or too fast.

According to Shouty Husband, his smoking, toking, and drinking were my fault. I used to buy his beer daily, then weekly, as it was easier. He always had a cupboard full of beer. I also bought his baccy every week, but not his dope, though I was around when his dealer came.

Shouty Husband told me he was a self-righting ship, and he'd stop when his addictions got too much, but that would never happen as long as I bought his beer and his baccy. But how could I not? I bought it because he told me to, and if I hadn't, then he'd have made my life a misery.

Then the unthinkable happened. I could not find the beer he liked anywhere. I hunted everywhere with no joy. It had simply disappeared; there wasn't a can to be had. I was worried he'd make my life hell without his crutch, but as it goes, I was wrong. I did manage to buy his beer in bottles for the weekend, but he was dry during the week.

Then, after about a month, the cans appeared back in the shops. I told Shouty Husband, and he told me not to buy any during the week – so I didn't. I just bought his weekend beer. Then he brought home a four-pack during the week. And then he'd buy one whenever he fancied, and before I knew it, his drinking was back up to where it had been.

Then his health problems kicked in, related to his smoking and drinking, and again, this was all my fault. I was only a baby when he started smoking at eight years old), five when he started smoking dope, and eight when he started drinking – so I really don't think so. But no, silly me – I bought him what he demanded each week, that's why I'm to blame...

Anyway, now that he's gone, my house doesn't smell of fags or dope, and my recycling bin isn't full of empty beer cans, and that's how it will stay.

The Sound of Silence - Disturbed

Today is DD Day - David's Death Day. He has two death days – the official one and the day I found out he had died. It's a bit like the Queen having two birthdays. He is no more; he is a dead David—I'm not being strange. I'm paraphrasing Monty Python, which David loved and quoted often.

I wore rose-tinted glasses for 26 years when it came to Shouty Husband. The glass was scratched, and I needed a new pair, but they were comfortable, and I hate change, so I just carried on wearing them.

Then, a year ago, a crack appeared on one lens that I couldn't ignore. In two months, they'd finally be discarded forever.

I am a fan of opera, and as I've said, my mum has sayings for every occasion. So, let's say the voluptuous lady is in the dressing room putting her face on. Soon she'll be practising her scales.

We'll have to wait a while before she takes the stage and sings, though, as this account of my journey seems to have taken on Wagnerian proportions.

So, a year ago, was when I saw Shouty Husband's true colours, in glorious technicolour and surround sound. To use one of my mum's muddled sayings, I put my foot down with a firm hand, and things began to change.

A year on, I've got my head around the fact David is gone. Even though I will see him or speak with him again, he is still with me and always will be. He's in my heart. But I will never forgive Shouty Husband for not being there for me. I will never forgive him for making it clear I wasn't important enough for him to sit and listen to, to comfort, as I grieved for my best friend in the world. Shouty Husband would say everything was my fault; well, I know this wasn't. I needed Shouty Husband to be there for me, as my friend and my husband, and he was sadly lacking.

A little bit of me died that day, too. But the good that came out of it was the strength to change my life. So, thank you, David. Thank you for being you. A year after my world collapsed, I am doing the same as I was then – drinking a glass of wine and listening to good music after lighting a candle for David to see his way to Valhalla.

Except this time, I am not alone. David is smiling at me from one of the only two 2 photos I have of him. I have friends I can call. I have my parents and my boys.

You did not break me, Shouty Husband. I am no longer your property. I am now the purple-haired warrior with knobs on, and I am living my life for me and nobody else.

And I'm doing a damn good job of it, too.

Purple Electric Violin Concerto - Ed Alleyne-Johnson

Time is rather wibbly wobbly, and I feel like it's just been me and the mad moggies forever. Today, I am listening to one of Shouty Husband's favourite albums. I love it as it brings back happy memories.

I've cleaned my house, cooked a roast chicken dinner, and spoken to Jordan. I've had great music on and made as much noise as I liked.

I keep a photo of Shouty Husband that I talk at. It's not always a rant, and today was a good chat. I can give him the look, tell him about my day, and tell him how I feel. I find it very cathartic.

Today I told him I have nothing to beat myself up over and everything was not my fault, as he always insisted it was. I bent over backwards, but things would never have gotten better; they'd have only gotten worse.

I suppose his health problems would have caught up with him eventually, but until then, I'd just have been existing, not living – walking on eggshells as 55 years of fags and 48 years of dope took their toll. Not forgetting the 45 years of alcohol, either.

Shouty Husband has asthma, COPD, and diverticulitis, as well as paranoia.

Before he left, I was already checking out the options I had for getting help, as I knew that at some stage he wouldn't be able to carry on working. I love my job, but it pays peanuts. I needed to work out how I could manage to live with an invalid who'd hate his situation and take it out on me; I knew I couldn't do it alone.

Well, now I don't have to. I can breathe again. I feel alive for the first time in ages. I can smell the coffee, hear the birds, and literally feel myself unwinding. I'm my own person again.

Mother - Pink Floyd

By now, you'll have worked out that I married a man with huge problems. Shouty Husband was a narcissist. He was also emotionally and physically abusive and used to gaslight me.

Some people are wired wrong from birth. Others are damaged by the ones that are supposed to love, care for, and protect them.

Shouty Husband was damaged by the person who was supposed to nurture him, love him, and make him the man he was supposed to be. Instead, he ended up with a thoroughly messed-up head and no emotional sense of how to love and be loved.

Shouty Husband was always fair when he talked about his mum; for every bad memory he told me about, he tried to recall a good one.

In the 1950s, a lot of Irish men and women came to the UK to find work and a better standard of living. Shouty Husband's dad and sisters were among them. His dad met his mum at a dance and the rest, as they say, is history.

We did have a photo of his mum and dad at their wedding. She looked great, though she was four months pregnant; it was a shotgun wedding. I guess it was never going to end well.

Shouty Husband was a breech birth at home, and his mum said he caused problems from day one. His two sisters arrived within just under four years.

Shouty Husband was three years old when his dad disappeared from his life. He does remember seeing him just before his fifth birthday, when he was promised a bike, then that was it for 48 years.

Shouty Husband's mum became a single parent with an Irish surname in the 1960s. They were the lowest of the low as far as the rest of society was concerned. Naturally, this had a major effect on them.

Shouty Husband said he would go to school in the morning and find they were moving again when he got home because his dad had found them. They spent a lot of time being put up by friends until his mum got a private rental, where they lived until he was nine.

One of Shouty Husband's first memories was the cellar which flooded with heavy rain. It had steep concrete steps and was dark and full of spiders. As a punishment, when he was little, his mum would make him sit on the top step in the dark and lock the door. He couldn't move in case he fell down the steps – he'd have broken his neck if he was lucky and his back if he was not. He'd sit in the pitch black with the spiders for what felt like hours.

I'll try to balance the bad memories with the good too.

Shouty Husband had to be circumcised when he was three because his foreskin was too tight, and he got regular infections. He told the nurse there was no way he was wearing a nightie as only girls wore them, so he went into theatre naked rather than wear an operating gown.

Having his dressing changed involved him sitting in a bowl of warm water to loosen the gauze, then the area was cleaned, and the gauze was replaced. It did stop the infections, though.

Shouty Husband also has very bad eyes and was registered as blind when he was little. There were weekly trips to the eye hospital where they'd put drops into his eyes that stung badly. If he cried, they had to wait a couple of hours to do them again.

So, on the way to the hospital, Shouty Husband's mum would take him past the toy shop so he could look at the Dinky cars. If he didn't cry, his mum would then buy him the toy car of his choice on the way back. He loved cars, so this worked well.

His middle sister, Sarah, was the runt of the litter, as he put it. She was ill a lot. Damp houses and no spare money for coal meant Shouty Husband and his sisters have chest problems to this day. Sarah got pneumonia every winter and Shouty Husband remembers walking up to the children's hospital every day to visit, no matter what the weather. It was about a two-mile walk, but bus fares were expensive.

There's no denying Shouty Husband was a handful as a child and his mum had another nasty punishment she used.

She'd get a garden cane, grab the wrist of whichever child was in for it, and make them run around in a circle while she hit them across the back of the legs. If they were lucky, it was only one circuit. The worst Shouty Husband ever got was four – he said the backs of his thighs were raw and bleeding by the time she finished.

Shouty Husband had grandparents, aunts and uncles who lived a bus ride away. Every Saturday morning, they went as a family to meet his nan at the café in his hometown. They always had toast with real butter and a cuppa before going shopping in the market and then back to Nan's for the afternoon and some tea. They'd get the bus home after listening to the day's football results.

Shouty Husband loved his grandad, who was the only male influence in his life. He was retired and spent a lot of time in his huge garden, where he had two greenhouses and grew prize-winning chrysanthemums. Shouty Husband was allowed in the greenhouse – this was a really big deal as his older cousin, who lived right next door, was not.

Going to his grandparents' house was a real treat for Shouty Husband because it was out of the city. He could play along the old railway lines and said it was like being in the countryside.

One Saturday evening, the bus didn't turn up, and he, his mum and sisters were taken home on his uncle's motorbike and sidecar. This was the start of his love of motorbikes.

Shouty Husband has always got up with the sun. Even with blackout curtains, as soon as dawn starts to break, he's awake. One of his first real memories was when he was five years old and 'escaped'.

The sun was up so he let himself out of the house and went for a walk. It was very safe where he lived, and as it was about 5 am, there was nobody about.

Eventually, a policeman found him. Shouty Husband had had his name and address drummed into him, so he was able to recite it. The policeman took him home and got his Mum out of bed.

She was horrified, but the policeman wasn't cross with her. He came back after his shift and put a big, heavy-duty bolt on the top of the door to stop it from happening again.

Another of his memories is when he learned nobody will help you – you have to do things for yourself. He'd have been about eight years old and in junior school. Because he was of Irish descent and from a one-parent family, he was bullied.

Five boys beat him up quite badly outside school one day. He went home and, in tears, told his mum what had happened. Her response was to shut him outside the back door and tell him he couldn't go back in until he'd sorted out every one of those boys.

He knew she meant it, so, as he put it, he hunted them down and hurt them all badly. He did miss one but got him at school the next day.

The headmaster called his mum in and told her Shouty Husband was an animal. In response, she pulled Shouty Husband into the office, pulled up his shirt and spun him around so the headmaster could see his bruises. Who's the animal, she wanted to know.

The bullies learnt that if they took on Shouty Husband as a group, he'd find them individually and hurt them ten times worse. Having a reputation as a psycho – his words – meant anyone with any sense left Shouty Husband alone. It's fair to say he's used being a complete head case to his advantage over the years.

I Wanna Be Somebody – Wasp

The house Shouty Husband remembers as his first proper home was condemned for slum clearance. Even though it was private property, the council rehoused the whole road into council houses.

So, along with the rest of the street, Shouty Husband and his family had to move. They left behind the terraced house with a toilet in the yard and no bathroom; 'bath night' meant a tin bath in front of the range on a Friday.

The new place was a brick-built council house, so they'd never have to move again. It had indoor plumbing, so his mum was over the moon. There was a huge garden, too, so she could have a vegetable patch. Shouty Husband was nine when they moved there; that means his mum has been in that house for 52 years.

It was cold, though; this was before the days of central heating as standard. There was a coke-burning potbellied stove in the kitchen, which produced gallons of boiling hot water and kept the back room warm.

Shouty Husband said he lived in the bath as it was the only way to keep warm.

His bedroom was at the front and was freezing, and Shouty Husband used to wet the bed, partly because of the cold and partly because of the stress caused by his mum and her rules. To deal with this, he was prescribed Valium, which he loved. But the doctors then didn't wean you off drugs slowly; they just stopped giving them, and you went cold turkey. As a result, Shouty Husband struggled with his mental health.

One time, Shouty Husband's mum needed knee surgery and had to stay in hospital. As his nan worked full time, one evening, the neighbour cooked tea for Shouty Husband and his sisters. The next night, the neighbour couldn't feed them, so Shouty Husband decided he'd cook for them all before his nan got there. Along with his sisters, he'd been taught to cook, sew, knit, embroider, black-lead a range, and get by on a budget of nothing. So, he thought he could easily handle making a meal.

Shouty Husband knew his mum put a pinch of bicarb in with white cabbage, so he did the same. Except he added half a tub. Neither he nor his sister Paula ate it, but Sarah loved it. She ate everybody else's as well as her own and ended up in the loo all evening. Shouty Husband still chuckles when he tells this story.

Shouty Husband's mum is of Welsh heritage. She's only 4ft 10ins tall, but she's fearsome; she doesn't have a fuse; she has an on-off switch (just like her son).

She came home from the hospital on crutches and with, apparently, a 'wicked' scar. One day, while Shouty Husband was playing with his cars in the back garden, he heard the front door being rattled like it was going to come off its hinges.

It was a neighbour from a street round, standing on the doorstep effing and jeffing that Shouty Husband had kicked his dustbin over. Now, Shouty Husband was no angel, but this time he'd done nothing wrong. His mum called him in from the back garden and told the man he'd been there for the last three hours. The man was very rude in response and implied she was a woman of loose morals.

That did it. Shouty Husband's mum chased the man down the road on her crutches, threatening him with a world of pain if she caught him. Shouty Husband said all the neighbours could see his mum protecting her family, and it made him so proud of her.

The neighbour got his six months later when, late one night, Shouty Husband put all his windows through with a catapult. Nobody had a go at his mum and got away with it. Soon everybody knew to leave her alone, or after they'd long forgotten all about it, there'd be consequences.

Shouty Husband is dangerous. He'll hold a grudge forever and always pays back any perceived slight to him or his family.

Summertime - Janis Joplin

Some of you will know how hard it is to be a single parent. Back when Shouty Husband was a lad, being a single parent of three children and surviving on National Assistance, welfare payments from the government, was incredibly difficult. On top of that, having an Irish surname meant other parents wouldn't let their kids play with Shouty Husband and his sister.

His mum was terrified of having social services involved in her life as they could take away her children. She brainwashed them as to what they should do.

If anything happened to her, he should stay with his sisters. If anyone tried to separate them, he should kick off big time and cause as big a fuss as he could. He must never repeat anything that went on at home outside the house.

When Shouty Husband went back to school after the summer holidays, all the kids were told to write a story about what they'd done over the summer. He always wrote, in capital letters, 'ASK MY MUM!'

They couldn't afford holidays, but Shouty Husband and his sisters did go on one.

The kids all needed new shoes for school, so his mum applied for a grant from the Welfare.

A lady was sent to see them, and while she was there, she asked about holidays. No, said Shouty Husband's mum. They'd never had a holiday.

So, they also ended up getting a fortnight in a caravan at Brean Sands in Somerset, paid for by social services. They even covered the train fare.

Shouty Husband said his mum put bits of shopping aside, so they had food to take with them. The whole family had the best two weeks of sun, sea and sand.

Shouty Husband's mum picked on Sarah more than she did on him and his little sister.

One afternoon, he watched his mum break plates over Sarah's back. He didn't know what she'd done, but whatever it was, she didn't deserve that.

He's always felt guilty because he did nothing to stop it; he was 13, so Sarah was 11. But he knew if he did, his mum would have lashed out at him. He didn't want to be a coward, but the backlash would have lasted for days.

Sarah also has an alpha personality, which is why she and her brother clash so badly. One day, when he got home from school, he found she was a bloody, beaten mess. She was just 11 years old, but somebody had beaten her very badly. Their mum told Shouty Husband to go and sort it, to give whoever it was the same amount of pain. The problem was, Sarah had been beaten up by a girl, an older one, but still a girl. And his mum was adamant Shouty Husband should never hit a girl, although it was ok to bully his sisters.

But, with his mum's blessing, he went out to find the girl who had hurt his sister. He found her brother first and hurt him. Then he found the girl with a gang of older boys. He would have taken them all on, but they were sensible – they let him hurt the girl. He was never happy about it, but his mum had told him to. If he hadn't done it, he'd have been punished.

Shouty Husband's mum did her best at Christmas, but money was always tight. One year, a neighbour with older children had a toy clear out; many had hardly been played with. Shouty Husband said he and his sisters had never had so many presents; he remembered them all and played with and kept them for years. Life wasn't always bad, he said.

Well, that takes us up to when Shouty Husband hit the teenage years – and then it all went to hell in a handbag.

Indiana Wants Me - R Dean Taylor

Shouty Husband wanted to go to the catholic school when he reached 11, but his mum wouldn't hear of it and sent him to the local secondary school instead.

He made the best of what he had and got into the 'A' stream and top set for all subjects. They pushed him, so he did well and didn't get bored. A bored, Shouty Husband is the worst thing in the world – that's when he gets into trouble.

Then, on Sarah's birthday, his world came crashing down.

It was a January night, dark and drizzly. Shouty Husband was pushing his bike across the road on his way back from the shop. He didn't see the car coming until it was too late.

He had a Pott's fracture and a dislocated ankle in one leg, and his other knee swelled up like a balloon. He ended up in hospital, terrified of what his mother would say.

After surgery to pin and plate his ankle, the hospital decided to feed him. It was the worst thing they could have done – he was still full of anaesthetic. He thought they'd given him cod roe, which he loved, but it was actually fishcakes. He was violently sick and has never eaten fishcakes again to this day.

Shouty Husband spent nine months with both legs in plaster and having multiple surgeries. They could fix the fracture, but then the dislocation would pop out.

One day he refused to go into surgery again and escaped down the corridor on his crutches – he was a whiz on them by now. His mum had to chase after him, struggling to keep up.

The main problem was that Shouty Husband wasn't allowed to go back to school; they couldn't have him there going up and down the stairs with both legs in plaster and on crutches.

Back then, there was no such thing as sending work home, so Shouty Husband fell behind and missed all the end-of-year tests. When he finally went back, he was put in what he called 'the dunce's class'. He asked if he could have the work the top sets were doing so he could catch up quickly and be moved, but the headmaster said no.

As a result, Shouty Husband spent the rest of his time at school fighting the education system - but more of that later.

The next step in the making of Shouty Husband came when his mother got involved with Joe, the man who became his stepdad.

After 14 years of trying, Shouty Husband's mother had managed to track down his dad and divorced him. (Here's what a nice man he was – every time she found him and tried to get child maintenance from him, he was happy to go to prison instead.)

So, there she was, 28 years old with three children. She wanted a man in her life. It was a shame it was Joe.

Once he appeared, Shouty Husband's world went from bad to worse.

Joe was not a good man, and Shouty Husband's grandparents did not approve of the relationship. So, they give their daughter a choice – Joe, or her family. She decided the man was worth losing her family for.

This was terrible for Shouty Husband. He adored his granddad, who was the only strong male influence he had in his life, his moral compass, and the person he turned to when life got too bad.

I was told Joe wasn't too bad until he managed to get a ring on Shouty Husband's mum's finger. He still wasn't who Shouty Husband would have chosen for a stepdad, though.

Shouty Husband's mum and Joe decided that, as they were going to get married, they should have a baby. That meant Shouty Husband's extended family cut them out, and instead, he got a very bad man who didn't want him or his sisters around. When his Mum got pregnant, Shouty Husband was pleased—he'd always wanted a brother and hoped the baby would be a boy. It was, but sadly, he only lived for 24 hours.

Shouty Husband went to the hospital to see them but was told he wasn't allowed in, so he threatened to make enough noise to wake the dead, never mind all the babies. His mum heard him making a fuss and told the ward sister he meant it, so Shouty Husband was allowed in under sufferance.

The news of his baby brother's death got round school, and the Buckley twins thought it would be fun to spread the story that it had happened because the baby was a bastard.

Shouty Husband wasn't going to school much at this stage; he was spending more time at home. He went in now, though. The twins didn't see what hit them when Shouty Husband went on the rampage – he got them both in an empty classroom and took out all his anger and frustrations on them.

His life had become terrible, and someone had to pay the price. After that, his attendance at school was even more hit-and-miss.

Bike - Pink Floyd

The one thing Shouty Husband loved was push bikes; as a teenager, he could build one from the ground up. He got into cyclo-cross racing and was very good at it, becoming a member of a team. It was a way to harness his anger, and winning was always at the forefront of his mind.

However, it was a sport that cost money, and he didn't have any. So, he needed to find a way to get some. Shouty Husband was always good at chasing money.

There was no money at home to buy him decent clothes or even to make sure there was plenty of food; there was a lot of making do. So Shouty Husband decided to rely on his own skills.

He did paper rounds and took everybody else's if they didn't turn up. He got a Saturday job in a garage, sweeping up and filling cars in the days when there was pump service. Those were the legal jobs, the ones that paid for his hobbies and his clothes. Shouty Husband did love his clothes.

Then there were the others, the ones that didn't make money but did make life easier for him and his sisters. He'd take a bucket with holes drilled in the bottom and a length of rope attached to the handle and go down the canal. Then he'd throw it in the water behind the coal yard. When the barges delivered coal, some would always fall into the water. Shouty Husband would pull out enough to fill a sack, then load it into an old pram and take it home. His mum would never ask where it came from, but she was glad to have it. Shouty Husband would do this all year round, so the coal house was full, and the house was warm.

And then there was the hooky stuff, like collecting copper wire from houses that were being cleared as part of urban slum renewal. The wire was stored at the electric yard, but it wasn't hard to get through the fence. Shouty Husband would 'borrow' it, burn off the insulating wire on the range at home, and then sell it to whichever scrapyard paid the most.

At this point, he was making more money than his stepdad and wore all the latest fashions. He even paid the electric bill when his mum was broke; she was wise enough to turn a blind eye to his shenanigans.

Crazy - Gnarls Barkley

Shouty Husband always said his mum had a cruel streak. Do you remember washing tongs? I do. (If not, then feel free to 'do the Google', as my mum says.)

If Shouty Husband was being cheeky while she was doing the washing, his mum would snap the tongs over his nipple and twist it. He'd be on his knees before she stopped, and he still has a scar to this day.

One of Shouty Husband's money-making schemes was to breed mice, as he'd worked out that the pet shop would pay him for them. The champagne ones made the most, so he soon worked out how to breed more of those; Shouty Husband loved science.

He also kept newts, not to make money but just because he liked them. I've told you Shouty Husband has a cruel streak and is one to bear a grudge; well, his mother was even worse. She took revenge to a whole new level.

One day, Shouty Husband came home to find all his newts dead - putting washing-up liquid in the water will do that to them. Somehow, the mice had all escaped from their cages, even though they were in a locked shed.

Then there was the wet fish incident. Have you heard the expression, 'hit round the face with a piece of wet fish'? If not, don't try this at home, kids.

Shouty Husband said something to his mum about being hit round the face with a piece of wet fish, and she happened to have some in her hands at the time. So, you've guessed it, she hit him round the face with it. It wouldn't have hurt so much if she'd already descaled it, but because she hadn't, it ripped the skin on his face. She laughed and still served up the fish for tea.

If I'd ever wondered where Shouty Husband got his cruel streak from, I know now.

Mama Weer All Crazee Now - Slade

When he was 13, Shouty Husband hated being at home; to his mind, standing on a street corner in all weathers was a better option.

The school youth club was great in the winter evenings - a couple of hours in the warm with a glass of squash thrown in. One evening, a local band went to play a gig there – Ambrose Slade had yet to make it big as the one and only Slade. Shouty Husband loved them and bought all their records.

Shouty Husband started smoking fags when he was eight years old. He was always clever at getting people to do what he wanted, so he had plenty of ways to fuel his addiction.

The working girls used to hang out at the bottom of his road, near the pub and the playing fields. It was a small red-light area compared to some, but as far as I know, it's still there.

Shouty Husband found that if he asked the girls for a fag, they might give him one as him hanging around put their potential customers off. If any of them told him where to go, he said he'd go and call 999 from the phone box – yes, it was that long ago – and tell the police they'd approached him. As that meant the police would come out and move the girls on, handing over a fag was the easy option.

Shouty Husband has an addictive personality, so he's been hooked on cigarettes for the past 53 years. When he got a job at the local newsagent, he'd spend his wages on them until he discovered the old stock in the back of the shop. This was the brands that didn't sell well or had been discontinued. Shouty Husband asked if he could buy them instead – at a lower price, of course. He worked his way through the Capstan Full Strength to Senior Service, and they must have been disgusting – they were old and dry. But still, Shouty Husband smoked them.

At school, he joined smokers' corner, where the rite of passage was being branded on the back of the hand with a fag burn. Shouty Husband's reputation preceded him, though, so nobody insisted on doing this to him. Nobody wanted to smoke his fags, either, as they were too strong, so both he and his cigarettes got a free pass. Smokers' corner became his home away from home.

He smokes roll-ups now, rolling them backwards as he just can't do it the right way. I was spending £60 a week on his tobacco when he left; as far as I know, he hasn't kicked the habit yet.

The Harder They Come - Jimmy Cliff

There were a few friends whose parents would let Shouty Husband go round, and he considered their homes a safe haven. One of those places was Brenda Millward's house; as Shouty Husband put it, she was as common as muck but had a heart of gold.

Brenda was on her own but had a Jamaican boyfriend. She was also a short-term foster parent, taking in black and mixed-race kids that nobody else wanted. This was the early 1970s, and racism was rampant.

Brenda understood that Shouty Husband needed a safe space and opened her home and her heart to him. She could never feed him as money was tight, but a cup of tea went down wonders.

Every Friday night, Brenda let her boyfriend and his friends have the run of her back room to play dominoes, drink rum and Red Stripe beer, listen to reggae music, and smoke dope. It was a place where they could safely be themselves.

Shouty Husband and Brenda's son would keep the rum glasses full and, in return, were educated about some really great music that he still loves today.

When the spiffs burned down to a couple of puffs, Shouty Husband would pinch them out of the ashtray when nobody was looking and share them with his mate. So, an addictive personality who already smoked tobacco discovered that dope calmed him down. The rest is history. A love of great reggae, ska, and dope started at 13 years old and endures to this day.

The Teacher - Magnum

Years ago, there was an advert to encourage more people to go into teaching. It featured famous people remembering great teachers. For Shouty Husband, it was his form tutor and deputy head, Mr Brucknall, his headmaster, Mr Hedges, and Mr Mallen.

Shouty Husband nicknamed Mr Hedges 'Batman' as he always wore a black gown. They may not have seen eye to eye, but Shouty Husband always talked about him with respect.

Mr Mallen was Shouty Husband's science teacher and the one who 'saved' him.

These men provided the male influence that helped Shouty Husband get through school when it wasn't a good place for him. He spent more time away from the place than in it until, at the age of 15, he found a way to be there and learn that worked for him. Shouty Husband clashed with any form of authority, and his form teacher, Mr Brucknall, was never happy with him. Things came to a head when Shouty Husband had a class with a newly qualified teacher. He'd gotten to the classroom first and chosen a seat at the front, ready to watch an educational film.

But the teacher told him he couldn't sit there; he had to go to the back. Shouty Husband refused; the teacher told him to move and, in the process, called him 'four eyes'.

Everyone went quiet. You didn't say that to Shouty Husband; he was sensitive about wearing glasses as he had to have the NHS ones with the thick frames and looked like Joe 90 in them. There was no money for expensive, stylish ones.

Next, the teacher grabbed Shouty Husband by his very expensive Shetland wool jumper. The class drew a collective breath and waited. Shouty Husband gave a final warning to let him go, but the teacher didn't listen and hung on.

He never saw the chair coming till he hit the ground. Shouty Husband then walked to the headmaster's office, found Mr Brucknall, and told him what he'd done. School policy at the time was not to suspend Shouty Husband as he was a ward of the court at that point and had to be in school. Instead, they would cane him.

Shouty Husband said if Mr Brucknall tried to cane him, he'd go back to the classroom and seriously hurt the new teacher. Mr Brucknall knew he meant it; he'd seen first-hand what happened when Shouty Husband was riled.

So, Mr Brucknall went to find Mr Hedges, and then Shouty Husband's mum was called in. Mr Mallen was there too, as Shouty Husband always went to his classes.

The upshot was that Shouty Husband spent the next two years in the science block, helping the lab technician. Mr Mallen was an old-style schoolteacher who'd clip you round the ear if you played up; he had huge hands, too. He only hit Shouty Husband once, and that was enough; Shouty Husband never played him up again.

Mr Mallen tapped into Shouty Husband's passion for physics and made sure he was kept busy and out of trouble. He taught him how to do weird experiments and furthered his love of science.

How Can I Tell You? - Cat Stevens?

The first time Shouty Husband got what you might call 'drunk drunk,' it was on dark rum. He drank the whole bottle and was extremely ill. Never mention dark rum in his presence – he still goes a funny shade of green.

He was 16 at the time, and after he made it home, he fell over in the hall. His mum wasn't happy and decided the best way to deal with a drunk teenager was to beat him across the shoulders with a metal coat hanger while he lay there retching.

Shouty Husband was convinced he was throwing up blood, rather than the dark rum, and thought he was dying. Afterwards, as well as having the mother of all hangovers, he was black and blue from where his mum had hit him.

That was also pretty much when Shouty Husband worked out that life was not going to plan. He realised that when push came to shove, his mum would always pick Joe over her children.

Joe liked the idea of having a son to carry on his name, and Shouty husband got a little brother who he loved and looked after. He did have a good side sometimes.

Living day to day with a toddler wasn't good for Joe, though, and he was a tyrant towards anything that upset his life! As a result, Shouty Husband spent a lot of time looking after his brother, diverting Joe's attention away from him.

Joe taught Shouty Husband how to box. They used to spar regularly – it was a way for Joe to get close and dig Shouty Husband hard in the ribs. One day, he let his guard down, and Shouty Husband hit him hard in the solar plexus. Joe went down like a sack of spuds and then threw up, all in front of Shouty Husband's mum, who wet herself laughing. I warned you, she told Joe, that one day he'd hurt you. Shouty Husband's days at home were numbered from that moment.

Then his little brother started crying, as toddlers do. Joe, still riled up, went to 'give him something to cry about,' but Shouty Husband wasn't having that and stepped in.

Joe wasn't going to take that lying down. He punched Shouty Husband and broke his nose, sending blood flying everywhere. Then he threw Shouty Husband out of the house and told him never to go back. His mum watched the whole thing and backed Joe up, which was why, at the age of 16, Shouty Husband ended up with a broken nose, no home, and nowhere to go. He spent a few nights sleeping in various doorways until the mums of a few of his friends let him sofa surf.

As he was working, Shouty Husband managed to get a bedsit of his own, complete with hot and cold running rats. The other flat was used by a pair of prostitutes who took Shouty Husband under their wing and kept an eye on him. He might have thought he was a hard man, but really, he was just a kid who'd suddenly realised his mum didn't care whether he lived or died. That was a hard lesson to learn, and it shaped the way he would live his life afterwards.

At the end of the month, his mum found him and asked him to come home. It wasn't because she cared; it was because she knew he got paid monthly, and she needed the money due to Joe's boozing and gambling.

He did go home, as Joe had been taking an unhealthy interest in Shouty Husband's sisters, and he was worried about them. An uneasy truce existed, and life went on, but Shouty Husband never got over his mum rejecting him, and neither forgave nor forgot.

Violence - Mott The Hoople

Shouty Husband had attitude in spades and a massive superiority complex. It got him into lots of trouble over the years, but at 16, he discovered he wasn't invincible.

Ok, so this is a very English thing – the pop man. Most areas had one. He'd travel round in his truck, selling fizzy drinks in big bottles – flavours like American cream soda, dandelion and burdock, and apple.

Shouty Husband got a job at the pop yard when he was 16 as a driver's mate, dropping off orders, collecting the money, and having a laugh with customers. It paid well, and he was happy.

Then he got on the wrong side of an older black man in his 40s who was known as Blackjack. He didn't find this cocky young upstart funny at all.

One day, after a particularly heated argument, Blackjack had had enough. He took a pop bottle, broke it, and pushed the jagged edge t into Shouty Husband's stomach. Apparently, being stabbed doesn't hurt, according to Shouty Husband. Watching your intestines fall out is interesting, and you don't feel a thing. Adrenaline is a truly amazing hormone!

After pushing his own intestines back into his body, Shouty Husband rushed at Blackjack, pushing him backwards into the pot-bellied wood-burning stove that was always running at full burn. He bent Blackjack over it, so his back was against the metal. It took three big men to drag him off.

Then, of course, the ambulances and police came, and Shouty husband and Blackjack were taken to hospital. Shouty Husband said the pain came about an hour later, but he held his intestines in and wouldn't let the ambulance men touch him.

The doctor who sewed him up did an amazing job, and after staying in hospital for a night under duress, Shouty Husband was allowed home with antibiotics and instructions on what to do if anything went wrong.

Blackjack had third-degree burns and needed skin grafts.

'Don't mess with Shouty Husband,' everyone said afterwards.

Shouty Husband still has the scar. Doctors always think it's from liver surgery, and he enjoys seeing the looks on their faces when he tells them it was a broken bottle. After that, you wouldn't go at Shouty Husband with a knife, or he'd hurt you.

Action - Sweet

The Tavern in the Town was well-known as a biker's pub. Shouty Husband was a regular as a teenager, and it was also one of the places where the Hell's Angels drank.

Shouty Husband was on nodding terms with some of them, but otherwise, he stayed out of their way.

Now, before you get to join the Angels, you must be a prospect. As Shouty Husband – and, more importantly, his reputation – was well known in the local pubs, it made him a magnet for every wannabe to have a go.

One prospect had had a few run-ins with Shouty Husband previously and lost big time, but because he was with the Angels, he decided to play to the cheap seats.

One of Shouty Husband's talents is to goad people. He pointed out to everyone in the pub that the prospect was only being gobby because he had backup from the Angels. One-on-one, he'd be beaten again, no doubt.

One Angel said they wouldn't do anything; the guy was a prospect and hadn't earned any respect. It gave Shouty Husband the green light.

It was a quick fight. The other guy ended up flat on his back over the pinball machine and was no longer a prospect.

The Angels asked Shouty Husband if he fancied trying out as a prospect, but he declined. He may have been a wild child, but he was self-aware; he knew he'd end up either dead or in prison.

Dedicated Follower of Fashion - The Kinks

Shouty Husband was immensely proud of his hair, which was long and blond with pre-Raphaelite curls that fell halfway down his back. He was also something of a clothes horse and always wore the latest fashions; in his own words, he was the bee's knees.

Always looking for ways to push the envelope, in 1970s Wolverhampton, he did so by tying his hair into a ponytail with a pink ribbon.

He knew somebody would make a comment about his sexuality, and that was all the excuse he needed to fight. He was addicted to the rush of adrenaline and serotonin that came with it.

He'd pull the ribbon out, shake his hair loose, and needle the other guy to start fighting – or, if he was sensible, to opt for 'flight' instead.

Word soon got around about the pink ribbon, so Shouty Husband started wearing a pink shirt. With his blond hair, fair skin, and oh-so-blue eyes, it really suited him. The ladies loved it, and he was in his element.

Shouty Husband would walk around like he owned the road because, in his mind, he did, and nobody was going to tell him differently.

The Spirit of Man – Jeff Wayne, War of the Worlds

As a teenager, Shouty Husband's tipple of choice was bitter with a splash of lime. The laws are much stricter now, but back then, pubs tended to turn a blind eye to underage drinkers as long as they were quiet.

His nickname in his local, which has since been converted into houses, was 'Black Bits'. This was because he complained his pint had black bits floating in it. Turns out there was nothing in his pint; he was just a bit drunk, but after he made a fuss, the name stuck.

Shouty Husband enjoyed drinking alone as well as with friends, and he liked to drink in the gay pubs in Wolverhampton because the beer was good.

He was something of a gay man's wet dream. He'd grown into his 5ft 7ins height, had that lovely long blond hair, and was slim-hipped with a great bum.

He always made it clear he was straight, but there was always someone ready to buy him a drink, even when he said he couldn't afford to buy one back.

Actually, Shouty Husband only ever got into trouble once. He'd had a skinful, and the guy who was buying cornered him in the loos and wouldn't take no for an answer; a nodding acquaintance had to come to his rescue.

After that, Shouty Husband became friends with Tony, who was very macho. He was also careful never to get too drunk in a gay pub again.

Coming Home - Scorpions

'No, son, but you meet it halfway.' Shouty Husband's mum on being told he didn't go looking for trouble.

Shouty Husband told me the best way to deal with people was to get inside their heads, and he could be very cruel.

Every week, he'd go to one pub with the sole intention of having a fight. He had a long-term grudge against the local hard man – no idea why; it could have been anything. So Shouty Husband offered him out.

Every week he was beaten, but every week he went back for more. The other guy couldn't understand why Shouty Husband kept taking the punishment, so he asked him.

Shouty Husband replied that one day he would beat him and beat him badly.

That night, as usual, the hard man and Shouty Husband fought. But this time, Shouty Husband won. He'd gotten into his adversary's head and made him feel vulnerable. That gave Shouty Husband the chance to destroy him.

Shouty Husband was exceptionally good at getting into people's heads. He was good at fighting, too.

I Fought the Law and the Law Won - The Clash

By his own admission, Shouty Husband was a wild teenager who ran with some bad boys.

When he was 17, he got caught riding in a stolen car and was sentenced to three months in a detention centre. At the time, that was considered to be a 'short, sharp shock,' kind of punishment. It worked for Shouty Husband; 45 years later, and he can still remember his inmate number.

Shouty Husband has a pedantic streak, which can get him into trouble. He refused to call the prison officers 'sir' on the grounds they hadn't been knighted. Instead, he would only call them by their names, which didn't go down well and meant he became a target.

At the time, he had hair down to his waist, and they cut it off. Then they took away his tobacco. On one occasion, an officer took offence at this refusal to play the game and got up in Shouty Husband's face while he was standing next to his bed waiting for a check. (The officers used to make sure everything was neat and tidy.)

Shouty Husband gets even more aggressive when he hasn't got his baccy; he made some smart comment, and the officer pushed him over the bed, resulting in Shouty Husband hitting his head on the metal bedside table.

He was put in solitary confinement as a punishment. Later, the officer concerned opened the cell door and suggested

Shouty Husband step outside to sort the problem out. As he wasn't wearing his uniform, Shouty Husband knew there'd be at least two more officers waiting to give him a good kicking, so he declined. Instead, he said, the officer could come in.

The officer thought better of it; Shouty Husband had nothing to lose and would have destroyed him.

Afterwards, Shouty Husband asked to see the governor and said he wanted to see his solicitor and submit a formal complaint against the officer. He knew his rights; they couldn't refuse. Instead, the governor suggested a compromise. The officer was nearing retirement, so if Shouty Husband dropped the complaint, the governor would make sure he was let out when his time was up; there'd be no addition to his punishment.

The officer went on gardening leave, and Shouty Husband was duly freed on Christmas Eve. While he was getting ready for a well-deserved piss-up, he found what he thought was a spot in his armpit and asked his mum to squeeze it.

Turned out it wasn't a spot; Shouty Husband had caught chickenpox. By the next day, he was covered head to toe and was really ill for two weeks. Christmas was cancelled.

Don't Go Breaking My Heart - Elton John and Kiki Dee

Well, you've made it this far, and now it's time to start introducing the supporting cast. You'll meet Vinnie, Karen, and the first Mrs Shouty Husband, Jinx.

I'm a firm believer in second chances, and Shouty Husband was definitely given a second chance to do something with his life. Shouty Husband had a job in a factory, working with metal. He enjoyed it and worked hard, taking every bit of overtime he could get. He was chasing money - he wanted a life.

Then, without warning, he found his job was being moved out of the area, and his world came crashing down.

The town of Telford came into being in the late 1960s. Before that, it was a cluster of little villages ripe for expansion.

New industry arrived, and big estates were built to house people who came to the area from Birmingham, Wolverhampton, and as far away as Scotland.

Telford offered jobs that came with homes. Bosses were offered cheap rents to open factories in the area. This was why Shouty Husband's job was moving. He wasn't sure what it would mean for him, but he decided to have a ride over.

He stopped at what is now Holmer Lake and looked at the new houses and flats that had been built. He loved how much green space there was – it was clean, no smog, and not a back-to-back house in sight. It was his idea of heaven.

Luckily for Shouty Husband, his boss knew he was a good worker and offered him a brand new flat with a job. All he had to do was move the 15 miles out of Wolverhampton.

Shouty Husband jumped at the chance, and, in May 1976, he moved to Brookside.

It was a fresh start.

Nobody knew him, so he could reinvent himself. And every weekend, he could go home and stay at his mum's, as the new place was on a good bus route.

The estate was clean, and since everybody had moved there from other areas and it was all new to all of them, there was a great sense of community. Every family received a welcome letter with useful information like phone numbers and directions to the doctor's surgery and the opening times of local shops and the community centre.

Shouty Husband loved his new home and soon made his presence felt.

When he was 18, Shouty Husband's best friend was Vincent, otherwise known as Vinnie.

Shouty Husband was something of an unknown quantity on the estate, as he'd only just moved to the area. The local hard lads weren't sure what to make of him.

They knew Vinnie, though, and he became Shouty Husband's first proper friend in the place. His mouth tended to get him into trouble, and Shouty Huband would sort it out. This meant he soon got the reputation of being someone who liked to fight and was more than capable of doing so.

It helped that he was a stranger; Shouty Husband made it known very quickly that it wasn't a good idea to kick his kennel, and people soon adopted the 'leave the nutter alone' attitude.

Still, there's always one who wants to have a go. Shouty Husband beat him, big time, in front of a crowd. So, he came back for a second go and lost again.

Teenage boys full of drink don't have the cleverest ideas. Even when they've been humiliated twice by an interloper, they still think they can come out on top.

On Friday nights, Shouty Husband and Vinnie always went to the local recreation centre for a piss-up. And there it was that Stupid Boy, who'd already lost twice in previous run-ins with Shouty Husband, decided the third time's the charm. After a run-in with Shouty Husband in the bar, he decided to follow him and Vinnie home.

Stupid Boy had worked out that he couldn't win in a straight fight, so he had a carving knife when he thumped on Shouty Husband's door. You've already learned about Shouty Husband's view on knives – come at him with one, and he will kill you.

Stupid Boy didn't know what hit him. Literally. And repeatedly. The neighbours called the police, Stupid Boy was taken to hospital, and Shouty Husband had a night in the cells. He was later charged with grievous bodily harm (GBH), to which he pleaded not guilty, claiming self-defence.

At that time, if you were on a low wage, you could claim legal aid. A young, hungry solicitor was assigned to Shouty Husband, and the way he put across his defence was nothing short of brilliant.

'An Englishman's home is his castle, and Mr Shouty Husband was defending his castle as is his right under law. The only reason that Mr Shouty Husband is here today is that he could defend himself better than Mr Stupid Boy could attack him!'

Shouty Husband walked from court a free man. His reputation grew, and Stupid Boy left the area. As for that hungry young solicitor, he's now a barrister.

Shouty Husband always said, 'the only person he was afraid of was himself,' because he knew the damage he could do to another human being.

Shouty Husband had been around the block a few times and always described himself as a tart. Sex put him in control, which he loved, and he wanted to be the best of the best. He was extremely competitive.

And, frankly, he was amazing in bed—at least until an excess of fags, dope, booze, and a life not-so-well-lived stopped it.

Shouty Husband and I had the same approach to sex. We were try-sexual – we'd try anything once, do it again if we liked it, and if we didn't, it was something to cross off the list.

Although he'd had plenty of girlfriends during his teenage years, he didn't lose his virginity until he was 18.

One night, a young mother of 23 decided Shouty Husband's cheek and self-importance were worth taking home. She offered him the world on a plate, and Shouty Husband was always too polite to refuse.

Finally, he could put into practise everything he'd read about in Fiesta and Razzle. He was never one for just sticking it in and wiggling it about.

Afterwards, the woman told him she'd never had a man who could go for so long, and that's when he learned that being able to stop ejaculation was a good thing. That would come back to haunt him, though – it's a form of impotence.

Shouty Husband would always rise to a dare, so at 18 years old, when he was challenged to get naked and have sex with a girl while riding a motorbike across a bridge, he jumped at it. He did it, too. I don't think the girl enjoyed it, but Shouty Husband had proved a point. He was the man, and sex was something he could control,

He always told me he was going to be the best at sex, and he did excel. Shouty Husband at his best was a hard act to follow, and I do miss that.

When it came to his relationship with Vinnie, Shouty Husband was the mentor as he was two years older. He was someone to admire and emulate. Well, that was never going to turn out well.

What would you learn from Shouty Husband's way of thinking – what was his moral compass, his work ethic? Well, you'd learn how to have front when you are bricking it. You'd know when to stand and fight and when to run.

The love of Vinnie's teenage life was Mags. It would never last; they were only 16 and 17 years old. But it meant the world at the time. Mags got pregnant. It happens, but remember, this was the 1970s; they were young and didn't know what to do.

So, Mags told her parents, who promptly threw her out. There was no way they were in a position to have the baby, so somehow, they found the money – and it was a lot – for her to have an abortion. No judgement here – again, it happens.

Mags still had no home, though. She couldn't stay at Vinnie's mum's place, so she ended up in Shouty Husband's spare room. She and Vinnie didn't survive as a couple. The pregnancy and termination were a lot to cope with, and ultimately, they were still kids themselves.

Shouty Husband and Mags got on really well. He always said she made the first move, but I know him – a troubled teenager would be fair game. Either way, she ended up in his bed and in his life.

He asked Vinnie if he minded, and even though he did, Vinnie said he didn't because Shouty Husband was the dominant one. Mags stayed for about six months before moving away from both of them.

After that, Shouty Husband and Vinnie worked as a tag team when it came to pulling girls. Maybe not every single time they went out, but they did ok.

Shouty Husband will tell you he's never gone to bed with a fat, ugly girl, but he has woken up with a few.

Darkness on the Edge of Town - Bruce Springsteen

Shouty Husband's drinking became a real problem when he hit 18. It takes a lot to scare him, but he was silly, and it finally caught up with him.

He went on a three-day bender with some friends and learned it's impossible to drink yourself sober when he nearly ended up with alcohol poisoning. The last thing he remembers is crawling on his hands and knees to a flat where he intended to carry on partying. Luckily, one of his friends was more sensible; they called an ambulance, and that was the last anyone heard of Shouty Husband for three days.

He was taken to the local psychiatric hospital and put on a ward where alcoholics could dry out in a safe space.

They took his clothes, so even though it was not a secure ward, Shouty Husband was stuck there. He said the vitamin injections they gave him to combat the DTs were horrendous. While he was there, he met a man whose weakness was strong, rough cider. He could stop for months on end, but then he'd give in and end up back on the ward to dry out. Shouty Husband decided he didn't want the experience, thank you.

As soon as he got his clothes back, he was off the ward, out of the hospital, and thumbing a lift home from the roadside. He never went on a bender like that again!

I'm going to tell you about Jinx, the first Mrs Shouty Husband. Shouty Husband loved her, worshipped her, and treated her badly.

Jinx came from a good family. She lived in a semi-detached house in a nice area with both parents and a brother. She had a decent education and got a good job in a building society.

She should have married well, had children, and enjoyed a happy life. Instead, she got Shouty Husband. I mean, that's not entirely a bad thing – life with him was never boring. But it was unpredictable, and surviving by the skin of your teeth isn't enough.

Stay – Shakespeare's Sister

While he spent Friday nights in Vinnie's company, Shouty Husband went home to Wolverhampton for the Saturday night life. Better clubs, old friends, and a bed to sleep in at his mum's.

She always put the bolt across at 11.30pm, though, so if he wasn't back by then, he was out for the night. Some nights, he got lucky. Other times he sofa surfed.

The day before his life changed for ever, Shouty Husband had his normal Friday night with Vinnie. By now, Brookside had a pub that was within walking distance of his flat, so they had a choice of two drinking holes.

I've said before that Shouty Husband always told people he never went to bed with an ugly girl, but he woke up with a few.

There was one there that Friday night. Shouty Husband got very pissed, didn't remember going home, then woke at first light to find himself in bed with, in his words, 'an ugly, fat girl.' He had no idea who she was or why she was in his bed and snoring like a warthog.

He wanted her gone so he could get the first bus to Wolverhampton. When he woke her up, she asked if he was going to have sex with her now, as he'd been too drunk the night before and had promised her the time of her life in the morning.

Even with the best will in the world and raging teenage hormones, there was no way Shouty Husband could perform after a skinful. He didn't want to, either, so he gave her a cup of tea and told her he had to catch the bus to Wolverhampton. It turned out she was going back to Shifnal, which was the same bus route, so he had to walk her to the stop and wait with her. He prayed nobody would see him, fearing it would ruin his reputation to be seen with a moose.

Eventually, she went her way, saying she'd love to see him again. 'Not in any lifetime,' thought Shouty Husband, as he went to his mum's to get ready for his next night out. He was young, single, with brass in pocket. One of his crowd asked him if he'd go on a double date. There was a girl he liked, but she wanted to bring a friend. Shouty Husband wasn't keen, but it was early doors, and he had an hour to spare, so he agreed. He was never one to stand in the way of a mate getting his leg over.

When Shouty Husband told me this story, he'd always have a smile on his face and a faraway look in his eye.

'I'm not dating her. She has red hair,' stated Shouty Husband after Jinx walked into the pub and his mate pointed her out. Still, she became part of the weekend crowd, and then she did the unforgivable – she found herself a boyfriend that Shouty Husband didn't like.

They weren't together, so why should it bother him? Well, turns out Jinx was everything Shouty Husband wanted in a girlfriend.

She looked like a lady, but she was a tomboy. She was a champion athlete in school. She rode pushbikes and was fearless. She was gorgeous, bright, and out of his league.

Shouty Husband bided his time, sure his moment would come. It did. One Saturday night, the boyfriend had a bad pint and didn't make it to the toilet in time. From then on, egged on by Shouty Husband, everyone called him Shit Leg.

Shit Leg wasn't interested in a long-term relationship. He just wanted to take Jinx's virginity, and after that, he got bored and moved on to the next gullible young girl.

Shouty Husband waited. He didn't want to be her rebound date. Eventually, he swooped in, and Jinx was his.

He did love her in his own way, but really, she was a trophy he had to have.

By now, Vinnie had met Karen.

Karen, who was in foster care with her sister, was a bright girl who was doing her A levels. Then Vinnie came along, and she had to choose between him and her education. She chose him.

Karen and Vinnie spent a lot of time with Shouty Husband and Jinx, who got the bus over every Wednesday to see him. She'd get the 9pm bus home, and, as mobile phones weren't a thing then, she had to call the phone box near Shouty Husband's flat from the phone box at the bottom of her road to tell him she was home safely.

She was a good girl, so she never stayed over. Her dad wouldn't allow it anyway. And then Shouty Husband got the flu. This was before the flu jab was available, and he was always really ill when he caught it. When Jinx went over, she found him in bed and truly sick, so first, she called the doctor out, and then she called her dad to say she was staying there until Shouty Husband was better.

I've looked after Shouty Husband when he's had the flu, and it's not a job I'd wish on my worst enemy. I have to feel for Jinx.

Kung Fu Fighting - Carl Douglas

Clubbing in our hometown in the '70s was a bit limited; it was much better to get the free bus to Shrewsbury or Wolverhampton.

One night, Shouty Husband took Jinx, Vinnie, and Karen over to Barron's nightclub, which was a tiny late-night drinking club with a small dance floor.

There was a taxi rank nearby, outside a men's clothes shop that had a huge plate-glass frontage. (It's a Subway now, but it's still got the windows.)

There was the inevitable queue for the taxis, and everybody was being very British and waiting patiently in line. The next taxi arrived, and two girls at the front of the queue went to get in when a guy came out of nowhere and pushed them out of the way. Vinnie took offence at this and told the guy so. He got a mouthful for his trouble, and they squared up to each other. To his credit, Shouty Husband didn't want any aggro because he had Jinx to look after, so he just gave the guy a push to move him away from the taxi and let the girls get in.

Unfortunately, the guy caught his foot on the kerb and windmilled backwards into the plate glass window, which broke under the force.

Shouty Husband grabbed Jinx and yelled, 'Run!'

They did. Shouty Husband never found out if the guy had hurt himself, and it was the first time Jinx had seen the damage Shouty Husband could do.

Sisters Are Doing' It for Themselves - Eurythmics & Aretha Franklin

Shouty Husband was brainwashed by his mum to look after his sisters if anything happened to her. I've mentioned them before – Sarah was so much like him but even more aggressive, all the time. She was known on the school run as the 'mad woman in the red mac.' She always frightened me, and I am glad she lives four counties away.

Paula, the youngest sister, was always good with me. I still wouldn't want to cross her, but she wasn't as bad as Sarah!

This next bit of my ramblings is all about the triangle of Shouty Husband, Sarah, and Paula. Does that sound like a Russian play? It is, really – lots of love, hate, and point scoring!

To say Shouty Husband and Sarah do not get on is the understatement of the century. They can't even be in the same room for more than five minutes without sniping at each other. Shouty Husband knows just what buttons to push and gets great pleasure from doing so. They're both alphas and complete control freaks – really, they should both have been only children.

When she was 18, Sarah got pregnant and married my lovely brother-in-law, Ed. Ten months later, they had another baby, so they ended up with what's known as 'Irish twins.'

She stayed local to her mum and sister, but her relationship with Shouty Husband was very on-off. Oddly, though, he always said she was the one who would help me if I ever needed it.

Paula is a different kettle of fish altogether.

Even though he can be cruel to her, she and Shouty Husband get on very well.

She's still selfish and self-centred, the same as the other two, but she hid it better, so I honestly thought we were friends. She's got as much depth as a puddle, though, and friendship was always on her terms; if you needed help, she'd run quickly in the opposite direction.

When she was still in nappies hanging down to her knees, Shouty Husband nicknamed Sarah 'Droopy Drawers.' He also used to call her 'Scrag' because she was thin. Sarah was extremely ill as a child and spent a lot of time in hospital. She was the runt of the litter, and nobody thought she would make old bones.

The day Sarah got married, Shouty Husband and his stepdad went on a pub crawl. Joe knew all the pubs that opened early to serve the market traders, and Shouty Husband was drunk and loud by the time he got to the wedding. Sarah has never forgiven him for it. Nor did his future father-in-law when he rolled up to collect the future Mrs Shouty Husband to take her to the wedding.

As it goes, Jinx got on well with her sisters-in-law, especially Paula, as they were the same age with lots in common. You Should Be Dancing – The Bee Gees

It's not very nice to be told that the wife who went before you was Wonder Woman, but that's basically what Shouty Husband did. He talked about Jinx more often than I care to remember.

He taught her to ride motorbikes and a motorbike and sidecar, and the first time the road came up to bite her, she broke her arm. It was her left arm, and she was left-handed.

She refused to have her leather cut off as it was expensive and instead gritted her teeth against the pain as she pulled it over her broken arm. Shouty husband was so proud.

Jinx was a biker but also a lady who wore heels, stockings, and skirts. She was, practically perfect in every way, to quote Mary Poppins.

The pedestal that Shouty Husband had put Jinx on was incredibly high, and he reminded me often that I should strive to be more like her.

One of Shouty Husband's favourite stories to tell me about when he was dating Jinx is the time he took her to the pictures to see Saturday Night Fever. Unfortunately, even though Wolverhampton had more cinemas than you could shake a stick at, every single showing of this must-see movie was sold out.

The only film they could get tickets for was The Stud. Well, Joan Collins was in it. It must be OK. In they went. Poor Shouty Husband. He'd so wanted to make a good impression, but he ended up taking his girlfriend to watch soft porn.

Jinx didn't know she was taking tests, but she passed them all anyway. It was one of Shouty Husband's habits - to make people jump through hoops. I got the ones ringed with flames, razor wire, guard dogs, and machine gun posts.

He always said they should have lived together, and the relationship would have run its course. They were both too young to get married, really. But Jinx was a good girl, and even if she was prepared to live with Shouty Husband, she'd never have gone against her parent's wishes.

Vinnie and Karen were married by now; Sarah had gotten married, and Shouty Husband wanted to keep Jinx.

He never told me how he asked her to marry him. He kept that private. (Everyone else was open for discussion, including their sex life, whether I wanted to hear it or not.)

Shouty Husband and Jinx were getting married, and the world knew it, but so far, there was no ring on Jinx's finger. She told him she wanted a pair of new boots, and, at the time, Wolverhampton had plenty of shoe shops. They walked round most of them, but Jinx wouldn't choose her boots, and eventually, his temper, and patience, ran out. That's when she told him that, actually, she'd seen a ring she liked but just didn't know how to ask him to look at it.

Being the great 'I am,' of course, Shouty Husband then took her to buy the ring she wanted. Now it was official— they were getting married.

Too Much Too Young - The Specials

The date for the wedding of Shouty Husband and Jinx was in June, midway between their birthdays. It was a register office wedding, a small affair.

After they did the deed and came out of the building, the bells were ringing. Not for Jinx, though – they came from the beautiful big church that she would have loved to have got married in, but Shouty Husband didn't agree. He won't do what other people want, not even for their wedding.

He didn't remember much more about the day. Apparently, they went back to the flat and had a nap; clearly, getting married is exhausting.

He did tell me he wondered if he had made a mistake, but he was never going to admit he'd messed up again already when he was only 21. Instead, he decided that he'd still be a single man, but one that was married and he would do what he wanted, when he wanted and Jinx would have to live with it !

Being married didn't really change much in Shouty Husband's life. He'd kept Jinx away from the crowd he knocked about with on Brookside, so this anecdote from the early days of their marriage always makes me smile. There is always the one that got away, so Shouty Husband's charm offensive didn't always bear fruit. There was one girl in the group who loved to flirt but wouldn't take it further. He told her that one day she'd want to taste the delights she'd heard of, but she never did.

Until she changed her mind and decided Shouty Husband was what she wanted, after all. She turned up at his flat and pretty much offered herself up on a plate. So he took her upstairs, made her a cup of tea, and introduced her to his wife.

He said he'd never seen anyone bolt down a cup of hot tea so quickly, and then she made her excuses and left. He still chuckles at her embarrassment to this day.

As time went by, two people living in a flat designed for one became increasingly difficult. Jinx wanted a house of their own and, after almost two years, the gods smiled on her.

Shouty Husband was a development corporation tenant now, so he could apply for a house. Then his rent increased to £30 a week, which was a lot of money then and more expensive than a mortgage.

Jinx worked at a building society that gave great rates to its employees, and the money was deducted from their wage packets, so it wasn't missed. It was also the time of the 'right to buy' scheme, and Shouty Husband would get the full available discount due to his tenant status.

They could get a three-bedroomed house at a ridiculously cheap price. It was the answer to Jinx's prayers. Jinx wanted a house on the road where Shouty Husband ended up living – more on that later – but that wasn't going to happen. Instead, they were offered a house in an area she didn't like, but as it was that house or nothing, Shouty Husband put his foot down.

He got a whole new area where he could make his mark and was happy in his 'single man that's married' mindset.

Faithfully - Journey

The sisters, Sarah and Paula, both lived in Wolverhampton and Shouty Husband and Jinx would go over to visit family every weekend.

Shouty Husband and Sarah weren't speaking again, which was a regular occurrence; their personalities clashed too strongly for them to be friends.

Shouty Husband went to visit both his mother and his mother-in-law, who he adored. He'd also catch up with Paula, who had moved into a flat but still went home regularly. Then the visits stopped, and her mother got worried. This was well before the days of mobile phones, and it seemed as though Paula had dropped off the face of the earth.

Shouty Husband had no idea where Paula might be or who her friends were; in fact, the only person that might know was Sarah. So, even though they weren't speaking, Shouty Husband and Jinx went to see her.

Little Ed, Shouty Husband's eldest nephew, got his dad once he'd opened the door and saw who it was. Ed told Shouty Husband he didn't want any trouble and said Sarah would be furious that Shouty Husband was on her doorstep. So, he explained about Paula being missing and needing Sarah's help and, for a while, it helped mend the rift between them.

Sarah knew all Paula's friends and where they lived, so off they went to track her down. It took hours of looking and knocking on different doors, but eventually they found Paula sharing a flat with a couple. She was being treated like a slave, made to do all the housework and shopping, and the woman was using emotional and physical abuse to keep Paula in line. Paula was simply too terrified to leave and felt she couldn't go home.

Shouty Husband got up in the guy's face and Sarah got Paula's stuff together. The woman became aggressive, insisting Paula owed her rent. Shouty Husband was all for squaring up to her, but Sarah stepped in to have words, then they took Paula home. Shouty Husband wasn't happy that the woman who had hurt his little sister was getting away with it, but as it goes she didn't - Sarah went back and sorted her out. Nobody messes with that family!

The recession stopped play in the early 1980s and Shouty Husband struggled to find work. Luckily Jinx had a job.

 He was resourceful, though, and worked out he could make a living cleaning windows. All he needed was a bucket, cloths and a ladder, and he carried them on his push bike; Jinx took the car as she had a 30-mile round trip to work. He built up a good business and got enough money to buy his dream car – a Reliant Robin, aka a plastic pig. He named her Edith, and he loved her, and it was the start of an affair that should have set him up for life. However, as you know, things don't always go to plan.

Shouty Husband had more work than he could handle on his own, so as Vinnie was unemployed, he asked him to help out. Cash in hand, obviously, so the dole office didn't need to know.

Vinnie shared Shouty Husband's 'single while married' philosophy, but took it a step further – he went catting and spent money like water, especially in the pub. Once he took him on, Shouty Husband always made sure Karen got Vinnie's wages so at least the kids got fed.

The window cleaning round went well until Shouty Husband fell off a ladder. He wasn't badly injured, but it was enough to stop him going up ladders; from then on, he'd only go up them if he absolutely had to.

Then he realised that with his gift of the gab, he could sell anything. He started working for Shop Check, what was kind of like a payday loan organisation before they were a thing. You borrowed money and every week Shouty Husband would collect it at 1000% interest. He rose through the ranks quickly as he was very good at getting money out of poor payers. Then his conscience kicked in and he quit; he never thought of himself as a tallyman and hated taking money from people who had nothing.

Instead, he decided door-to-door selling was the way to go. Again, he did well and soon became a team leader. His sales team would start the process, then he'd go in to seal the deal. One lady he worked with, who was only young and gullible, fancied him. And Shouty husband did like to flirt. It had to be pointed out to the young lady that Shouty Husband was that rarity, a married man who stood by his vows. He did love Jinx and would never have slept around.

The job lasted until, again, Shouty Husband's conscience kicked in. This became a recurring theme through his whole life – the great jobs he had and why he had to walk away from them.

The Snake — Al Wilson

It's a very small world sometimes. Without either of us being aware of it, some friends of Shouty Husband's also became mine. Tracey was one of them.

Shouty Husband was working for a local free newspaper. He loved being able to ride his bike around to collect advertising payments, though the newspaper shut down quite quickly. It was another job that didn't last, but he enjoyed it at the time.

Tracey worked in the office. She was lovely but very insecure, so Shouty Husband took her under his wing. She was in the minority of women who never fancied him, seeing more instead as a big brother.

Tracey's boyfriend was into bikes, so Shouty Husband invited them both over to the house. They even made it inside, as Tracey and Jinx got on. Usually, other men only got as far as the garage.

 Well, it turned out that Tracey was in trouble, as her boyfriend was emotionally and physically abusing her. They lived together and Tracey felt she couldn't go home, so she stuck it out. Then, one day, the bad boyfriend held her hand under the grill for not cooking his fish fingers properly.

She broke down during a visit and told Jinx everything, and of course she told Shouty Husband. The bad boyfriend's days were numbered, as Shouty Husband had very definite rules about hitting women. (Yes, I hear you. He was a bad man and cruel, but he regarded Tracey as a little sister.)

I never found out what he did to the bad boyfriend, but Tracey escaped to London and became a nanny. Then Shouty Husband lost track of her and that was that, until she popped up at a women's group, I went to about fifteen years later.

Days - The Kinks

Shouty Husband has always had animals. Even though feeding them was a problem, he still collected them. So, once he and Jinx were settled in their own home, he wanted a dog. Time to say hello to Kelly the collie.

In those days you could buy a puppy from any pet shop. Shouty Husband and Jinx went looking for a bitch – he said female dogs had better temperaments than males.

Kelly was a ball of fluff that instantly melted the stone swinging on a brick that passed for Shouty Husband's heart. Wherever he went, Kelly went with him. I If he climbed a tree, Kelly followed him. I think he loved that dog more than he loved Jinx!

Never one to do things by half, Shouty Husband increased his pack until, at its heyday, there were six dogs. All very well – until life and work got in the way and the responsibility of looking after them fell to Jinx!

One of These Days - Pink Floyd

Jinx wanted all the normal things other people had, such as holidays. Shouty Husband didn't do holidays, but he loved Jinx, so he was open to suggestions.

He'd got rid of his long hair as she didn't like it. And, after his trip to the alkies' ward, he'd knocked the beer on the head. He was a new man, his wife was his life, and so for a while he did what she wanted.

To pay for their honeymoon, he worked picking potatoes. (I know first-hand that this is back-breaking work.) The best he could offer at the end of it was a few days in a tent in Wales, so they packed up the bike and sidecar and off they went to Barmouth.

On the way, the sidecar tyre blew. They found a garage, but the owner said it was too bad for a repair – they'd need a new one. He had one, but Shouty Husband would have to hunt for it in a whole pile of tyres. Then he charged them a fortune for it, which took most of their spending money. Still, they were nearly there now so they carried on.

At the campsite they met a group of bikers from Merseyside, who were far from impressed with how Shouty Husband and Jinx had been treated by the garage owner. Shouty Husband was able to enjoy drinking with them as Jinx wasn't keeping track of him, and he was always good at acting sober when he wasn't.

The weather was overcast but still lovely, so Shouty Husband and Jinx went for a walk along the beach. Jinx got burnt, what with having red hair and fair skin. At one point, Shouty Husband put his arm round her and accidentally burst a blister on her shoulder; Jinx levitated, and he felt so guilty!

When the bikers left, they gave Shouty Husband and Jinx all the food they had left, so the two of them had a great few days even on a shoestring budget. Bikers help bikers, wherever you come across them.

The next time they went away was to Brean Sands, which you may remember was where Shouty Husband went as a child. This was a better holiday, though, as nothing went wrong. After that came a bike rally.

This wasn't Jinx's idea of a holiday. She wanted what her friends had – plane journeys to hot, exotic and beautiful places. Sadly, all Shouty Husband offered were camping and bike rallies. Take it or leave it.

Mama, I'm Coming Home - Ozzy Osbourne

Shouty Husband's sisters were also trying to make lives of their own. Sarah was living with her boys near her mum's place, while Paula had a job and a bad boyfriend.

Sarah was the first sibling to incur the wrath of their mother. She was on the bus one day with her boys, who were both aged under five at the time, when her mother got on. The eldest, Little Ed, shouted hello to his nan.

Everyone on the bus knew who he meant and, as many of the women had had run-ins with her before, they were all keen to see how she reacted. Very badly, as it went. She looked at Little Ed, then at her daughter, and then told everyone on the bus they were nothing to do with her as she turned her back on them. And that was the end of Sarah's relationship with her mum. I have no idea why it happened, or if Sarah had done anything to cause her mum to disown her in such a vicious and public way. But that was more than 30 years ago, and they've not spoken again since.

Meanwhile, Jinx decided she'd had enough of being on her own and gave Shouty Husband an ultimatum – it was her or the job. He wanted to keep his wife but could see their marriage was heading towards the end, so he visited his mother for some comfort.

Yes, I know – she hadn't been much of a mother to him so far. She wasn't then, either.

When Shouty Husband told his mum he thought that his marriage was over, she told him he wasn't moving back home so he'd better find a flat. All he wanted was a hug and some sympathy – for her to hug him, pat him on the back and say 'There, there – it'll be ok.' No. That was never going to happen.

The irony is that when I learned David had died, all I wanted was a hug and some comfort, but Shouty Husband turned into his mother.

Anyway, he never forgave her for it. Their relationship carried on for a while, but eventually she cut him out of her life, as she had with Sarah.

I have only seen my mother-in-law once. We were in Bilston market and Shouty Husband was standing in the way of a little old lady. He wouldn't move, which wasn't like him, and the little old lady was forced to walk around him. When I asked him about it, he said that had been his mum – he hadn't seen her for 25 years, but she'd still blanked him completely.

Blackbird - The Beatles

Jinx found a lovely flat back in Wolverhampton and finally left. Shouty Husband helped her move and kept in touch; he really thought she'd come back after some time apart.

He'd always trusted her so, while he was in London, he'd give her a signed blank cheque every Sunday that she could use to get money for housekeeping. They agreed a set amount and, as far as he was concerned, it worked well.

After Jinx left, he had the dogs to look after, so working away all week wasn't an option. He decided to stay home and find a job, and in the meantime he would refit the kitchen.

Shouty Husband had no real need of cash; he used his credit card to pay for running the bikes and Jinx took care of the day-to-day expenses. So when he went to get some money from the cashpoint for his kitchen project, he was rather surprised to see a message telling him he had 'insufficient funds'.

There should have been thousands in that account, but it was nearly empty. He went into the bank to sort it out.

It turned out Jinx had been slowly draining the account as she quietly planned her escape. Shouty Husband went through paperwork she'd left behind and discovered she'd been putting in lots of overtime while he was away. It was all part of her escape to a new life – one that didn't include him.

This was a problem, as he still loved her and wanted her back, but he didn't think it was insurmountable. After all, they still spent time together and he had the house, so there was still hope – or so he thought. He couldn't forgive her for stealing his money, but he would put it behind him.

Two years on, they were into the divorce process. Shouty Husband wanted to keep the house so he was doing everything in his power to get enough money together to buy her out. Jinx had had enough of waiting, though, and her solicitor sent Shouty Husband a nasty letter saying the house would be sold if he couldn't find the money. Shouty Husband was seething and decided the solicitor would feel his wrath; he made it from Telford to Wolverhampton in 18 minutes on his motorbike, which is giving it large. It was to no avail, though. Shouty Husband couldn't find the money in time and ended up losing the house. This set him on a very dark path of self-destruction, and he was lucky he didn't end up either dead or locked up. Nobody ever talked about Jinx apart from Shouty Husband, it's almost like she only existed in his head. It means don't know both sides of the story, sadly.

I do admire her for escaping Shouty Husband, though.

Crazy in Love - Beyoncé

After Jinx left and before he went over to the dark side completely, Shouty Husband had a few girlfriends. I use the term very loosely.

We used to see one of them while out shopping; she always looked terrified when she spotted him and would never speak. Shouty Husband told me she'd once come to spend the weekend, never said a word the whole time and then disappeared. It sounds incredible now but at the time I didn't think this was strange. My alarm bell was on mute, as it was for more years than I care to remember.

Anyway, on to the fight to end all fights.

Shouty Husband was still living in the house he had shared with Jinx. He was totally messed up after she left, which made him dangerous – after all, he had nothing left to lose.

His live-in girlfriend, for want of a better word, had left another man to be with him. Unsurprisingly, the other man wasn't happy about this, and he and Shouty Husband had several run-ins. He wanted to destroy Shouty Husband and his reputation as someone not to be messed with, but he didn't want to get his own hands dirty.

Enter The Patsy – a hard man without the intelligence to know he was being played.

His first mistake was to phone Shouty Husband to tell him he was coming round to sort him out.

As far as Shouty Husband was concerned, his home was his castle, and he would defend it to the death.

So off he went in his £30 old banger to head off trouble before it arrived. He and The Patsy met on the road outside and The Patsy thought it would be a good idea to play chicken with his car. Shouty Husband didn't care about his car – the insurance would pay out more than it was worth – so he wasn't going to back down. The Patsy, who had decent wheels, lost that one.

The Patsy's second mistake was to go at Shouty Husband armed. You just don't. He had a tree branch, so Shouty husband grabbed a tyre iron.

By this time, they had an audience, but nobody tried to stop the fight.

Shouty Husband wanted to put The Patsy down as quickly as possible, without too much blood spilt. He recalls going very cold and feeling like everything happened in slow motion.

The Patsy was big built but slow. Even so, he put up a good fight and did Shouty Husband some damage. There was blood over the front of the Patsy's car afterwards, but whose it was Shouty Husband couldn't say.

At one stage The Patsy managed to hit Shouty Husband's wrist with the branch. His wrist swelled up and he thought it was broken at first, but it turned out his Timex wristwatch – which he loved – had taken the brunt of the blow.

After what seemed like hours – but was probably minutes – a taxi driver called Tony, who knew both of them, intervened. Shouty Husband walked away; The Patsy was still standing but had taken a lot of punishment.

When the police came, Shouty Husband said he'd go quietly after telling his girlfriend what was going on. The younger officer was having none of it, but his sergeant stepped in. Yet again, Shouty Husband got his way.

The case went to court but was eventually dismissed after being adjourned for months, which was great news for Shouty Husband. It turned out The Patsy had a heart condition and died fourteen months later, leaving a wife and child. Shouty Husband didn't know if the fight contributed to his death, but he did feel guilty.

His girlfriend's former fella heard about the fight and went toe-to-toe with Shouty Husband, but declined when he was told he could have a pop if he thought he was hard enough.

The only part of the whole situation that really bothered Shouty Husband was that his neighbours avoided him like the plague after they saw him fighting. Not long after, he left the house to move back to his.

The First Time Ever I Saw Your Face - Roberta Flack

When I married the boy's dad I moved to the other end of Telford and my friends were two bus rides away. He had friends as he was from that neck of the woods, so I ended up becoming friends with their wives and, in turn, their friends.

Jordan was born in mid-December, so there was no way we could party on New Year's Eve. Then, out of the blue, Donna – the Queen Bee of the group of friends - told us Karen was having a party and we could go if we fancied.

I sort of knew Karen and Vinnie but with a new baby that was breastfed, and having to get taxis, it really wasn't viable as far as I was concerned. The boy's dad really wanted to go, though, and Donna told us it was ok, all the kids were going. There were enough bedrooms, and it would be 'sleep where you drop'.

I was fat, frumpy, felt like a walking milk bar and my stitches were bothering me. The last thing I wanted to do was go to a party. But I didn't want to stay home on my own, either so I agreed.

Karen put on a good spread, to give Karen her due. And when you have a new baby at a do like that, you can play invisible – hide in the corner and watch what's going on.

After finally getting Jordan asleep and into his carrycot, I had something like 20 minutes of adult conversation before he cried to be fed again. He was only two weeks old and that's all I knew to do – he cried, I fed him.

Donna proclaimed him a sucky baby and said he needed a dummy. They were the work of Satan, according to my health visitor, but Donna was a mum of two, so surely, she knew best. She went upstairs and got a spare dummy, washed it under the hot tap, dipped it in a glass of Baileys, and shoved it into Jordan's mouth. My jaw dropped. Jordan was quiet. He went back into his carrycot out of the way, and I was able to breathe.

That lasted until the dummy was lost and the shawl, he liked to be wrapped up tight in came loose. He needed me – I was his world.

The problem was, I needed the loo and every time I tried to put him down, Jordan went puce from screaming. Everybody else was either dancing or outside. I was tired, hormonal and stuck on my own in a strange house.

A guy called Don appeared to have moved into the downstairs loo after ignoring the warnings about Vinnie's homebrew. His wife, Liz, was furious – but at least their baby was six months old and asleep.

Eventually, when I was on the point of bursting, I went in search of the boy's dad. I found Dawn, Karen and Vinnie's neighbour, very drunk and sitting on a bar stool. She was a horrible woman with a mouth like a sewer; she'd already had a run-in with Liz earlier in the evening when she picked up Liz's son and wouldn't give him back.

Then in walked a stranger, who smiled at me as he leant back on the sink. Honestly, I can remember this like it was yesterday.

Shouty Husband was dressed to kill in a black, double-breasted suit (he never wore any other type of jacket – easy to get out of in a fight) with a brilliant white shirt, scarlet tie and gleaming black shoes. His long blond hair shone, and his smile lit up the room.

I had a choice. Wet myself where I stood, give my son to the drunk neighbour so I could go to the loo alone, or take him with me and hold him as I tried to levitate to avoid peeing on my stitches. Or, alternatively, I could trust the stranger with the wonderful smile not to run away with my baby boy instead. Decision made.

I walked towards him, said, 'Hi, my name's Anne, please can you hold my son for me, I have to go to the loo! 'Then I thrust Jordan into his arms and ran up the stairs.

I think that was both the longest and quickest trip to the loo I have ever had. When I got back downstairs, I found Jordan still lying quietly in the arms of the nice man.

Shouty Husband and I went to sit behind the dining room table, and he even found me a cushion. He introduced himself and asked if he could carry on holding Jordan, who was still asleep, as he was enjoying it.

Neither the boy's dad nor I had any idea who Shouty Husband was at that point, or that he'd ruffled a fair few feathers simply by turning up.

He was interested in talking to me and made me feel special. He told me I had the glow that only pregnant women and new mums had, that I looked beautiful. When you're feeling like a dairy cow the size of a small house, noticed by nobody, that's really something.

Sadly, it ended when Jordan woke up, decided it was supper time, and headed for the nearest nipple. Shouty Husband ended up with a perfect mouth-shaped patch of drool on his beautiful shirt.

I had no idea Shouty Husband was completely off his face after two bottles of champagne and a load of dope. He'd been to the pub and already partied hard before turning up in a coal lorry.

It was the day he'd received the letter telling him the court case over the fight he'd had was being dismissed. He was celebrating and had only come to the party to make mischief. I had no clue about any of this; he just seemed like a nice man who made me feel I counted.

Meanwhile, the boy's dad was having a great time, looking at Liz's (admittedly great) legs, shown off in a very short skirt and following Donna around with his tongue hanging out. She looked amazing in a blue wraparound dress and was very slim with a great smile. How could I compete?

At midnight, the bells rang and everyone sang Auld Lang Syne while I watched from my corner of the living room, Jordan in my arms. Then everyone kissed each other, as you do, and Shouty Husband did what none of the other men were brave or stupid enough to do, and kissed Karen in front of her husband.

She told me later that the world stopped, and she was one with Shouty husband and the kiss, I found out later what she meant, Shouty husband could kiss!

Vinnie had a New Year's Eve tradition where all the men had to wear one of his large collection of novelty G-strings and run out of the back door, around the three houses in his block, and come back in through the front door.

Shouty Husband refused; he'd hit 'full' and needed a quiet place where he could come down. The problem was, he was in a room full of men who wanted to put an axe in his head so even in that state he was hypersensitive and dangerous. No, I didn't have a clue at that point what a dangerous combination that was.

The boy's dad, who'd had more than a sniff of the barmaid's apron, found Shouty Husband sitting on the floor in the room the kids were in. Feeling brave, he decided to say something. Shouty Husband got in his face and the only reason that he didn't throw the boy's dad down the stairs was because he knew he didn't have a clue who Shouty Husband was or what he was capable of.

Shouty Husband had just lost Jinx and was in the process of losing his home. He had nothing left, and the boy's dad doesn't know how lucky he was.

The party was winding down and I was on my cushion with Jordan when suddenly all hell broke loose.

The woman Shouty Husband was living with when he had 'the fight' turned up and started mouthing off at Karen. Donna tried to calm things down, to no avail.

Karen ended up pushing her into the Christmas tree in the living room and it all kicked off. Shouty Husband appeared – his woman, his mess. He left, Karen threw the woman out, and then the party carried on. I wanted to go to bed, but that wasn't going to happen – there was nowhere for me to go. So, instead, I went to find myself a quiet corner.

Karen's house had a porch with a built-in bench. It was out of the way in the corner, covered in coats, so I got my cushion and made a nest away from the noise. Jordan and I dozed for a couple of hours, then the next thing I remember was hearing the boy's dad talking to Donna. They had no idea I was there. I heard him saying he was going on a fag run to the garage and did she want anything and then, the immortal words: 'I married the wrong person, I should have married you. ' We'd been married for 18 months and had a brand-new baby. I never forgot that or forgave him for it.

Eventually, Karen fed us bacon sandwiches and we got a lift home, and life carried on. But I never forgot the stranger and the kindness he'd shown me that night. Who knew, 33 years ago, that something as banal as needing the loo would change my life?

Shouty Husband had a motorbike and side car when he was with Jinx, and he wasn't the only one – it's time to say hello to Little John, who became a good friend when he needed one.

After the house went, he was a bit stuck. He stored some of the furniture he'd saved in his old bedroom at his mum's place but going back to live there wasn't an option. Other than that, he only had on old van he could keep his bike in. He went back on the road - London called and Shouty Husband answered. For a while he'd come home every weekend and crash at Little John's.

Little John was a single dad, but unfortunately, he loved to drink – in the same way a fish loves water. Shouty Husband could put it away, but next to his mate he was a non-starter.

Some years later, Little John and Shouty Husband were having a chat and, forgetting I was there, the story about 'the Lizzy toilets' came up.

The Lizzy, as it was known, was a pub called The Elizabethan. On Friday nights they used to have live music – some of the singers were pretty good and Shouty Husband did love to dance.

The guy who sent The Patsy to fight Shouty Husband was still out for blood. He'd put the word about that Shouty

Husband needed to feel some pain, so every wannabe was up for putting him in his place.

Now, when he went to the toilet in the pub, Shouty Husband would never use the urinals. He said you never knew who was behind you, so he always went in a stall.

One night, as he was washing his hands, he could see two guys behind him who'd followed him in. He just knew they were going to have a go, so he got in first.

He used their heads to break the basins and left them in a bloody heap on the floor. Then he went back to the dance floor and asked if anybody else fancied having a pop at him.

Nobody did. Very sensible of them.

'Forbidden love provides happiness when there is no happiness.' Unknown.

After New Year's Eve and the world-stopping kiss with Shouty Husband, Karen's life was no longer enough for her; she'd tasted forbidden fruit and wanted more.

Even though Vinnie was his best friend, Shouty Husband was more than happy to oblige and the two of them began an affair.

I found out later that Karen had abandoned Vinnie and their two children and run off to live with Shouty Husband in his flat above the cobbler's. He was couriering out of Birmingham at the time so got home every night, although not always early. Karen got a throw away job. Shouty Husband said she was like a baby bird that always wanted feeding; she was great if she had money in her purse – a lot of money, his money!

Karen was one of those who always thinks the grass is greener on the other side, but then finds out it's just different. Once she realised life with Shouty husband did not live up to expectations, she decided to go home.

However, in the meantime Vinnie had realised the grass could be any colour he wanted it to be – it just had to be young, female and willing!

Karen wasn't going to give up that easily. She was sly, crafty and always looking out for Number 1, so she came up with a cunning plan. (Here's a tip – never get stoned with me and tell me your darkest secrets; I have a memory like an elephant's.)

She went to the library and researched how to take a paracetamol overdose and survive. She decided she could cope with getting her stomach pumped in hospital as a means to an end, downed a lot of pills, and rang for an ambulance. She even left a note for Shouty Husband.

He went to the hospital, of course, but when the nurse asked Karen if she wanted to see him, she said no and asked for Vinnie, loud enough for Shouty Husband to hear.

Her plan worked – Vinnie agreed to take her back and she left Shouty Husband. That wasn't the end of that little ménage à trois, though.

We're an American Band - Grand Funk Railroad

Even though Shouty Husband was making money hand over fist, for a few months he lived out of the back of a van with his motorbike. Weekends, he could spend on the floor at Little John's.

It seemed he was on a destructive path from which there was no return – but it's funny how the world can intervene.

Paula had met a lovely man, Bill. He had an ex and two children but he earned good money, so Paula decided he was the one.

Bill and Paula had decided to get married and wanted a house of their own. They both had good jobs and could it, but day-to-day living was difficult; Bill's ex-wife had her begging bowl out and there were two children to think about.

Shouty Husband was working out of Birmingham. He wouldn't be there much, but he needed a base – somewhere he could sleep and eat.

The world turned, the planets aligned, and Shouty Husband ended up living with Paula and Bill. This arrangement lasted quite a while and was the catalyst for him getting his life back together. He always says Paula was what saved him.

It worked well. He took every couriering job going and, by the time he got home, Paula and Bill would be in bed. His dinner would be in the microwave and all he had to do was heat it up. There'd be coffee ready in his mug, too, but that was the last thing he wanted – he preferred whiskey. At that time, he was drinking a bottle a night, sometimes two.

Paula was worried; it was pretty much guaranteed he was riding his motorbike while over the limit. One night she poured all the whisky down the sink and told him to get his act together; he was slowly killing himself, she said, and Jinx wasn't worth it.

In turn, Shouty Husband helped her and Bill. He was making more money than he'd ever dreamed of and always carried a wedge that could choke a donkey. He always paid his way and, when Paula was struggling due to an excessive electric bill, he just pulled out the cash and sorted it out.

My brother-in-law Bill was lovely and used to share his memories of life with Shouty Husband before me. He told me about a shopping trip where Shouty Husband walked along the racks of clothes, pulling out shirts, trousers and underwear in his size in every colour; he spent £2000 in half an hour.

Bill was gobsmacked, but Shouty Husband had always been a clothes horse. He'd also decided the way to get over Jinx was to start clubbing and sleeping around, and he was eager to get back out on the town.

I Will Survive - Gloria Gaynor

Shouty Husband's big dream was to have a piece of the world that was all his. Jinx put a halt to that for a while, but before long 'One day I will have my own house again' became his mantra.

As he was raking in the money and things were going well, he decided to see if what was around. His plan was to buy a fixer-upper for cash and have somewhere to call his own.

He got himself on the mailing lists of a few High Street estate agents and, in time, went to have a look at a terraced house not too far from Paula & Bill's place.

They were asking £6,000 – worth a look, though it was a bit cheap. He found out why when he saw it – it was a disaster. It was subsiding and you could feel the living room floor dip by 45° when you walked across it.

So much needed doing, it would be a money pit. Shouty Husband could afford to pay for it, though, so when the agent called to see if he was interested, he offered £3,000 thinking they'd never accept. When they called back ten minutes later to say yes, he realised the place had major problems and declined.

Three months later, the council bought the whole road under a compulsory purchase order so they could knock it down for a new bit of the ring road. They paid the full price of £22,000 and Shouty Husband would have made a killing if he'd gone ahead, but it wasn't to be.

Instead, life went on at Bill and Paula's. Then the wheel turned again, and the courier work dried up. Shouty Husband needed a new support network and got back into the groove of 'if it moves, try to get it into bed'.

Louie Louie - Motorhead

For Shouty Husband, giving a woman pleasure was a power trip which is why he loved it so much. He'll tell you himself, he's always been a tart.

He'd made some new friends and, through a couple called Karen and Trev, he met Margie; she was Karen's sister-in-law. Margie was up for anything and, as she was married, she wouldn't want anything serious. That suited Shouty Husband just fine.

She was a bunk-up after the pub on a Friday night and, knowing her reputation, Shouty Husband decided a condom was in order. (He rarely used them; he could never come with one on.)

At that time, Shouty Husband had a big draughtsman's table that he used for doing his art. Shortly after his encounter with Margie, he was sitting there and realised his nether regions were very itchy. He stripped off to have a good look and found little black bits in his pubic hair. He assumed they were blackheads, which he was prone to, but then one of them moved. After levitating with shock, he got angry and grabbed a compass to dig them out. It turned out that Margie gave him a dose of crabs.

Off he went to see the doctor and told him he thought he had pubic lice. When the doctor asked how he knew, he pulled out his baccy tin and opened it – he'd kept all the crabs he'd dug out of his groin!

At the time, Shouty Husband had long hair and a full beard. He's lucky he didn't have a hairy chest too, otherwise he'd have had to shave his whole body from his nether regions to the top of his head.

Some very smelly cream and boil-washing his clothes and bedding soon killed the little buggers off, but he wasn't going to leave it there. Shouty Husband went to visit Margie, who thought he'd come back for a bit more fun. When he told her he had a present for her, she looked happy and drew closer as he pulled out his baccy tin. Then he told her she could have her crabs back and threw the lot full in her face. Her expression was priceless.

Shouty Husband turned and walked away, and Margie made sure to steer well clear when they were both in the pub at the same time in future.

Bedsitter - Soft Cell

It's time to introduce Shouty Husband's cousins. They really come into their own in this bit. The twins, Charlie and Tommy, arrived when Shouty Husband was 13, followed by Billy a year later.

When the work dried up and staying at Bill and Paula's was no longer working, it was time for Shouty Husband to find a new home.

But, before I tell you about the joys of bedsit land, you should know about the ménage à trois that was him, Vinnie and Karen.

Shouty Husband and Karen carried on their affair after she went back to Vinnie, and then she found out she was pregnant. So – who was the daddy? He knew she'd stay with Vinnie, so Shouty Husband went back to Wolverhampton and that's where he ended up in bedsit land.

This was the time of the new support group; he's always had one, one way or another. Eventually he either walks away or drives them away with his attitude and behaviour.

I feel lucky that I met them all and am still friends with some of them.

Shouty Husband ended up living in a series of big Victorian houses that were made into bedsits, mostly to cater for the university students. He was free, single and could drink and smoke himself to death if he wanted to – what could be better?

Rock and Roll Queen - Mott the Hoople

Because his cousins, Charlie and Tommy drank it, Shouty Husband got into drinking Kestrel super-strength lager. In his heyday he could down around 15 cans, and he still loved his dope, too.

Over the years he bought his dope from lots of different people. He hated using street dealers as you never knew what you were getting, and instead had a regular network of dealers he considered 'safe'. Sometimes, though, needs must when the devil drives.

Some parts of Shouty Husband's hometown were rough, such as the flats at Blakenell. There were always dealers hanging around outside one particular block so, if his regular dealers weren't around on a Friday night, he'd go there to score.

This particular Friday night, Shouty Husband had his cousin, Tommy, riding pillion on the bike. Tommy went off to a quiet spot with the dealer while Shouty Husband stayed with bike; not a good idea to leave it unattended there. Having spent the last £10 of Shouty Husband's money, Tommy handed over the lump of dope so he could check it and make sure he'd got a decent amount. It turned out that Tommy had bought a lump of liquorice. In his defence it was dark, and he hated going there to score. Shouty Husband always described it as 'black man's land', and Tommy was a white skinhead with the politics to match.

Shouty Husband told Tommy to stay by the bike and be ready for a quick getaway while he went to talk to the dealers.

They laughed when he demanded either his money back or a proper lump of dope. The dealer who had dealt with Tommy looked Shouty Husband up and down, sucked his teeth (the biggest insult going at the time) and said: 'You can't do anything to a black man on Blakenell. '

It was a red rag to a bull. Shouty Husband gave the dealer a Wolverhampton kiss, headbutting him with his motorcycle helmet still on. The dealer went down like a sack of spuds while his friends looked on, astonished. Before they could react, Shouty Husband was back on the bike.

He got the front wheel up in the air, with Tommy hanging on behind for grim death, and gunned it out towards the ring road. As they pulled out, a police car coming the other way clocked them doing their impression of Barry Sheene[*] and turned around to give chase.

Shouty Husband knew how to take the racing line. The bike was leaning until the foot pegs touched the road, and Tommy said later he was just clinging on, hoping he wouldn't fall off and praying it wouldn't go down.

The chase was short. Shouty Husband knew every rat run and alley in Wolverhampton, so he shot down a backstreet

---

[*]   Barry Sheene was a professional motorcycle racer, greatly admired by Shouty Husband

where the police car couldn't follow. Then he went back to his bedsit via a roundabout route.

He knew he was safe. Even if the police had clocked his number plate, it didn't matter – he always used a set of fakes if he was up to anything hooky.

Gimme Shelter - The Rolling Stones

Shouty Husband was still spending time with Little John. He loved to tell the story of the time they went to the Southwest Custom & Classic Bike Show, with Little John riding pillion.

Every few miles, he noticed the back end of the bike was stepping out. It took a while for him to realise Little John was taking cans of Guinness out of the panniers, drinking the contents, then waiting to throw the empties into open car windows as they passed by!

Shouty Husband didn't go to bike rallies run by the Hell's Angels; he said they were trouble waiting to happen. Nobody told him the Southwest was an Angels-run event but, since they were there, they decided to enjoy it.

Shouty husband got very drunk and very stoned in the beer and music tent, and his internal indicator hit full big time. The last thing he remembered was praying he didn't throw up as he was lifted over someone's shoulder. He assumed it was a Hell's Angel who'd picked him up, and vomiting down his back would have ended in a good kicking. Actually, it was Little John – he carried Shouty Husband back to the tent like he weighed nothing.

Then there was the one about the washing line and the sword. Little John had found himself a missus by now and she wanted a washing line in the garden. Since Little John was as useless as Shouty Husband at doing odd jobs around the house, she was waiting a while.

One day, Shouty Husband and Charlie decided they had enough petrol to come over from Wolverhampton and go up the Wrekin. (If you haven't heard of it, it's a famous hill above the Shropshire plains.) They had enough dope for one big spliff and felt like sitting on a hill in the sunshine while they put the world to rights.

On the way home, Shouty Husband decided to go and see if Little John was about. They turned up hoping for a cup of tea, but Little John offered them beer. Shouty Husband explained they had no money, but Little John said the session was on him.

By the time they got back to Little John's house they were all the worse for drink and feeling hungry. Shouty Husband loved that Little John couldn't cook and just had a pan on the stove he referred to as 'stew'. This is what he was given, though I'm not sure he was brave enough to eat it.

Charlie, as a long-standing vegetarian, was another matter. Little John's solution was to go outside to the cold frame, put his foot through the glass, pick a handful of parsley and dump it on a plate – with the roots, dirt and all - for him.

Then Little John got his samurai sword out and was showing what he could do with it. Shouty Husband, well pissed by now, decided he wanted a go. First, he chopped down the washing line and then he decided to attack the post it was attached to. By the time he'd finished it was all a bit of a mess. Little John's missus was not happy, and Shouty Husband stayed away for quite a while after that.

I always enjoyed it when Little John came over to visit Shouty Husband. He swore like a trooper and always had great stories to tell. The funny thing was he was always very respectful when he spoke to me, with no bad language at all. Then, as soon as he turned back to Shouty Husband, he was effing and jeffing like there was no tomorrow.

Sunday Morning Coming Down - Kris Kristofferson

When Shouty Husband was after money, he put his all into it. He's always been a grafter. He didn't want to stay in bedsit land for ever, so he got on with it.

Wolverhampton in the early 1990s was full of students and Shouty Husband became friends with Cal, a lad who lived upstairs. Since Cal and all his friends toked, Shouty Husband got into buying a big lump of dope – not dealing, exactly, but for them all to share. Once you'd divided it up there was always some left over, so Shouty Husband got to keep toking and the students got their dope without the risk of buying it themselves. Everyone was happy. In another life, Shouty Husband could have been a very successful businessman – or criminal.

He worked at any job he could get, but the best at that time was running a hot dog van outside a night club.

He did this alongside Charlie, and together had a great time and made a lot of money. They were both high on dope and their banter had plenty of customers wanting to watch the show.

The best story I heard was about the woman who wanted a vegetarian hot dog. Bear in mind this is a two-bit hot dog van outside a nightclub in the '90s. Vegetarian sausages were rare enough in the shops, never mind a hot dog van.

She was drunk and arsey and was holding up the queue, which meant Shouty Husband was losing money. The only veggie things they had on the van were the buns and the onions, so Shouty Husband showed her the ingredients list on the tin of sausages but covered up the last one – mechanically recovered meat. Seeing they apparently had no meat in them, the drunk woman bought two.

Shouty Husband could have sold sand to the Arabs. Even when stoned, he was still full of charm and very quick witted. At that time, he was also going through women like they were about to become extinct. Jinx had broken his heart and damaged his ego, and his head was in a dark place. He decided the best way to get over her was to get over and under as many other women as he could.

Then he met the one who got away, the one he believed could stay with him for ever, the one that got him because she was just like him. This was Greta or, as he called her, Gritty.

Gritty was a German student and lived in the same big Victorian house as Shouty Husband. She had no intention of stopping in England long-term; she planned to return to Bavaria, where she had a boyfriend, and run the family business. Shouty Husband was just a pleasant distraction, a friend with benefits.

He always said she could make a great meal from nothing more than a few bits of old veg and some rice. She was his ideal woman and he always talked about her fondly with a faraway look in his eyes for what might have been.

Red Light Spells Danger - Billy Ocean

Deciding he'd had enough of his bad bedsit, Shouty Husband moved to another big Victorian house on the next road over. And that's when he met Graham, who became his mentor, father figure, best friend and saviour.

Shouty Husband was heading for either death or prison, and Graham saved him from either fate. In return, he needed a big friend and Shouty Husband had a need to protect someone. They had a great relationship for years until the Bony One took Graham away.

They were both out of work, so a lot of their time was spent trying to find ways to make money.

Graham got a short-term job in an office and bought a Mini that Shouty Husband, a dab hand with a welder, was going to do up for him.

The problem was that the car was more rust than metal. Shouty Husband went round it with a screwdriver, swearing as he poked holes in the bodywork. In order to weld, he said, you needed metal to weld to. Nobody in their right mind would buy such a heap of junk. That said, he still worked wonders on that Mini and got it roadworthy.

One day, the bailiffs came round. Graham had run up debts and they wanted to collect, even though he had nothing of any value. They still took everything that wasn't nailed down, even a coffee jar that was full of 2p and 1p pieces. Graham was left with nothing, and Shouty Husband wasn't letting that one lie. Graham was more than capable of taking care of his own problems, but not with violence; he was more devious. His mantra was that you could rule the world if you used your mind.

Shouty Husband found out where the bailiffs' offices were and learned they had very expensive cars parked outside. In the wee small hours of a rainy night, Shouty Husband and Graham went out on the bike armed with a catapult and ball bearings.

It took Graham a mere two minutes to fire the ball bearings. He took out every window in every car and damaged their paintwork. He paid that debt back with interest.

Not long after, Graham introduced Shouty Husband to Squeaky Trev, as he's always affectionately been known.

Trev owned a butcher's shop and on Friday nights he drank in The Alexandria, which at the time was a spit-and-sawdust pub. first night he met Shouty Husband

Shouty Husband had got some couriering work down in Bristol. Hans the German was hitchhiking and, since Shouty Husband always carried a spare helmet, he offered him a lift and they went to the pub.

At the time Trev was seeing the barmaid, Karen. Shouty Husband thought she was a bit of all right and chanced his arm but got nowhere. He'd known Trev was interested in her but hadn't realised they were already a couple; after all, they were both married to other people.

Trev and Karen stayed friends with Shouty Husband for 30 years until he finally turned on them. You'll have to wait for that bit of the story, though, as it involves me – and I'm not around at the moment.

Standing In My Light - Ian Hunter

If he can possibly help it, Shouty Husband does not go to weddings or any other formal occasions. He did make an exception for Trev and Karen, though.

(Trev is an incurable romantic, by the way – he won't mind me saying so. Never forgets birthdays or anniversaries, there with the flowers and presents – he's the real deal.)

Trev and Karen's wedding was one of two that Shouty Husband says were memorable for the right reasons. The other one was ours.

Anyway, they got married on Valentine's Day in a leap year, Karen ignoring Shouty Husband's last-minute offer to take her away so she could be his.

The wedding reception was at KFC and Trev put sugar on his fries instead of salt, causing Shouty Husband much mirth. He told Trev that, since it was a leap year, he only had to remember his anniversary once every four years.

Even though it was Trev and Karen's big day, Shouty Husband still had to be the centre of attention.

Peek a Boo - The Stylistics

If Shouty Husband got into trouble, Trev and Graham were always the ones who patched him up afterwards.

On a dark and rainy Friday night in October, Shouty Husband was riding his motorbike homewards, looking forward to for a bath, clean clothes and a spliff before heading to the pub for plenty of beer.

Luckily, he was riding through a built-up area, so he wasn't going too fast when a car door opened into his path suddenly, knocking him over. After killing the engine and taking off his helmet, Shouty Husband picked up his bike and went over to sort out the idiot who hit him.

He wasn't in the mood for a discussion, so Shouty Husband just grabbed the large Asian guy who had knocked him off the bike. After pinning him up against his car he got him across the seats inside and started punching him.

Next moment, Shouty Husband is grabbed by the legs and hauled out by two of the driver's friends. Then, to coin a phrase, he took a beating.

Afterwards, Shouty Husband could barely see. His head was so swollen he couldn't get his helmet on, and his leg had ballooned. Luckily, he'd reacted like a hedgehog and curled up, so otherwise he got away with two broken ribs and bruising.

He manged to ride his bike home, where Graham and Trev cleaned him up and took him to the hospital. He was black and blue for weeks and nearly lost the sight in one eye.

Shouty Husband was never one to take a beating lying down, so he planned his revenge. He staked out the houses where the incident happened, knowing the car belonged there somewhere. He found out where the Asian guy lived and worked out his routine. He really should have tried out for MI5!

He learned that the guy went to the pub every Friday night and got home around the same time each week. So, one rainy evening, Shouty Husband waited patiently until his target returned and then smashed him over the head with a plank of wood. He got in his face to make sure the guy knew who had hit him; after all, said Shouty Husband, what was the point of getting anybody back if nobody knew who it was?

I'm Waiting for the Man - Velvet Underground

Always open to new experience, Shouty Husband would try anything that was offered. That included LSD: at the time he was with Charlie and Charlie's missus in their flat. Shouty Husband was having a great trip until he looked in the mirror and paranoia took over. He could see two Charlies – a nice one, reflected in the glass, and an evil one who was in the room behind Shouty Husband. He decided he had to get away and go home.

Unfortunately, Shouty Husband lived on the other side of town. It was too far to walk, so in his infinite wisdom he decided to get the bus.

So, there he was at the bus stop, off his face on acid, by the side of a busy main road. Even he realised this wasn't his best idea when he nearly got run over after thinking he could simply pluck cars off the road.

Ok then, maybe a taxi would be better way. Shouty Husband made it to the taxi rank and managed to give them his address, and off they went. The meter was ticking when his paranoia kicked in again. Panicking that he wouldn't have enough money to pay the fare, he got the driver to stop half a mile from home. Then he threw some money at him, got out, and started to walk.

He still can't remember getting home, but he did wonder about his actions when he finally came back down to earth. To this day he gets flashbacks to that first trip and laughs as he wonders how he didn't end up dead.

I am the Walrus - The Beatles

As Shouty Husband had missed out on his education, when he learned the DSS[*] would pay him to attend college he thought it was a good idea. It would certainly boost the pittance of dole money he usually got.

He ended up doing the pure maths course. He had a head for numbers and loved it. The weird thing was that he transposed his numbers – always has – so his working out was wrong, but he always got the answer right. It confused his teacher, but he was having fun and it stopped him being bored.

Then Shouty Husband had a chemical romance, one of those moments that became folklore. Charlie's best friend, Nigel, had a knowledge of drugs and their chemical makeup – both legal and illegal – that was second to none. He should have become a chemist.

Shouty Husband got into hallucinogens. His favourites were magic mushrooms, but the problem with those is they have a very short growing season, are hard to find, and the growing areas are generally kept a closely guarded secret.

---

[*]   DSS – Department of Society Security, the government department formerly responsible for benefits payments. It ceased to exist in 2001.

Charlie and Nigel knew where they were and would pick and dry them for later use. They'd always give Shouty Husband a bag which he'd make into tea to get the full effect. A few mushrooms went a long way.

After happily tripping one night away on mushroom tea, Shouty Husband woke up late. Unfortunately for him he was due in college and attendance was monitored as his dole money relied on him being there.

He grabbed the nearest cup of liquid and drank deeply while trying to get his head together. Turned out it was magic mushroom tea that had steeped all night.

So, after downing a very powerful hallucinogenic, Shouty Husband went off to his lecture. The trip began about an hour into the session; everyone there melted into one big psychedelic swirl and his paranoia kicked in. He made his excuses and left, making it home eventually via the park so he could hide and enjoy the unexpected trip.

He realised the park was a good place to trip in and went there a lot – as you'll read later.

High Energy - Evelyn Thomas

Work was hard to come by, so Shouty Husband did odd jobs for the little old ladies who lived in the old folks' flats opposite. He would work for a dinner and the little old ladies loved him, so he ate very well.

Then the world changed and the then-Prime Minister, Margaret Thatcher, introduced the poll tax to replace domestic rates. There were widespread protests and thousands of court cases against non-payers; most were fined, but some were jailed. As he was on the dole, Shouty Husband couldn't afford to pay his rent, eat and pay the poll tax, so he didn't bother with it. The law caught up with him after a while and he went to court to join the queue of people who were in the same boat.

Bored of waiting, he decided to sit at the back of the court to get an idea of what would happen. He said it was like a kangaroo court, with people sent to prison for 28 days if they couldn't pay.

One poor man had only got a job two weeks before. He'd paid his rent and filled his pantry so his children could eat, but the court decreed paying the poll tax should have come first. He got sent down there and then.

Shouty Husband was determined he wasn't going to prison. He agreed with everything that was said in court about payment, said 'Yes sir, no sir' as required, then went home and moved bedsits.

He ended up in another big Victorian house, a real dump where he had to pay cash, with a nutty landlady aptly named Hazel.

There was a residential home next door which housed five men with learning difficulties. In charge was Tilly, who came from Indonesia. She kept an eye on Shouty Husband and would feed him in exchange for odd jobs. She'd also make him toast when there was nothing for him to do, which was very welcome as there wasn't much left of his dole money for food once he'd paid his rent.

One day he put his back out and was bent double in agony. Tilly took him into her living room, put him on the floor and walked up and down his spine. She was only a tiny lady, and Shouty Husband said it was amazing – his back stopped hurting.

When she decorated her living room, Tilly gave a huge white woollen rug she didn't need to Shouty Husband. It lasted him 20 years, by which time it was threadbare. It was a lovely rug to walk and lie on, and I know quite a few women – me included – had some good times on it.

Even though he was paying cash for his room, Shouty Husband decided to claim housing benefit. The problem was, that as the council didn't know Hazel was renting out rooms, officials were sent round to have a look. When they saw the state of the place – there was raw sewage running down the walls – they condemned it as unfit for habitation and all the residents were told to leave.

Shouty Husband, who by now had all his important belongings stored at Graham's new flat, took his sleeping bag, a camping stove and his dog and camped out in the council offices. He said that since they'd made him homeless, it was their responsibility to rehome him. He stayed there all day and said he'd keep coming back until they found him a home.

His tactic worked. The council gave him a flat in a converted house, in an area with predominantly black and Asian residents. It was on the top floor, and he loved it; the living room windows were huge and caught the sun, so Shouty Husband grew plants and turned it into a veritable Kew Gardens.

The day he moved in, Charlie came to help and trouble naturally followed. A guy in a BMW came and said they needed to move the van they were unloading as it was in his way. Charlie went and hid as Shouty Husband lived up to his name; he knew how he handled this situation would define life in the new flat. Kicking off from the start meant he'd be left alone in future.

Life on Mars - David Bowie

While Shouty Husband was welding, Sue - the neighbour - brought him garlic sausage sandwiches. Not his favourite thing, but food was food. A tiny tabby cat wandered over and watched him. It looked thin so he threw her bits of garlic sausage.

Afterwards, it jumped up onto Shouty Husband's shoulder and stayed there, even while he was taking his equipment back upstairs. Back in the flat, the cat jumped onto the sofa and started purring. Mum Cat lived with Shouty husband for 16 years. We never knew how old she was, and she was always tiny, but she loved Shouty Husband dearly – she'd chosen him as her human.

One of the funniest stories was how, one Sunday morning, Mum Cat was spotted dragging an enormous, cooked chicken across the car park. Someone must have put it on a windowsill to cool. It was bigger than she was, but she was determined to have it. Mum Cat ate very well that week and Shouty Husband kept very quiet about what she'd done or they'd both have been in trouble.

Shouty Husband loved living at that flat, but all good things come to an end. Karen appeared and life took an interesting turn, and the flat had to go as he got into rent arrears.

The Bitch Is Back - Elton John

I met Shouty Husband again when Karen was pregnant with who he thought was his son. The rest of the crowd except me played bingo on Tuesday nights, so I was babysitting for Donna. I only lived eight minutes away, but she'd always make sure her then-husband walked me home when he got back from work at 10pm.

Shouty Husband turned up to see Karen and offered to walk me home. I was pregnant with Luke at the time and wanted to get back, and he remembered me from the infamous New Year's Eve party.

He was very attentive all the way to my house, and I enjoyed our chat. At the time I was still in the dark about his ménage à trois with Karen and Vinnie and just enjoyed his company. I had no idea he'd be back a couple of years later, and that my life would never be the same again.

Fight the Good Fight - Triumph

Eventually, Karen and Vinnie broke up and Vinnie moved to Wales. He remarried further down the line. In the meantime, the bank repossessed their house and Karen — plus her three children — had to go into a private rental. She was friends with another woman I knew, which is how I got to know her, although not too well until she remarried.

We ladies all went to the wedding. We knew the marriage would end in disaster but, like those women who sat by the guillotine during the French Revolution, we couldn't resist a good show. Marry in haste and repent at leisure, so the saying goes, and Karen certainly did that. Her new husband had five children and wanted a housekeeper, not a wife. Karen lasted six weeks before she walked. Of course, the house she'd been living in had been re-rented by then, so she needed to find a new one. In the meantime, she and the kids moved in with the Boy's Dad and me for a couple of weeks; by this time, I thought we were best friends. (Another of my mistakes.)

At the time, we lived in a three-bedroom terrace, so three adults and five kids — aged nine, seven, five and two three-year-olds — squashed into that space made for interesting times. Karen did give us some money towards the food bill, but we were left well out of pocket by the experience.

Every evening she'd spend time with Thom, an old flame. I knew him and he was lovely; he also had a wife and daughter, both of whom he loved dearly, but he liked to have a mistress. As long as you understood the rules, Thom was fun to be around and Karen had filled the role for a long time, on and off. She needed money and he always had spare cash, and he helped her get a home for her and the children.

If she'd left Mr Wrong a day earlier, she'd have got her old place back. Instead, she ended up on an estate a few miles away from me. Her neighbours were called Max and Sharon, and that's how they came into our lives – more on them later.

Tainted Love - Soft Cell

I realise that so far, I haven't put any flesh on Karen's bones, as my mum would say. I'll put that right now.

Karen was five years older than me. She stood 5ft 4ins and was of tiny build, about a UK size eight. (Or, at her worst – which she hated – a size 12. She didn't diet, she starved herself.) She was perfectly normal-looking, with mousy collar-length hair, and she wore glasses. I learnt the hard way that she only cared about herself.

Karen and Shouty Husband are really peas out of the same pod. They both took advantage of me, and I let them. However, the one thing he taught me was how to take someone's head. Sometimes you're in the right place at the right time with the right information, and you get your moment. Don't hate me, but you'll have to wait a bit longer to hear more about that.

Back to Karen. She knew Shouty Husband was using me in the game that was their relationship – it was all about one-upmanship. Shouty Husband wasn't a tactile person – more wrapped in razor wire – whereas she was more like ivy – she clung. She desperately needed reassurance that she was wanted and loved. She also needed a man in her life to validate her existence. In all the years I knew her, she went through an endless cycle of having a man in her life, ending up alone, then desperately hunting for the next man who could fill the void. The sad truth was the only person who could really do that was Vinnie.

Rockin' in the Free World - Neil Young

Time for some memories of Max and Sharon now. They played a big part for a short time in this story and made a real impression. It will all make sense in the end, I promise.

While Shouty Husband was with Karen, he spent a lot of time with Max. They'd get up to no good as they'd egg each other on. Max knew all the fun places to go where it was fine to drink and toke, something Shouty Husband appreciated as Karen was against him doing both; it took his money out of her pocket.

Shouty Husband was never one for video games, except for one Christmas when Max took him to the bowling alley. It happened to be open, and it served beer, which was how they ended up there. There was a shoot- 'em-up video game and, since Shouty Husband was well pissed, he decided to have a go. He was a good shot even when drunk. He spent a fortune, got very aggressive, and – when he got too loud – he was asked to leave.

He was incapable of getting home under his own steam, so Karen had to pick him up. He made her drive all the way home at 20mph because he was doing his best not to throw up. (This was something that rarely happened, so he must have had an absolute skinful, and probably a load of dope too, knowing Max.)

Karen was going over the speed bumps so slowly, a snail could beat her. She got pulled over by the police who thought she was the one who had been drinking – until they took a look at Shouty Husband, who by now was a funny shade of green. They laughed and Karen made his life a misery for the next couple of days, but Shouty Husband said it was worth it as he'd had a great time.

As far as the rest of the world was concerned, Karen and Shouty Husband had the perfect relationship.

In reality, Shouty Husband was playing the long game because he had nowhere else to go. He knew that if he gave Karen hope for the future and kept her happy, life was sweet. He had a home, a quiet life, could drink and smoke as he wanted and there was sex on tap.

Karen couldn't wait to tell me when Shouty Husband decided they should get married. She'd been sterilised previously, but she announced she planned to have the procedure reversed so they could have more children.

I believed her; they were still in the first flush of romance, and she had fallen for the dream. It was time to go dress hunting.

Internet shopping had yet to take off in the mid- '90s, so Karen looked at beautiful dresses in wedding magazines and used the Yellow Pages to track down fancy bridal shops. She was on Cloud Nine, which meant Shouty Husband was happy too, and even the kids picked up on the good vibes and behaved well.

I went with Karen to the wedding dress shop she'd chosen, one of those posh, expensive places that don't put the prices on anything. It was in Newport, a nearby market town, and when we walked through the door there was a

Pretty Woman moment – the smile dropped from the assistant's face when she saw us and I honestly thought she'd refuse to serve us. I guess she remembered that you can never really tell who money might have, though, because the next minute Karen was being addressed as 'modom' and we were looking at dresses.

Karen picked out a pink dress with a huge underskirt and lots of layers of pinned tulle and net. It was so big I could get underneath to puff out the underlayers. She looked like a giant pink meringue, but she loved it – as far as she was concerned this was the one – a dream dress for her dream wedding. The fact it cost £2,000 – and at that time you could buy a new car for that amount of money - was irrelevant. She could picture herself floating down the aisle in this dress and no other.

You've probably worked out by now that what Shouty Husband promised and what he delivered were two different things. So, I don't think I'm spoiling the plot by revealing that Karen never got her pink meringue dress, and she never married Shouty Husband, either.

Lay it on the Line - Triumph

Life was going okay in the Shouty Husband and Karen household, but then Shouty Husband showed his true colours by getting to fall-over-in-a-heap drunk and letting Karen down big time.

Super-strength lager had become his tipple of choice after being introduced to it by Charlie during his stint in Bedsit Land. Usually, he didn't drink or toke to excess in public; he'd do it quietly in the garage.

But then Impecunious Hero needed a new part for the head gasket, so Shouty Husband took it to pieces and went over to Wolverhampton on the bus to get it fixed.

After visiting the bike shop, he always used, he went to The Alex to meet up with old friends. After a skinful of beer on an empty stomach, he made it back to the bus stop and settled in for the journey home. The bus driver wasn't happy about taking him when he was so drunk, but Shouty Husband promised to behave. Unfortunately, the amount of booze he'd had didn't mix well with the rural roads and he soon felt sick. The only option was to throw up into the bag with the head gasket in. So, he did.

Once in the town centre, he waited for the next bus that would take him home. He ended up on his hands and knees, throwing up into the gutter. He wouldn't normally have been that sick after a belly full of beer, but he'd been drinking nowhere near as much in recent times and it affected him badly. Finally, he managed to get home, four hours later than planned. Karen would have been annoyed at the best of times, but on this particular evening they were supposed to be going to an open evening at the secondary school her middle son, Will, attended. The idea was they'd show the school they were a normal family unit and it had been on the calendar for weeks.

Instead, Karen called me to say Shouty Husband had got pissed and let her down, and could I go with her instead.

At the time I had very short hair and, as it was such short notice, I had no time to change. I wore jeans and a t-shirt, while Karen had made an effort and looked very pretty in a gypsy skirt and flattering top. She looked very feminine, and I looked very masculine.

After the tour and a chat with the teachers, we were talking to the headmaster when he commented that Will should keep quiet about his mum being in a relationship with another woman as children could be cruel.

It took us both a minute to realise he'd assumed Karen and I were a couple. Being naughty, we didn't tell him any differently.

Shouty Husband was in the doghouse for a long time after that – and then things went really wrong.

Live It Up - Mental As Anything

After Shouty Husband's drunken episode on the night of the school open evening, the cracks in his and Karen's lives started opening up again.

First the heating went wrong, and the friend who owned the house had to pay silly money to get it fixed. Then the job in Germany that was supposed to last five years fell through, so they faced being homeless when he wanted his house back.

Karen went back to the letting agency she'd used previously, and they found her another house on the same estate so the kids could carry on going to the same schools.

The problem was the previous tenants – who'd been evicted – had been druggies. They'd painted on the walls and the woodwork, and it was a mess. There were bags of crap everywhere and the place wasn't fit for any kind of human habitation, never mind kids.

But beggars can't be choosers, and Karen agreed to take it as long as it was decorated. The agency offered her a grant for materials if she did it herself, and so began two weeks of renovation. Armed with heavy duty gloves, Karen and I set to work. The environmental health department gave us sharps bins and tongs, and we disposed of 200 used needs. We cleared bin bags of old clothes, pulled up the carpets and got the place as clean as possible. My mum would babysit the boys every evening so the Boy's Dad and I could help Karen with painting.

I can't deny part of my motivation was the chance of seeing Shouty Husband. I can remember one evening as though it were yesterday, not 28 years ago – spending a couple of hours with him as we painted the ceiling – badly, in my case. I had his full attention and made the most of it. It was obvious I was in heaven, and neither Karen nor the Boy's Dad were happy. But she needed the help, and she got to have a laugh at my expense with Shouty Husband after I'd gone home.

A fortnight later, Karen, her kids and Shouty Husband all moved in, and it was the beginning of the end. He had no choice but to be there as he'd lost his flat by now, and Karen stopped trying so hard to keep their relationship alive.

Little Girl Blue - Janis Joplin

Not long after, Shouty Husband got really sick – as in, he ended up in hospital. As you might imagine, he was the worst patient ever. He didn't like being woken up in the middle of the night to have his blood pressure taken, and he said the food was terrible. The poor nurses had to put up with him for a week.

In that time, his friend Graham visited and took him food. That's when I first met Graham; he'd come to take Karen to visit Shouty Husband in hospital, so I went to babysit for her.

When they got back, he offered me a lift home and, as he seemed to be a perfect gentleman, I accepted. Little did I know Graham would become a good friend to me.

Shouty Husband was finally diagnosed with glandular fever; the consultant said his tonsils looked like a bird had shit on them. Who knew? Lots of junior doctors had already looked at Shouty Husband's tonsils.

Shouty Husband was off work for a month, which he struggled with. He didn't get much sick pay, Karen always had her hand out, and he wanted peace and quiet rather than a house full of boisterous kids.

Then, shortly after he went back to work, he lost his job. I was never entirely sure whether he was sacked or walked out as I only ever heard his side of the story.

The next bit of the tale didn't come from Shouty Husband; I only heard Karen's side, but Steve was there and also told me about it years later.

Shouty Husband had had enough and wanted to leave, but Karen didn't want him to, so she got in the way. To say that made him cross is an understatement; he went out of the front door, Karen behind him still shouting, and punched the fence that ran down the side of the house. The planks were an inch thick and overlapped, so it was strong. Still, when Steve heard banging, he looked out of his kitchen window to see Shouty Husband destroying it .

Afterwards, Steve went out to see if he was ok. Shouty Husband was in that danger zone, where the adrenaline rush makes him hypersensitive to light and sound. He feels completely alive and invincible, with complete clarity of mind.

Karen had heard he could get like that but had never seen it before, so she didn't know that shouting at him and getting in his face was the worst mistake she could make.

He went to get his stuff, but she wouldn't let him back into the house. So he got into his Mini, drove it through the gate – which was shut – and aimed straight at her.

Luckily for Karen, the garden was on a steep tiered slope and Shouty Husband stopped before he damaged his car.

Then he reversed and drove off, while Karen was still frozen to the spot.

A few days later, Shouty Husband went back to fix the fence and gate. Steve went over to help him and then, once it was done, Shouty Husband was gone.

They Don't Know - Tracey Ullman

Luckily, his cousin Tommy had moved in with his girlfriend, leaving his flat empty, or Shouty Husband would have had no place to go.

Meanwhile, Karen didn't let the bed go cold before Thom – remember him? – reappeared for a while. The Boy's Dad and I went to a great country pub with them on a double date, but we didn't think Thom would stay around for long – Karen tended to get clingy and demanding.

We were right. Before long, Thom vanished, and Karen was back on her own again.

It's a Mystery - Toyah

Shouty Husband decided some time out was the best way to keep Karen under his thumb. Tommy's flat – on the seventh floor of a high-rise in a rough part of Wolverhampton – wasn't ideal, but it was better than staying with her.

Karen was left to stew and Shouty Husband went back to life on his own, taking his anger out on anybody who got in his way.

For someone with bad eyesight, Shouty Husband is an incredibly good shot – he always hits the target, whether he's using a catapult, crossbow or an air rifle.

His prized possession at the time was his motorbike, Rocky, which he kept chained to the railing's downstairs in front of the flats.

To be honest, it was a heap that nobody in their right mind would try to ride. It had temperamental brakes and handled badly, but Shouty Husband loved it.

He'd put a cheap alarm on Rocky, just in case somebody was stupid enough to try and mess with it and kept a loaded crossbow by the window.

One time, when the alarm went off, Shouty Husband grabbed his crossbow and looked out of the window to see two lads messing around with Rocky. He decided to teach them a lesson; he aimed at the pavement and hit the spot he intended as the target, but of course they didn't know that. They just thought the nutter on the seventh floor had shot a crossbow bolt at them and missed.

The incident established Shouty Husband's reputation and, after that, everyone left him – and Rocky – alone.

While he was away from Karen, Shouty Husband got a job doing piece work.

If you don't know what that is, it means you're paid by the amount of work you produce – so, the more you work, the more money you earn.

The flat below had an amazing stereo and played old school reggae which Shouty husband loved – usually. However, it lost its charm when he was overtired, had no dope and needed to get up for work at stupid o' clock.

One night, the bass was turned up so high Shouty Husband's floorboards were shaking with the vibration. He decided to do something about it; he was reputed to be a nutter, after all. So, he pulled on some jeans and went downstairs.

Shouty Husband was always reasonable to begin with, so he asked the guy who answered the door nicely if they'd mind turning the bass down a bit. The guy sucked his teeth, said 'We will see ', and shut the door in his face.

Shouty Husband went back to his flat and hoped. After about ten minutes, the bass was turned down and he got some sleep.

The next day, he shared the lift with the owner of the other flat who told him there'd been six big guys in there and it wouldn't have ended well for Shouty Husband if he'd been aggressive about the noise.

Shouty Husband explained that he loved the music, but he had no dope and had needed to get some sleep. His companion turned out to be the block's top dealer and, what's more, he knew about Shouty Husband and the crossbow.

Shouty Husband was invited in for a drink and a spliff. He acquired the taste for very good brandy, and from then on was never short of dope the whole time he lived in Tommy's flat.

Tom Sawyer - Rush

Deciding life without Shouty Husband was not worth living, Karen went to eat humble pie after giving him some time to calm down.

She got her sister to drive him to the flats at Blakenell; she didn't know exactly which one he was in but had a feeling somebody would be able to tell her.

Unfortunately, the car had three aerials sticking out of the roof as Karen's sister had a car telephone fitted as part of her job. The dealers thought this meant she was a plain-clothes policewoman and gave Karen grief.

Luckily, Shouty Husband looked out to see what the commotion was in case anyone was messing with his bike and saw her. A week later, he moved back in, and things were better between them – for a while, anyway.

Love Shine a Light - Katrina and the Waves

The first time Shouty Husband entertained the Boy's Dad and I, he told us to come for dinner and said he'd cook.

He made his famous spaghetti bolognaise with homemade garlic bread, and I was on Cloud Nine at the prospect of a whole evening with him. I dressed for the occasion in a tartan skirt that stopped just above my knees. (Usually, my skirts graze my ankles.) was given the ring binder in which Shouty Husband had listed every vinyl record he owned so I could pick the mood music. According to Karen this was an unprecedented honour – usually, he picked it himself.

My one and only choice from the binder was an album I already had and loved.

He regaled us with the story he told everyone when he cooked spaghetti bolognaise for them – how, when he was with Jinx, his sister Paula had gone round for dinner. When he brought out the dish of home cooked spag bol, Paula looked at it and said the immortal words: 'I thought it would be Heinz out of a tin. '

I'm writing this with a smile on my face, as I loved every moment of that evening. Shouty Husband seemed interested in everything I had to say, and I gloried in the attention.

Paradise by the Dashboard Light - Meat Loaf

Now it's time for the tale of the first time I stood up to Shouty Husband. They say hindsight is a wonderful thing and I should have listened to the inner voice that spoke to me back then.

My first boyfriend's mum died and, as she and I had always got on, I planned to attend her funeral with my parents. Karen agreed to have Luke for me, and Shouty Husband was due to be working, so no problems there. Or so I thought.

He was in one of his 'had enough of living in a mad house' phases and feeling Karen didn't appreciate him. He walked in from his shift while I was sitting there and, instead of taking his fury out on Karen, he directed it at me. He told me I was destroying his relationship with Karen by always being around, and he had had enough, and I had to go. Well, even though I wasn't the Purple-Haired Warrior with Knobs On back then, I still had a temper, and I wasn't putting up with his crap. I drew myself up to my full height of 5ft 2inches, pulled my shoulders back and gave him both barrels.

I poked him in the chest and told him he knew Karen was minding Luke for me as I was going to a funeral, that whatever his problem was it was not my fault, and that he was a bully. I was going now, I said, but I'd still be around as Karen was my best friend. (Got that one wrong, but never mind.)

Shouty Husband looked at me, boiling with rage, and then laughed and told me he was waiting for me to grow a spine and tell him off.

I had it right then - he was a bully. But love is blind and, even though I never thought we'd end up together, he was all I wanted. I loved him even then – so how dare he have a go at me!

A Face in the Crowd - Tom Petty

I never found out just what problems he was having with Karen, but before long Shouty Husband was back in his cousin Tommy's flat.

Karen was having a night out with her sister – they'd planned to get their hair done in an expensive salon, followed by a meal and drinks. The kids were at their dad's, so the house was empty.

Shouty Husband rang me that morning and told me to tell Karen he was coming to collect the rest of his stuff. The house always looked like it had been burgled after he did this because he had so much furniture, plus his stereo.

I knew that Karen was due home that morning and his tone of voice made me worried for Karen. I tried to find her sister's number, but she was ex-directory and people didn't have mobiles then. I didn't drive, so I took a taxi the six miles to her sister's house. Karen wasn't concerned at all; she drove us both back to her house to find it tidy, though all Shouty Husband's stuff had gone.

Thom appeared again after a week and, as it was coming up to mine and the Boy's Dad's wedding anniversary, he suggested we all went for a meal and then to the cinema to see Jurassic Park, that summer's blockbuster movie.

We had a great night, but I could tell Karen was still working out how she could get Shouty Husband back.

In the event, she decided to write him a letter. We went to his workplace s and she left it on Rocky, the bike.

Everybody knew not to go near Shouty Husband's bike, so he heard some woman had left something on it before we were even out of the car park.

He made her suffer for another week before he came back, though. And in the meantime, she'd realised she needed to buy a potato peeler as he always his with him when he left!

I Only Want Be with You - Dusty Springfield

Karen's birthday is over Christmas, so she always had a party around then. We went to two while she was with Shouty Husband.

Steve and his then-wife, who lived opposite, were also invited. I knew her but had never met Steve – just heard about him as part of the fence and gate incident.

After introducing himself, he asked his favourite question: 'Do you have any Brummie in you? No? Do you want some? ' I howled with laughter, then we got on to music and found we liked the same artists, and before I knew it two hours had disappeared.

By now, Shouty Husband was lying on the sofa, drunk and stoned. When I went in he asked me if I could get him some jelly and ice cream – preferably his favourite, lime jelly.

I did as I was told and then, because he was comfortable, he asked me to feed him. So I did, in front of the Boy's Dad and Karen. I didn't care. I was in a bubble with him, and I loved it.

Young Hearts Run Free - Kym Mazelle

Shouty Husband took Karen and the kids away for a long weekend to Brean Sands. Being blond and fair skinned, he got sunburned and, when they got home, Karen asked if I could take my aloe vera gel round for him. Well, of course – it meant I could spend time with Shouty Husband. I found him lying on the sofa and legs were so red, I could feel the heat coming off them. He asked me to rub the gel into his thighs, but there was no way Karen would let that happen. She all but pushed me out of the door, telling me they were in a really good place so she wouldn't be around as much for a while. I should stay away, and she'd call when she was available.

When she did need me again, I went running back; as well as wanting to spend time with Shouty Husband, I missed the person I regarded as my best friend!

Shouty husband had his bike Rocky, but Karen needed a car to get around, so Shouty husband found a mini, but he did not have the money till payday. Karen told him that I had savings and would lend him the money for a few days if he asked.

So Shouty husband came round to ask the boys Dad if it was ok for him to borrow the money for a few days. The boy's dad said yes and Shouty husband gave me his bank card and told me that I should get the money out when he got paid.

I took the money £200 to Karen and on pay day I went to the cash point and got my money back. I never looked how much he had in the bank and told him that. The one thing that Shouty husband always said about me was I was trustworthy.

I Am What I Am - Gloria Gaynor

He was useless at the here and now, but Shouty Husband always had an eye on the future and a long-term plan. His mantra at this time was, 'One day, I'll get my own house again '.

Karen was also looking ahead; in her heart of hearts, I'm sure she knew she wouldn't be making old bones with him.

 Her dream was to be a maths teacher. As she'd abandoned her 'A' levels to be with Vinnie, the best way forward was to do a one-year access course and then go to university.

At the time, having a job myself was out of the question as I spent a lot of time taking Luke to hospital appointments due to his autism. However, the boys' school welcomed volunteer mums to help with reading, so I signed up for one morning a week. I loved it, the teachers loved having me there, and I was given small groups to work with. Since I had no clue how children learnt and wanted to help them properly, I thought about doing a training course.

It so happened that the local college had an open evening. Karen wanted to find out about access courses and didn't want to go alone, so she asked me to go with her.

When she spotted me looking at a City and Guilds learning support course, she laughed. 'You'll never be able to do that, ' she said, in a derogatory tone. So, I signed up, just to prove her wrong.

Karen moved to a different college for her course, as she didn't like the first one, but I continued going to my sessions every Thursday night. I was driving by now and had a car for two hours a week so I could go and learn how to be a teaching assistant. I put in more time at school to get the necessary hours in, and I really enjoyed it. One evening it had snowed heavily. I'd never driven in snow and was apprehensive; when I told Karen how nervous I was, she volunteered Shouty Husband to give me a lift as he was going to Wolverhampton to visit family.

He dropped me off and told me he'd be back for me at 9pm. Unfortunately, I was the only person that made it, so the class didn't go ahead, but with no way of contacting Shouty Husband I was stuck for the evening.

My mum's house wasn't far away, but I didn't fancy the idea of trudging through the snow. So, I did the only sensible thing and went to the nearest pub, where I drank two halves of lager and lime and hand-wrote my coursework. When Shouty Husband collected me, he laughed when I told him what had happened. If I'd only found a phone, I could have called him and gone home. Incidentally, I passed the course with a distinction and have gone on to take many more since. One good piece of advice Shouty Husband gave me was to get the pieces of paper that would help me get a job. As a result, I've been a specialist teaching assistant working with autistic students for the last 13 years. I still love it.

So much for Karen telling me I was wasting my time!

He might have been playing happy families, but beneath the surface was the real Shouty Husband, the one with a violent streak who did not suffer fools. Then came the incident with the window cleaner, which brought out his true colours.

When Karen's window cleaner knocked to ask for his money, Shouty Husband answered the door and asked when the windows had been cleaned. The man told him two hours earlier, which Shouty Husband knew wasn't the case as he'd been in all day.

He asked the man if he'd cleaned the patio door windows and, on being told yes, Shouty Husband pointed out a muddy mark from a football that was still there.

An argument followed, with the window cleaner demanding his money and Shouty Husband telling him he was on private property and needed to leave or else, as per the law, after two warnings he'd remove him.

Moving quickly, he puffed his chest out, so it knocked the window cleaner backwards. The man ended up on his backside on the grass, to the amusement of the kids playing outside on the green. Getting up, the window cleaner said as Shouty Husband had hit him, he was calling the police.

Two police officers, one male and one female, duly arrived. Karen invited them in, and the policewoman told

Shouty Husband she thought he was dangerous. Still wound up about the whole thing, Shouty Husband told her she wasn't welcome in his house and should leave. A bit of a standoff developed, but fortunately the policeman was a reasonable person and said he'd handle it. He listened to Shouty Husband's version of events, warned him not to do it again, and the matter was dropped.

As far as he was concerned, Shouty Husband was just defending his home and his family, as was his right. It took him a while to come down from the rush of allowing his true self to show, though.

Geno - Dexys Midnight Runners

You already know Shouty Husband liked people to know it was him when he got his own back on people, else it was no fun. He also believed in the saying that revenge is a dish best served cold.

This is the story of him, Pat Conner, and a paraffin lamp.

Vickey, Karen's daughter, was running wild with a group of bad kids when she was thirteen. Their leader was a boy, also thirteen, with looks and attitude she couldn't resist.

He thought it would be fun if he and Vickey jumped all over a car. Why, I have no idea. But it was Pat Conner's car, and they dented the boot and trashed the paintwork.

Pat Conner knew where Vickey lived so he stormed round and confronted Karen on the doorstep. Shouty Husband, woken from a deep, lager-induced sleep as a result, stormed downstairs ready to create hell. He saw Pat Conner laying down the law to Karen and it took a moment for the penny to drop. He knew him. They'd had a few fights as teenagers, which Shouty Husband won. Pat Conner didn't recognise him, though.

Karen said she could see the light bulb go on above Pat Conner's head when Shouty Husband reminded him of the past. He calmed down and explained what had happened, and Shouty Husband went to look at the damage. Deciding it was fixable, he told Pat Conner he'd sort his car out for him and spent the whole of Sunday pushing out dents and polishing the bodywork. Pat seemed happy enough with it.

Then Shouty Husbands' bike was stolen out of the garage. He asked everyone if they knew who'd taken it but came up blank, until a car thief from another estate got caught and held his hands up to it, among his other crimes. The police passed on the information to Shouty Husband, who paid the thief a visit. And he learned the man had been paid £20 by Pat Conner to pinch the bike.

So Shouty Husband decided to get his own back, which involved a small paraffin lamp like the ones used to warn of roadworks back in the day.

He lit the lamp so the flame was exposed, then placed it under Pat Conner's car near the petrol tank. The petrol expanded and went bang, flipping the car onto its back. (Don't worry, nobody was hurt – it was away from people, houses and other cars.)

The police were called, along with the fire brigade, but as Pot Conner was the kind of man who made enemies rather than friends, the list of suspects was endless. Pat Conner got his car replaced through his insurance, and life went back to normal.

Then, a few months later, Shouty Husband made a point of walking into the rough pub Pat Conner drank in. When he was halfway down his pint, he quietly told Pat it was a shame about his car, but he had enjoyed the blaze. Then he said if Pat wanted to play again, they could go outside together and sort it out like men there and then.

Pat Conner finished his half of bitter and left.

Everyone heard about how he'd taken on the wrong man, and Shouty Husband was given a wide berth by the whole estate.

Do You Really Want to Hurt Me - Culture Club

Karen had an abnormal cervical smear and, after lots of tests, the hospital decided she needed a hysterectomy. She was only 33.

Shouty Husband was working weird hours and, when Karen got home, she got a lot of grief from Vickey; got to love teenage hormones. After a week, Karen decided her daughter should go and stay with her dad in Wales. (Harry was already there. Will was allowed to stay at home as he wasn't causing any problems.)

So, on a Sunday night five months after I passed my driving test, I drove Karen and Vickey the two hours to a small village in South Wales, where we had a cup of tea before returning. It was both terrifying and fun.

By coincidence, about another week later, I also ended up having a hysterectomy. I was 28 at the time. I realised Karen must have got through that journey on sheer willpower as, a week after my operation, I wasn't fit for anything except lying on a sun lounger at my mum's.

What a fun summer that was!

Perfect Day - Lou Reed

The first time Shouty Husband went to a proper dentist, he was 16 years old. (I'm not counting the school dentist.) He got a real butcher who gave him eight fillings in one go without any novocaine.

The experience meant regular future visits were rather hit and miss, mostly miss.

He wasn't brilliant when it came to dental hygiene and he ate too many crisps, so it wasn't much of a surprise to anyone – except Shouty Husband – when he got an abscess under one of his back teeth.

Karen, having had enough of him acting like a bear with a sore head, made him an appointment with the emergency dentist, who told Shouty Husband the tooth needed to come out. However, what he didn't say was that the abscess was still there, and really Shouty Husband needed antibiotics before the tooth was pulled.

He didn't use enough novocaine, then the abscess burst during the procedure, and Shouty Husband hit the ceiling with the resulting pain.

While he climbed down, muttering dire threats about what he intended to do to the person who'd caused it, the dentist backed off and wrote a prescription. Shouty Husband, with a half-pulled tooth and still mad with pain, stormed off with Karen to collect his painkillers from the chemist's. He dry-swallowed two without even knowing what they were, then went home and took to the sofa with more pills and his super-strength lager. Karen left him to it.

Shouty Husband liked the pills. They took away the pain and put his head in a good place. So, he kept taking them.

Karen got up the following morning. She still wasn't happy, so she made a lot of noise, but Shouty Husband decided he was in too nice a place to object. He could just shut her out, drift off, and never come back.

And that's when he realised, he was dying. Part of him was okay with this, but the essence that is Shouty Husband kicked and fought to hang on to life. He managed to shout to Karen to call an ambulance, and then collapsed before it got there.

He was blue-lighted to hospital, where he woke up to find people hitting him to find a vein, then a burning sensation, and then boom – he was back in the room.

Turned out the tablets were DF118s – dihydrocodeine tartrate – which are now banned as it's so easy to overdose on them. Shouty Husband had taken twenty one tablets in the space of twelve hours. He said he just wanted to stop the pain, but the hospital thought he'd tried to kill himself and sent a psychiatrist to talk to him.

Shouty Husband was released the following day, equipped with antibiotics and less lethal painkillers, after the hospital dentist pulled the tooth and packed it properly.

On his next visit to the dentist's chair, he needed to have all four wisdom teeth removed. They did it in one go and gave him intravenous diazepam, which he loves. He had a wonderful trip and even tried to tip the dentist afterwards.

He also decided he was hungry and insisted on getting a bacon sandwich. I know, but you couldn't stop him. He thought he had red sauce on his sandwich at first; then he realised it was blood and he was chewing the inside of his own cheek.

(We Are) The Road Crew - Motörhead

You might recall Shouty Husband's mantra – that one day he'd have his own house again. After talking about it for years, he decided it was time to do something about it.

He was over 30, looking ahead at years of dead-end jobs, and knew he was reliant on Karen for the roof over his head – and let's face it, life with her had its ups and downs.

So, he set to it. He was used to piece work, so working hard for good money was no hardship. He reckoned all he needed to get together enough for a mortgage was six months of full-time employment at a decent rate.

The only place in the area offering the kind of money he needed at that time was Borgers a factory where they made injection mouldings of car parts – the dashboard and all the plastic bits.

The problem was it was a hell hole with an abysmal health and safety record. It was a standing joke that the fire brigade was called out there at least once a day.

There were accidents. People got hurt. But it was a big company, so it had money to throw around and, if someone did decide to go for compensation, the lawyers were clever enough to tie them up in court proceedings for years.

Shouty Husband knew all this, but he had his heart set on his own house. Karen, who was now at university studying for a maths degree, had no idea he intended his dream home would be just for him – not her and the kids as well. After proving to the recruitment agency that he wasn't scared of hard work, he got taken on full time. He did 12-hour shifts, four days on and three off – horrible hours and a mix of days, nights and afternoons, which didn't do his temper any favours.

Still, he was raking in the money; every week he hit his productivity targets and got full bonus. Shouty Husband worked out the maximum mortgage amount he could get, and Karen decided to go house-hunting; they looked at some beautiful houses, though none of them ever came to anything.

At this time, she had her head in a book every evening, studying hard while she listened to John Goulding. It was the tape of his music that Karen kept when the end finally came for her and Shouty Husband. I spent 20 years trying to replace it, but I did it.

So, while Karen dreamt of being a teacher, Shouty Husband was working himself into the ground, saving every penny he could, and searching for his ideal home. They might have been together, but their heads weren't even in the same library, never mind on the same page.

As far as Shouty Husband was concerned, though, his plans were on track. Then the universe decided to get involved. The machine he operated essentially poured molten plastic into moulds for car parts. To keep workers safe, it had a laser light that, if broken, stopped the machine working. Did I mention health and safety at that place was dire? One day, while Shouty Husband was feeding the machine, it malfunctioned. The laser light also failed, the machine kept going, and he got pulled in!

He squealed like a stuck pig – hardly surprising when you've suddenly got full thickness burns down your face, neck and arm from molten plastic and a dislocated shoulder. We heard about it when he and Karen turned up on our doorstep. Shouty Husband was all bandaged up and fully dosed with strong painkillers. He'd been told he'd be scarred.

There was a silver lining, though. Borgers didn't want Shouty Husband to go down the legal route with a claim for compensation as Karen had been in touch with the Health & Safety Executive (HSE) and told them the factory was dangerous.

Instead, he was called in to a meeting with the men in suits, where he was made an offer, he couldn't refuse; full pay and full bonus for as long as he was off sick and, within reason, that could be pretty much as long as he liked. In the event, he took twelve months and then went back. With hindsight that was a mistake, as psychologically he still wasn't healed. Still, once the physical pain subsided it meant he had plenty of time to look at more affordable houses. His face and neck healed well, and, in the event, there wasn't any scarring there. He did lose a chunk of muscle on his forearm and ended up with a dent which did scar, but it became a source of amusement – Shouty Husband could always prove who he was at parties.

Two Out of Three Ain't Bad – Meat Loaf

The bank turned Shouty Husband down when he applied for a mortgage, so he went to a broker instead. On the day of his interview Karen was at university and Harry was home ill with a cold, so Shouty Husband took him along to the meeting.

It turned out to be a smart move. The mortgage advisor was a woman, so he played the family card for all he was worth, saying he wanted to marry Karen, be a great stepdad and provide a lovely home. The mortgage advisor lapped it up and Shouty Husband got his mortgage offer; now he just had to find a house.

He had a list of the features he wanted – a garage, three bedrooms, and not being overlooked. Karen was looking at properties at the top end of what they could afford, including her salary as a teacher, but he was looking at houses he could afford on his own.

He found one that needed some work. It had the garage and three bedrooms, but was overlooked at the back – not badly, but you couldn't have sunbathed nude without the neighbours seeing.

The owners wanted a quick sale as they were getting divorced, but Shouty Husband needed time to get things organised. So he made them an offer they couldn't refuse – he'd rent the house from them until the sale was finalised. That way, the house would be lived in and heated and, if it all fell through, at least they'd have got some income out of it. They agreed, but initially wanted a ridiculous amount in rent. Shouty Husband said he'd pay what his mortgage was going to cost him and no more, and eventually they agreed. Shouty Husband was happy. He'd made good on his mantra and got a house to call his own again.

I Am (I'm Me) - Twisted Sister

As Shouty Husband was at home and Karen was at university, I didn't see much of them for a while.

So, imagine my surprise when my doorbell rang one rainy Wednesday afternoon. With only half an hour to go before the school run, I was going to tell whoever it was I didn't have long. Then I opened the door to find Shouty Husband bouncing up and down on the step like a three-year-old on a sugar high.

Waving a bunch of keys around, he told me excitedly that I had to go with him to see his new house. Ok, I said. Why me? Because I was the one who'd believed in his dream, he said. That meant I should be the first person to see it. Me, not Karen. Boy, did I feel special! I grabbed my coat and handbag, and two minutes later we were at Shouty Husband's new house.

It needed work, it had the most horrible stone-clad fireplace, and whoever had decorated it needed their eyes testing. But Shouty husband's enthusiasm was infectious, and I fell into the moment with him.

It had been a long time since any man had made me feel special or seemed interested in my opinion – and he made me go weak at the knees into the bargain. Shouty Husband started living at the new place in the week and spent weekends at Karen's. She was waiting until the mortgage came through to move in. Shouty Husband was on top of the world. He'd got what he wanted. But we all know what happens when the world turns...

While he was with Karen, Shouty Husband bought himself a Vauxhall Chevette. It was in great condition for its age, and he loved it.

One day, Shouty Husband was coming back from Wolverhampton. He had a full tank of petrol and was following a car pulling a trailer which decided to turn without indicating. The trailer flipped. Shouty Husband swerved but clipped it. The Chevette rolled over three times and ended up in a ditch on its roof, with Shouty Husband held in upside down by his seat belt while petrol spilled out. He was convinced he was going to burn to death.

 He managed to get the seatbelt undone, bashing his head as he fell. The other driver stood at the side of the road and did nothing to help, apart from calling the police. He also tried to blame Shouty Husband for trying to overtake him. He might have been dazed and confused, but Shouty Husband knew he wasn't at fault.

Unfortunately, his solution was to get aggressive which didn't go down well with the police, who threatened to arrest him. The Chevette was taken to the impound yard and declared a write-off. With Shouty Husband and the other driver blaming each other, the insurance companies decided they could both wait while it all got sorted out. Meanwhile, Shouty Husband had to buy a cheap banger to get to work and the impound fees for the Chevette went up daily.

The insurance company finally paid up, but Shouty Husband was still seriously out of pocket. He never told me what he did to the other driver; he just said he'd sorted it and it had cost the other guy more than the value of the Chevette.

Mistletoe and Wine - Cliff Richard

At the time, I didn't see Shouty Husband's cruel streak or dark sense of humour. Hindsight is wonderful, as they say.

It was coming up to Christmas and the Boy's Dad invited Karen and Shouty Husband to come to his works' party with us. He worked at an army base – he's done so for the past forty years - and I was looking forward to it as I'd never met his colleagues.

Shouty Husband decided to play with the Boy's Dad's head and act all camp, making advances towards him. As the Boy's Dad is a homophobe, it went down like a lead balloon.

Karen and I thought it was a laugh and joined in, and the Boy's Dad's friends worked out it was a bit of fun and played along too.

Now, of course, I can see it wasn't just a bit of fun. It was Shouty Husband's way of deliberately humiliating the Boy's Dad. But at the time, under his spell as I was, I had no idea as I was, I had no idea

Night Owl - Gerry Rafferty

Shouty Husband's mortgage arrangements were a bit dodgy, he said, but it was the only way he could get it.

He'd signed up for the personal protection payment. Technically, this meant the policy would cover his mortgage payments if he got sick; in reality, he knew it wasn't worth the paper it was written on. He needed to pay a deposit of £1500 for the house and when the mortgage went through, he would get it back as the money was to pay the mortgage broker in case he pulled out. The mortgage broker would be paid more from the mortgage company as they were used.

So, he had the money in the bank, but Christmas was coming, and Karen's university grant wasn't due until the second week in January.

Shouty Husband offered to lend her £1,000 to make sure it was a great Christmas for the kids, as long as she paid it back when her grant came in. If she didn't, he said, he'd lose the house.

Well, it was shopping spree time. Karen and I went to Wolverhampton with envelopes full of cash. (I should say I was only there to carry the bags.) We shopped at Beatties, renowned as 'the posh shop' and she bought me lunch – chicken supreme and a pint of lager and lime, and very nice it was too.

They all had an amazing Christmas and Karen got a great birthday party into the bargain.

But...by the time Karen's grant came through, she'd found out Shouty Husband intended to live in the house he was buying alone. So, she did what any aggrieved woman would do, and put a spanner in the works.

 Shouty Husband needed the money back in his account twenty-four hours before the deposit was due. Instead of making the payment, Karen went to see him at the house and told him she wasn't giving him the money. She loved him, she didn't want to lose him, and this was the best way she had of making him see they belonged together.

Unsurprisingly, he didn't agree. In a fit of temper, he pushed over the glass dining table that he loved, smashing it into a thousand pieces. Then he picked Karen up and threw her bodily out of the house.

She ended up at mine and the Boy's Dad's, where she told us what had happened and cried over the end of her love affair. The Boy's Dad laughed and told her she'd broken a cardinal rule – never steal from Shouty Husband!

As for him, he was panicking as he had twenty-four hours to find the money he needed – he only had £500. Well, thank the gods for Graham, who came through with the shortfall. Shouty Husband signed the papers, the house was all his, and he paid Graham back when the money hit his account. And Karen? She was history – or so we all thought...

Sugar Sugar - The Archies

The kids went to a childminder after school while Karen was at university. One day, after picking them up, she noticed Harry had a bad bruise just above one hip. He'd been seen falling into a chair a few minutes earlier, but the bruise came up too quickly to be ignored.

The Boy's Dad offered to feed and take care of the other kids at our house so I could go to the hospital with Karen and Harry. Once there, they noticed other bruises under Harry's socks; Karen was terrified they were about to accuse her of abusing him.

Many tests later, they diagnosed Harry with immune thrombocytopenia, or ITP; essentially, it's an autoimmune condition characterised by a decrease in the number of platelets in the blood. This can lead to easy bruising, bleeding gums and internal bleeding. It's a chronic disorder to it can't be cured, only managed, but it sounds worse than it is. Harry was admitted and hooked up to a drip, and we kept Vicky and Will so Karen could stay at the hospital with him.

Karen rang Shouty Husband to let him know what had happened. He went to the hospital but, of course, Karen had also called Harry's dad, Vinnie. When Shouty Husband arrived he was there, playing happy families at Harry's bedside, so he walked away. Karen chased after him, but he didn't want to know.

Life carried on. After he was discharged, Harry had to have regular hospital appointments every six months to make sure he was okay.

It's fair to say I was in something of a rut until my thirtieth birthday. I wasn't bothered about doing anything; life was dull.

Living with the Boy's Dad was like watching a heart monitor flatline. I felt like I was a single parent who happened to be married, and I was just going through the motions.

I was ripe for an adventure. And boy, I got one.

My birthday celebrations involved nothing more exciting than a night out with Karen and the Boy's Dad. But, as they say, the best laid plans of mice and men often go awry...Harry being in hospital meant my night out would be a night in; Karen obviously couldn't come along, and the Boy's Dad didn't have anything else lined up. The day before my birthday was Saturday. That evening, while I was doing nothing much, the phone rang.

It was Shouty Husband. He'd invited Steve and his girlfriend, Lottie, over for a few drinks and a smoke. As it was my birthday eve, would the Boy's Dad and I like to come and party in his new house?

I agreed in a heartbeat. Turning thirty was a milestone and I was fed up of living a half-life. The Boy's Dad wasn't bothered, but I bullied him into going. I called my mother-in-law and asked her to babysit, and then I put on a skirt and makeup. I knew Steve from Karen's parties, but not Lottie.

She turned out to be a very young sixteen-year-old in love with Steve, who was nineteen at the time. (She also ended up being infatuated with Shouty Husband for almost twenty years, and he wasn't kind to her – but more of that later.)

I had a great time, though the Boy's Dad wasn't enjoying himself much. When the beer ran out, he agreed to go to the off-licence with Steve for fresh supplies, leaving me to bask in the sunlight of Shouty Husband's attention.

He told me that if stayed until midnight it would then be my birthday, and he'd give me a kiss to celebrate. Well, having heard Karen talk about what a stop-the-world experience that was, I was keen to find out for myself. So, I agreed.

The Boy's Dad wasn't very happy about it; he and Lottie had been the butt of Shouty Husband's cruel streak all night. I didn't notice at the time, and his barbed comments went straight over Lottie's head, but the Boy's Dad felt every single one. Would I have cared if I'd realised? I was in my happy place – I'd had a drink and a smoke and was with Shouty Husband. When the Boy's Dad made noises about getting back to his mum could go home, I told him to go ahead; I was staying. He left, and Steve and Lottie hung around until about half past eleven.

I watched the hands on the clock – an adapted seven-inch single – move towards midnight, agonisingly slowly. Sweet Caroline by Status Quo was playing, and I could feel the anticipation through my stoned, drunken haze. I was finally going to kiss Shouty husband! I'd wanted to do that ever since I'd met him, and it had been a long time coming.

When midnight finally struck, he was close to falling over. But he took me in his arms and kissed me, and it was everything I'd dreamed of and more. The world exploded and all I wanted, right at that moment, was to have rough, dirty sex with him on the hall carpet. I tried to make it happen, believe me, but Shouty Husband very gently told me no. It would ruin a great friendship, he said. I should go home, and he'd see me again soon.

It's fair to say I floated home on Cloud Nine. I went to the park first, where I sat on the swings and sang Happy Birthday to myself. When I got back, the Boy's Dad was already in bed and gave me the cold shoulder. I didn't care; all I could think about was Shouty Husband.

My thirtieth birthday might have started with a kiss, but the day itself was a damp squid. I worried that I'd made a complete fool of myself and lost Shouty Husband's friendship. So, I called him that afternoon to apologise, to throw myself on his mercy and ask him to forgive me for being a wanton hussy.

His reaction wasn't what I expected. He laughed, told me it was ok, and said if I went round in the week, we could have a chat about where we went if I wanted it to go further. Friends with benefits was what he was offering; it was up to me whether I accepted. I jumped at the chance and said I'd see him later in the week when I could think of an excuse to visit. That kiss was the best and worst birthday present I've ever had. It changed my life, for better and worse, but one thing's for sure — it wasn't flatlining anymore.

Goody Two Shoes - Adam Ant

After what had happened, I was in a whirl. I wanted to see if Shouty Husband would be true to his word, and I was giddy at the thought of being with him. I had no clue where it would lead, but I was fairly sure it would change my life – and let me live again, rather than merely exist.

On the Wednesday night after my driving lesson, dressed for the occasion in my best short tartan skirt, I made an excuse and went to see him.

Max was there, so Shouty Husband gave me some of Karen's stuff – making out it was why I'd turned up – and, as he said goodbye at the front door, told me to go round on Saturday night if I wanted to have some fun.

I had new neighbours at the time, Michelle and Bob. They were a military couple – RAF – who lived off-base.

Michelle and I were good friends. She didn't know anyone and couldn't drive, so we went out and had fun together, walking in the woods and taking the boys to feed the ducks. She knew Shouty Husband, and she also knew I wasn't happy with my lot. I told her everything over coffee and she encouraged me to do whatever made me happy.

Well, that meant being with Shouty Husband, in whatever way I could. So, over the next days, Michelle and I worked out how to transform a frumpy mum of two into a sex kitten. We went budget shopping. New underwear from

Primark – white with purple spots. (I loved purple even then.) Then to C&A, where we picked a red, short-sleeved jersey top and a red and white spotted wrap-around skirt. We topped it off with some hold-up stockings from Debenhams, where she also told the ladies on the Chanel counter that it was my thirtieth birthday and asked if they could give me a makeover. By the time they'd finished I looked amazing.

As a treat to myself for my birthday, I went to HMV and bought The Fine Young Cannibals, Finest album and 'Dreamland by Robert Miles.

They were the soundtrack to the start of my life. They ended up leaving with Shouty Husband, but they still remind me of my thirtieth birthday, when my life was turned upside down and inside out.

So - I had the clothes, the makeup, and I felt and looked amazing. I was ready to live the dream.

Michelle and I had come up with a plan so I could get out of the house. I'd tell the Boy's Dad I was babysitting for Karen, and I'd tell Karen I was going out with Mick the Sav and ask her to cover for me with the Boy's Dad.

It was all set. I was careful, even walking the long way round to Shouty Husband's house in case the Boy's Dad was watching from the kitchen window. That extra five minutes gave me time to wonder what the hell I was doing; I had no idea, but I was going to do it anyway.

I wasn't sure exactly what Shouty Husband was offering me or where it would go, but it was a chance to rediscover life and I was grabbing it with both hands. When Shouty Husband opened the door, I thought he looked like sex on legs. He was wearing a very white shirt with tight jeans, and his curly blond hair was halfway down his back.

He was very honest about what was on the table. He enjoyed our friendship and I if I wanted to sleep with him, that was ok with him. He'd still be our friend; he'd still hang out with me and the Boy's Dad – nothing would change. There'd just be some no-strings sex added on. I thought all my Christmases had come at once. If he he'd told me a condition of it happening was that I had to run along the road naked, I'd probably have done it. I was desperate to bask in his light. I was bored, I'd just turned thirty, and I wanted some fun.

Moods - Various Artists

Shouty Husband had a tape named 'Moods' that became the soundtrack to our relationship. It was playing while Shouty Husband was putting me at my ease - a spliff and some great music were his 'get you into bed' head trip.

There was no television in the bedroom but he couldn't go to sleep without noise, so he always had the radio on. I remember that 'Breaking Point' by Etta James came on, and so did 'I Want to Wake Up With You' by Boris Gardiner. I lay there in Shouty Husband's arms, feeling safe and loved, and I never wanted to leave.

Be careful what you wish for, lest it come true – as the saying goes.

You already know this won't be a happy ever after. Karen was still around, and so was the Boy's Dad.

But right then, I didn't care. They say it only takes one lungful of crack to get addicted. Well, I was on my second – and I was hooked on Shouty Husband, whatever happened next.

Bad Medicine - Bon Jovi

I spent every spare minute I could with Shouty Husband. I still saw Karen and would listen to her planning she'd get him back. At that stage, I really didn't know him well enough to guess which way he'd jump; I wondered whether she'd manage it. Then she decided it was time for a big, make-or-break gesture, for which I never forgave her. It was Easter. David was coming to visit, and I was looking forward to some 'us' time – we always had fun together.

Karen, struggling to cope without Shouty Husband and looking gaunt and ill, asked if I could look after Will for a few days so she could go away. Harry would go to his dad's, and Vicky could stay with her best friend. It would be four days, tops.

I wasn't best pleased about it, but she looked pretty rough, and I also felt guilty about being the one in Shouty Husband's bed now, so I agreed.

On the Friday afternoon, Karen rang to ask if I'd call Shouty Husband for her. She was in Torquay, quite a distance, and was in a bad way. She wanted to come home and needed him to fetch her. At the time, Shouty Husband was working all the hours he could in a steel rolling mill. I pushed a note through the door when I found he wasn't home, and he called me later to say he didn't care about Karen and wanted nothing more to do with her.

When Karen rang me back, I gently explained she was on her own. She seemed to take it okay; she told me not to worry and said she'd be home on the Saturday. This was important; David was coming, and Will was in the bed I needed for him.

I was collecting David from the train station when my phone rang. On the other end of the line was a nurse who asked me if I knew Karen as she'd been admitted to hospital. She'd given them my number as she couldn't remember Shouty Husband's.

It turned out that Karen had overdosed on paracetamol. Her liver was badly damaged, so they were keeping her in. I remember telling the nurse who rang me that if Karen had tried to kill herself and failed, that I would kill her instead. But really? Well, I realised that even though she had taken a lot of pills, Karen had made sure she'd be found. This wasn't a cry for help; it was her last gasp attempt to win back Shouty Husband.

But, because her had was in such a bad place, she'd misjudged how many paracetamol tablets she'd taken. She'd realised she'd genuinely overdosed this time and was in real danger of checking out for good; it nearly was 'Goodnight, Vienna'.

She went home four days later, looking like she'd been through the ringer and with her arms were black and blue from where they'd taken blood and given her injections.

I told her no man was worth dying for and asked how she could do that to her kids. She needed a wake-up call, and I gave it.

I kept Shouty Husband in the loop, but he was adamant he wanted nothing more to do with her. Slowly, Karen recovered and realised he wasn't coming back. And then I had my moment – are you ready for the Purple-Haired Warrior to make her first appearance?

Head Games - Foreigner

You might remember me mentioning the women's group I belonged to. It applied for lottery funding to pay for a holiday as, apart from two, they were single-parent families. For three years, the Boy's Dad, the boys and I had a caravan holiday with friends on a Haven Holidays site. The year of Shouty Husband, Karen, the overdose and me was no different – except I could drive now. No coach journey for me!

The caravan park in Prestatyn was booked and we were all looking forward to a week away. Driving to Wales was a huge deal as I was only used to driving around my hometown and was still getting used to having the boys in the back. I had the Boy's Dad, a map and directions from my dad, and I was a nervous wreck by the time we arrived.

We'd already unpacked and were thinking about a chippie tea by the time the coach arrived with the rest of the ladies. I gave them a chance to settle in before going to see if we were all going to the club that evening. That was the usual form – we'd get together as a group and keep an eye on all the kids together while we enjoyed a drink and a laugh.

It didn't take me long to realise I was being given the cold shoulder. So, wanting to know why, I went to see Maureen – she was the queen bee, in charge of the group, and she'd know what was going on.

It turned out the ladies had taken sides. Karen had played the victim card and, as the Boy's Dad and I hadn't turned Shouty Husband away, we were now persona non grata. Nobody had said a word to me. They'd heard Karen's side of the story and turned their backs, and it was a real shock to be blanked by women I'd thought were my friends.

At least having a car meant I could drive us somewhere every day. In the evenings, rather than endure the ladies' hostility at the site's club, we went into Prestatyn.

I wanted to get my own back on Karen, but even then, I knew enough from watching Shouty Husband play with people's heads to realise I should bide my time. I was sitting on a juicy piece of information that would really mess with her, but I had to get the timing right.

The night before we went on holiday, Shouty Husband and the Boy's Dad went to the pub. Shouty Husband got chatting to a German lady and, at the end of the night, he offered to walk her home as she lived about twenty minutes away. He tried to persuade the Boy's Dad to go with him, but he wouldn't; he made an excuse and left Shouty Husband to it.

The Boy's Dad told me what had happened, and I was terrified Shouty Husband had found someone new, and I'd be out in the cold.

I needn't have worried. He called me the morning we were going away to tell me about it. The German lady had a husband and children, and he really did just walk her home. Karen didn't know that, though. On the Thursday night, I visited Karen in her caravan. She gave me the full force of her anger, telling me how Shouty Husband had ruined her holiday because she was still in such a bad way. She ranted as though it was all my fault and then came out with the immortal words: 'What have you ever done for me? 'It was the final straw. I smiled and told her about Shouty Husband and the German lady. How he'd walked her home. That's all I said, but it was enough to get into her head. The look on her face at the thought of Shouty Husband with other women was priceless. She yelled at me to get out and I did so, quietly, while she screamed like a fishwife.

Next day, I decided to brave things out to gauge the mood of the ladies. You could cut the atmosphere with a knife; it was clear they had decided I was not welcome any longer. The group I'd been a part of for eight years was finished with me. It wasn't really a problem. I'd already seen the writing on the wall and knew I didn't need them anymore. But I'd still wanted to take my boys away, and it was all worth it for the look on Karen's face.

Maureen and Connie, two of Macbeth's witches, said it would be better if I stayed away for a while until Karen was in a better way.

The next day I drove us home, and that was that – at least, it was the end of the group. Not the end of Karen, as you'll find out.

Ooh Aah... Just a Little Bit - Gina G

My first proper date with Shouty Husband happened the day I got back from that fateful holiday. He was a huge fan of the opera Carmen, so when the English National Opera were performing it in his hometown theatre, he wanted to go. A funny thing – he wanted to see it, he wanted to take me out, but I ended up paying for our tickets. They weren't cheap, either.

I'm an eternal tomboy, but I put on a dress and heels, and even did my face. Shouty Husband was dressed to the nines in a suit and his hair, long and blond at that point, looked fantastic. I noticed other women glancing at him appreciatively as he walked by.

I drove us there. We parked a mile away, so we didn't have to pay and then walked to the theatre. I hate walking in heels, but this was the first time I could hold Shouty Husband's hand in public and I basked in his light. I felt alive and wanted, which is a heady combination when you've been starved of affection.

Carmen wasn't an opera I was familiar with, but the performance was amazing, and Shouty Husband was happy, which meant I was, too.

Afterwards we went for a drink. I was on Cloud Nine and all I wanted was to stay in that bubble. At that point, for me, happiness was being with Shouty Husband.

Thunder in My Heart - Leo Sayer

To stay in Shouty Husband's world meant jumping through various hoops of his choosing. The first one was to meet and gain approval from people who were important to him.

I'd already met Paula and Bill while he was with Karen and, although I also kind of knew Graham, I didn't realise at that point how important his opinion of me was to Shouty Husband.

When he invited me to meet him properly, I was flattered; I knew from Karen that Graham was the man Shouty Husband went to for advice. What he thought mattered.

He'd always like a gentleman. I didn't know that the meeting was a chance to put me to the test – how I reacted would determine my relationship with Shouty Husband.

Karen had failed spectacularly. Now they wanted to see if anything was more than a silly lovestruck girl who could be taken advantage of.

When I met Graham, I found him kind. He listened to what I had to say and made me feel comfortable. It was like chatting with a favourite uncle.

Then the mind games began.

At that time, a film called Indecent Proposal was a big hit. The central premise was this – would you let your wife sleep with another man in exchange for a million pounds?

Graham had already used it to play with Karen's head, asking if she'd sleep with him for that much money. Thinking it was a joke, she agreed. Graham had said that now he knew what she was, they just had to agree a price. Shouty Husband thought it was hilarious and Karen, oblivious to the dark side of the comment, thought Graham liked her.

Now it was my turn to be asked the same question, and I didn't react well. I was furious and told Graham he was out of order in no uncertain terms.

I was really upset – I liked Graham and thought he liked me in return. I was about to walk out when he apologised, giving the deep belly laugh I remember him for.

Shouty Husband explained it was Graham's way of making sure I was the right one for him; I was still fuming – and they knew it – but I was also happy I'd been accepted. Graham remained a good friend to me until it was time for his walk across the black sands with Death. (More on that later.) I'd passed that first test with flying colours, but still there were hoops to jump through – some ringed with fire, others with razor wire or over a bed of hot coals.

Yet however tough the challenge, I never questioned it. I worshipped Shouty Husband and would do whatever he asked.

Lady in Red - Chris de Burgh

By now, I was now totally enthralled by Shouty Husband and wanted us to do something special.

He always loved summer solstice and said if I could make it happen, we could go away together for the weekend.

It wouldn't be easy. I needed a good excuse to leave the boys with their dad and would have to book a B&B without the help of the internet. I was determined, though, and came up with a great plan.

Shouty Husband wanted to stay in Swindon, so we could use it as a base to visit the standing stones at Avebury. My former neighbour, Michelle, had been relocated to the airbase there; we were still in touch, so a weekend at her house was the perfect alibi. I cleared it with the Boy's Dad, found a place to stay, and planned my escape with military precision.

When I picked up Shouty Husband that Friday lunchtime, I felt like the heroine in a spy film. My subterfuge had paid off and I would have an illicit three days and two nights with my leading man. The bed and breakfast turned out to be a dump, but I didn't care; I was with Shouty Husband, everything was new, and I was loving the adventure.

That first night, we ended up in a pub with a great jukebox and slow danced to Lady in Red in the empty lounge. I wanted that moment to last forever.

The following morning, we visited a car boot sale in Swindon. There was a good market there too, and a junk shop for Shouty Husband to browse around. He found a NAD amplifier he had to have; this meant nothing to me as I wasn't into hi-fi equipment, but he knew what he was looking at. It cost him £35, a lot of money then, and it was all the money he had for the whole weekend. He still bought it, though, and it lasted him for fifteen years before it finally gave up the ghost.

Salisbury Hill - Peter Gabriel

It was late afternoon when we drove to Avebury to see the standing stones. The atmosphere was fantastic, and we really got into the spirit of the summer solstice, watching the hippies dancing and enjoying the music.

As it got towards dusk, Shouty Husband decided we were going to climb Silbury Hill. There's no public access allowed to this historic mound, but as ever – you try telling him he can't do something.

Silbury Hill dates back thousands of years. It's man-made, with steep sides and a flat top.

When we got to the top, Shouty Husband pulled out the three-skin spliff made with Arley's weed. We sat on the top of Silbury Hill in the dark and got stoned together, and the memory still makes me smile all these years later.

Shouty Husband stood on the edge of the hill and leaned into the wind, his long blond hair flowing out behind him, and his arms outstretched. It was so strong. He was lucky it didn't drop; he'd have gone headfirst over the edge.

We thought it was just us up there, so we got a fright when another couple popped up and said hello. After that, Shouty Husband's paranoia kicked in, so we climbed back down. Well, he did – I went down on my bum with my skirt rucking up.

We listened to music on our Walkman's on the way back to the car park, Pink Floyd for him and the Rocky Horror Picture Show soundtrack for me. Shouty Husband was getting increasingly paranoid and was so busy checking behind him that he didn't notice the white-robed druids until they were right on top of us.

As we went through the middle of them it was like the parting of the Red Sea – a very surreal experience indeed!

Over at the Frankenstein Place - Rocky Horror Picture Show

By now, Shouty Husband had the munchies. As luck would have it there was a butty van at the side of the road, and a quarter-pounder with all the trimmings was just what we needed.

Then he got an idea in his head for a painting, and he had to do it now. He had paper from the burger, but nothing to draw with.

We stopped at a garage so he could buy sweets, and he offered the shop assistant £5 of my money for his nub of a pencil. The guy wouldn't budge, though, and respect to him – I don't think I could have refused Shouty Husband in that mood with his hair everywhere! Eventually we got back to the bed and breakfast and found a pencil – but by then, Shouty Husband had forgotten what it was he'd needed to draw so urgently.

Rebel Yell - Billy Idol

The following day we took the scenic route home and stopped off at an antiques centre in Fairford.

Shouty Husband loved finding interesting, inexpensive items and ended up buying – with my money – a frog-shaped candle holder made out of metal. The back leg was broken, so it was only £3.50.

Then we enjoyed a good Sunday lunch in a pub beer garden before going home – the end of the first weekend I spent with Shouty Husband, and I was well and truly hooked.

The frog with the broken leg still lives with me, a reminder that life with him wasn't all bad.

Those Were the Days - Mary Hopkins

Work was still a bit hit and miss for Shouty Husband, so I'd go and spend time with him during the day if he was free.

The house needed some TLC. The dining room was easy – it got a coat of green paint over the woodchip wallpaper and some cheap carpet.

The living room needed a bit more attention, though. It had a horrible stone-clad chimney breast and shelves that took up too much space.

Rather than take time to prepare, Shouty Husband took the sledgehammer approach – literally. He knocked out the shelves, which left lots of rubble. His solution for that was to get me to help him dump it in the garden.

And so, the rubble mountain was born. It got bigger over time, especially when Shouty Husband decided he wanted to get rid of the concrete area outside and have a proper garden. Over the years, it became a home to insects and bees, and I'll tell you more about it later.

The living room looked good once it was finished. It was painted in various shades of lilac with some cheap carpet, a white rug, a cheap sofa and some house plants. Oh, and don't forget metal racks to store his collection of vinyl. Shouty Husband found some cream curtains in a charity shop that he said he could dye, and a men's dressing gown in a Paisley print that the Boy's Dad told him I'd love.

Shouty Husband laughed and said I'd never get it, but I did – I wore it until it was so thin, it was see-through.

The curtains were regularly dyed dark blue over the years. It would have been cheaper to buy new ones, but that wasn't Shouty Husband's way.

He loved to draw after Jinx left, so he had his drawing table in one corner. He put his art on the walls, along with lots of mirrors to make the room look bigger. I'll give him his due – when it came to interior design on a budget, he knew what he was doing.

Hells Bells - AC/DC

With interest rates – and his mortgage – going up, Shouty Husband decided getting a lodger was the way to go. I put an advert in the local paper for him, and that's how Bruce ended up sharing his space.

Bruce and Shouty Husband were chalk and cheese. Bruce was a lecturer at the local sixth form college and had lost his wife, daughters and his nice house after being caught playing away from home. He stayed for six months.

I liked Bruce and, since he paid his rent-on time, so did Shouty Husband. A few years after he moved on, we got a postcard from Canada, telling us that he was alive, well and happy with a new wife. That was nice to hear.

For the next two years, on and off, my relationship with Shouty Husband was both fantastic and painful. He was hurtful, kind, deceitful, funny and so much more, but I can't deny he did teach me how to make things happen and how to channel my strengths to be a better person. In hindsight, he was laying the foundations for the person I am now. That sounds funny, I know, as I was his doormat for so long.

At that time, my youngest son had been diagnosed with autism and I was struggling to get him support at school; it was easy for Shouty Husband to embed his thumbprint in the top of my head.

He listened to me when I had a victory over the education department and again when I lost the battle. He offered advice and built up my confidence, helping me believe I could do anything I wanted to.

The educational psychologist told me Luke needed an hour a day of one-to-one support at school as he was two years behind other students his age. Even though I worked with him at home, I took this on board and applied to the council for some help.

Getting support was a long, tedious process but Luke needed help there and then, so I offered to pay for a teaching assistant myself. The headmaster – who frankly

had had enough of me, as I was like a dog with a bone –
agreed. Now, I just had to find the money.

Shouty Husband suggested I should try relevant charities
to see if they could help. This was in the days before
crowdfunding became a thing, and also before the
internet. I had to do things the old-fashioned way, so I
went to the library and took out a book that listed every
charity in the UK. Education wasn't a well-supported area,
but I found a few that might help.

I handwrote letters to the tax office, the Vincent de Paul
Society and my dad's work as he paid into the charity arm
of the company. I raised £2000, which paid for Luke to
have a whole academic year of support.

The Boy's Dad thought it was a waste of time, but Shouty
Husband encouraged me. He was there for the good bits,
the bad bits and the mother-in-law from hell bits. He was
my rock and taught me how to be persistent. I've always
been single minded, but he helped me channel it and
become stronger, whereas the Boy's Dad just left me to it
and never backed me up.

So, I owe him a huge thank you, for being my cheerleader
at that time and pushing me as he did. It did backfire,
though – because eventually I was able to be strong with
him, too.

Ain't Too Proud to Beg - The Rolling Stones

Just like the wind, Shouty Husband could blow hot, cold and cruel. He'd shine his light on me until I basked in its warmth, and then push me into the darkness to freeze. I'd live like this for the next ten years.

Christmas 1997 was a time of darkness. He'd still call round every Friday to go to the pub with the Boy's Dad, but he wouldn't talk to me. It was midnight on Christmas Eve when the phone rang. A call at that time would usually mean something was wrong; it was Shouty Husband, saying he needed to talk to me, and he was on his way to our house.

I got out of bed and went to open up. I knew that cold tone – it meant whatever was wrong was something bad. I also knew it could be nothing I'd done.

It turned out he'd spent the evening with Graham, who'd let slip Karen had been in touch to find out Shouty husband seeing it was Christmas. She missed him, she said, even though they lived within ten minutes of each other.

Rather than ruin his evening with Graham, he decided to come to me afterwards. He was at his most dangerous when he arrived – cold and polite. He didn't need to be angry to scare me. He told me – he didn't ask – to call Karen on Christmas Day and tell her to not bother either him or Graham ever again. If she did, there would be consequences. He didn't elaborate on what these would be, and at that point I didn't know him well enough to realise he likely wouldn't have done anything – it was one of his mind games.

After issuing his demands, Shouty Husband – who was very angry, very drunk and very stoned – tried to leave. Unfortunately for him, getting out of my house was like Escape from Colditz as we'd replaced the doors and locks after a failed break-in. He wanted to make a grand exit, but there were two doors and numerous locks to get through, and he got stuck in the tiny porch. I reached around him to undo the top lock, and that kicked off his paranoia. Convinced I was trying to keep him in, he headbutted the door of the bin cupboard but managed to hit the heavy-duty hinge instead of the wood. When I opened the door to let him out, blood was pouring down his face. He has the scar on his forehead to this day.

Anyway, I did as he asked. On Christmas morning, after fortifying myself with a slug of brandy, I rang Karen and told her Shouty Husband wanted nothing to do with her and she shouldn't poke the bear. I hated doing it, but I knew it was the only way Shouty Husband would shine his light on me once more.

It worked. I was part of Shouty Husband's life again - for a while, at least.

You're in My Heart - Rod Stewart

On Friday nights, Shouty Husband would go down the pub with the Boy's Dad. On Saturday nights, I went to his place to smoke dope and have Shouty Husband time.

The Boy's Dad never objected. As you've probably realised, there was nothing left between us, and it was just a matter of time until we were over.

Saturday nights were always fun. On one of them I was put under the 'are you good enough?' spotlight again, this time with Cousin Tommy. I liked Tommy. He was Charlie's twin – who also featured sometimes on Saturday nights – and was great fun with a wicked sense of humour.

When I was married, on nights out with the ladies, we'd sometimes go to see a male stripper. It was ok, but what I really loved were the drag acts – the effort they put in on their looks amazed me.

Tommy loved hearing about them. He said he'd always fancied being dressed up as a woman and would I help?

I thought it would be fun, so I hunted out my frilly underwear, dusted off my make-up bag, and took my best party dress and a new pair of hold-ups round to play with Tommy.

Shouty Husband lay on the sofa while I transformed 6ft 4inches of wiry male into a woman. Sadly, I didn't have a wig and my shoes were nowhere near big enough for him.

So, there was Tommy – a skinhead in women's clothes with full make up, flouncing around Shouty Husband's living room on some great dope. The photos got lost in my various house moves, but I still smile at the memory.

Tommy walked over the black sands with Death some years back, but I'll always remember him that way – posing in my best party dress with socks for boobs, smiling.

White Lines (Don't Do It) - Grandmaster Flash and the Furious Five

Next on Shouty Husband's pharmaceutical chemical romance list were amphetamine sulphate, pure base, speed, Billy Whizz and pink champagne.

Speed increased his paranoia and aggression, and he really should keep away from it. The first time he did it with me, he was in a good mood to begin with. There was super-strength lager and dope to bring him down when the rush got too intense.

It was a Friday night with Tommy, who was a fan of speed and brought some with him. I wasn't a fan, having tried it before, so I stuck to my dope and coffee.

Taking speed made Shouty Husband want sex but frankly, unless you start as soon as you snort, it's not going to happen. The spirit might be willing, but the flesh will be weak. Shouty Husband let his mind run wild and came up with all kinds of fantasies to encourage Boris Becker the Bionic Pecker (his pet name for his penis) to work.

Now, I'm broad-minded, but he had a very vivid imagination. There was no way I was doing some of the unusual and downright strange things he came up with. Nothing worked, but before I went home Shouty Husband asked me to give him my knickers. When he finally came down from the speed, his head would still be full of fantasies so he thought lacy underwear that smelt of me would help him finish himself off.

The next time Shouty Husband tried speed with me around ended very badly – but you'll hear about that later.

Soon after came the Night of the Custard – which Shouty Husband never let me forget. He'd started a cold and was worried it would go onto his chest, as he'd be really ill. He was doing his dying swan act on the sofa and said he fancied some custard. The powder was in the cupboard, and he knew I could make it, so he was willing to let me loose in the kitchen. Well, I was off my face on weed, but I'd do my best.

It looked like custard. It smelt like custard. But it had a life force of its own. It solidified in the bowl with the spoon stuck in - Shouty Husband got it out of the bowl in one piece and when he dropped it on the fake marble hearth, it bounced!

We fell about laughing and the Night of the Custard was born. I'd invented a new dangerous substance and it made Shouty Husband laugh, so it was all good.

Tribute - Tenacious D

I said Shouty Husband used to go out with the Boy's Dad on Friday nights, and Max would go with them. One of their favourite ways of letting off steam – though the Boy's Dad was far too sensible to join in - was roof-rack surfing down country lanes at high speeds before slamming on the brakes.

On Shouty Husband's 38th birthday they all went out and got very drunk. Shouty Husband decided he wanted to take a 'men at work' sign from the side of the road home with him. Max and the Boy's Dad tried to stop him, sitting on him until he let go, and they ended up rolling around on the grass and getting dirty.

They were like a bunch of teenage boys, and Shouty Husband got to take his road sign home in the end.

Max loved to play with people's heads in the same way Shouty Husband did. On the night of the party, he rolled fags for Shouty Husband and the Boy's Dad but, instead of baccy, he just did them with dope.

The fag-come-spliff knocked Shouty Husband over and he was used to it. The Boy's Dad never stood a chance.

He got very aggressive and decided it was a good idea to sleep in the bath, so I left him to it. (Obviously, it was empty – I'm not that mean!)

Handbags & Glad Rags - Rod Stewart

Sadly, my time in Shouty Husband's light passed and I found myself on my own again. Karen came back into my life then. We'd see each other on the Beavers run when we took Luke and Harry, and she decided to offer an olive branch.

She had a new man, unsuitable but very good-looking, was coming to the end of her university course and was happy.

Each year the Scouts did a lads-and-dads camping trip up the Wrekin. Harry was allowed to go without a dad as there were enough people to keep an eye on him, so Karen invited me down for the night. We could go out, have a few drinks, and I'd stay over. Why not?

I overdid it on the lager and lime, not to mention the dope, and after the pub we ended up at a very posh house that belonged to someone Karen babysat for as a teenager. Karen had had an affair with the dad, and they'd stayed friends.

I had a glass of wine, and the world went full tilt, and I threw up all over a beautiful solid oak table.

It wasn't far to Karen's, but there's no way I could have walked so she got me into a cab for the five-minute drive. I hung my head out of the window and threw up all down the side of the taxi, and then spent the night on Karen's sofa with my head in a bucket.

The following morning, I went to go home to recover before I went to pick up the boys and their dad from the camp – and realised I'd left my handbag in the kitchen at the posh house.

Karen drove me round and I knocked on the door with trepidation. The wife appeared and threw my handbag at me before slamming the door in my face. The husband hadn't cleared up after I vomited on the table, which wasn't a pleasant surprise for her. I don't know if there was any damage; I do hope not.

I managed to pick up the boys, despite feeling fragile. Karen moved to a new house not long after so I didn't see her for a while. Don't worry, though – she'll be back.

Ain't No Love in the Heart of the City - Whitesnake

Shouty Husband and I were in one of our 'not together' phases, so Mick the Sav was back in my life. He was living with his daughter at the time and for a while we had a friends-with-benefits arrangement. (This was something that happened quite a lot over the years when Shouty Husband pushed me away. Sometimes you just need to feel skin.)

Then Joy arrived on the scene, and Mick was smitten. She never took to me – hated me on sight, in fact, as she thought I was a threat to their relationship. I wasn't, but she never believed it.

Mick brought Joy round to meet me and the Boy's Dad, and the Boy's Dad called Shouty Husband as he'd always said they'd get on. So Shouty Husband came round and yes – he and Mick got on like a house on fire and their bromance was born.

Funnily enough, it was Mick who the Boy's Dad had a problem with as he thought if I was ever going to leave him, Mick would be the reason. That was never going to happen – we're great friends, but that's all we'll ever be.

The story of Joy and Mick and the aftermath of their relationship though – well, that's a whole other tale yet to come!

When I Need You - Leo Sayer

Friday nights meant time to myself. Shouty Husband and the Boys' Dad would go to the pub, the boys were in their bedrooms, and I'd enjoy bath night – an hour on my own with a face mask and a tape player (yes, it was a while ago) singing along to something like Bread or ELO. Shouty Husband and I weren't together at that point, but we were talking, which was something. On this particular Friday – October 18th, 1997 – they went to the pub as normal. I had my bath, watched some television and went to bed – so far, so normal. I often did this if they weren't back by 11pm – sometimes Shouty Husband would come back to ours, sometimes the Boys' Dad would go to his.

But the next thing I knew, I was woken by the phone ringing. The clock told me it was 1.20am, and there was Shouty Husband on the other end of the line, saying he'd been beaten up, he was at the hospital, and please could I pick him up? I called him all the names under the sun while I dressed. He didn't want to be with me, but he called me when he needed bailing out. And yes, I'd go running. Then I realised the boys were fast asleep in bed – I couldn't leave them alone. I'd forgotten to ask about their dad, too.

Luckily my neighbours, Jodie and Jon, were young – they'd see the dawn on Friday nights. Jodie was happy to stay with the boys, so I went on my way.

At the hospital, I saw Shouty Husband hobbling towards me. When I got him in the car, he told me he'd been beaten up by an ex-lodger with the help of the ex-lodger's brother-in-law, and they'd used a crowbar.

The doctor who'd examined him assumed Shouty Husband was under the influence of drink and drugs and that it was just another Friday night punch-up. He hadn't been sympathetic, so Shouty Husband decided he was going home.

I told him I was going back into the hospital to find out how badly hurt he was – there was no way he was dropping dead in my living room with my kids upstairs in bed! As an afterthought, I asked where the Boys' Dad was. Apparently, he'd stayed in the pub with Jayne, one of Shouty Husband's occasional friends with benefits. So, still half asleep, with my hair sticking up in horns – it's always had a life of its own – I charged back into the hospital and spoke to a lovely ward sister who told me Shouty Husband was being unreasonable.

She also said someone should keep an eye on him overnight, and he should go back in the morning to get checked over.

I took him home with me, where I found the wonderful Jodie still babysitting as there was no sign of the Boys' Dad. I put Shouty Husband in my armchair, covered him up with an orange blanket, and warned him one of us would shake him awake every 15 minutes to make sure he was okay. If we couldn't rouse him with shaking and shouting, we'd be calling 999 for an ambulance.

The Boys' Dad rocked up at 2.30am; turned out he'd been at Jayne's, having a good time. He was very drunk, so we sent him to bed. Jodie and I needed to stay awake but, this being 1997, all-night television was limited. I had a video player, though, so we watched the Boys' Dad's porn collection and took the piss out of the décor and furnishings while Shouty Husband dozed. Coffee and cigarettes kept us going.

At 7am, Shouty Husband wanted us to go and check his house and fetch his phone. We walked round there and banged on the door like we were the police; the cowardly lodger – who'd been present the night before and no use whatsoever – wasn't pleased to see us. He'd been up all night with the police and had to go to work.

I was ready to rip him a new one, but Jodie got in first. She told him he was a coward, that it was no thanks to him Shouty Husband was still alive and ordered him to let us in so we could collect some stuff.

Shouty Husband called Graham to take him back to hospital for a check-up, and I went along too. Turns out he had a hairline skull fracture, fractured vertebrae in his neck, two broken ribs and heavy bruising.

Shouty Husband nil, crowbar one. Turns out he's not invincible after all.

Graham was amazing, telling me all kinds of amusing stories while Shouty Husband was being examined. And it meant my place in Shouty Husband's life was assured, too – Graham could see I was willing to keep an eye out for him, and his opinion held a lot of sway.

Take Me Bak 'Ome - Slade

Shouty Husband was always capable of taking care of himself. In his younger days, Friday nights meant a skinful and a fight. He always said the buzz he got from fighting was better than any drug and, though he'd calmed down a lot, he could still be dangerous when crossed.

Shouty husband had a lodger who arrived just before Christmas. He stayed just a week before leaving to dog-sit for friends until the new year...but although he'd left a room full of stuff, he never came back. His phone number was disconnected, and we assumed that was the last we'd see of him.

Until six months later, when he got in touch to say he wanted his stuff back. No problem, said Shouty Husband, but he still owed two weeks rent. Pay up and you're welcome to take your stuff.

Again, there was radio silence...Until one night, drinking in the pub with the Boys' Dad, Shouty Husband had a call from his new lodger saying somebody was outside the house, shouting and kicking the porch door.

The Boys' Dad didn't want to get involved, so Shouty Husband left him to it and went home. All seemed quiet and he wondered what the fuss was about – when suddenly there was a loud, hard knock on the door.

The old lodger was kicking the door and demanding his stuff. Shouty Husband was drunk, stoned and not in the mood. Then the old lodger's brother-in-law waded in and there they were, all three of them.

Shouty Husband has never had a problem with two against one, and ordinarily he'd still have got the better of them. However, one of his faults was his inability to put things away after using them. And it so happened he'd been knocking out a stone fireplace and left a crowbar lying around. For eighteen months. And it nearly cost him his life. He was getting the better of his would-be assailants when the ex-lodger decided to grab the crowbar and whack Shouty Husband across the back and shoulders half a dozen times. When he managed to get into the kitchen, and the ex-lodger and brother-in-law decided they'd won and left, and he was able to crawl across to his neighbours' house and ask them to call an ambulance. (Meanwhile, his current lodger was still hiding upstairs; he'd kept well out of the way throughout the whole thing.) The ambulance came and so did the police, so Shouty Husband gave a statement and waited to see what would happen next.

Crocodile Rock - Elton John

On the Saturday night, I told the Boys' Dad I was staying at Shouty Husband's so I could keep an eye on him. I pulled the armchairs together and fell asleep watching the Blues Brothers – I was there if he needed me. I wrapped his heavy-duty painkillers in a tissue and wrote down the times he could take them and made sure there weren't any left lying around for him to find. He had lots of visitors that first week, and it so happened I was there for all of them. Graham was there a lot too, and as far as he was concerned, I was the best thing since sliced bread – Shouty Husband would have been much worse off without me. When the Boy's Dad came, he was shocked to see what state Shouty Husband was in, Graham took the piss out of him for not helping.

Paula and Bill dropped by, as did Mick who also called every day for an update. His friendship with Shouty Husband was absolutely firm now.

It took three weeks of heavy-duty painkillers and not moving from the sofa before Shouty Husband recovered, and I went up three times a day, every day, to make sure he'd eaten and had everything he needed.

Separate Tables - Chris de Burgh

Shouty Husband needed to go shopping after his enforced rest on the sofa, so one Sunday afternoon I offered to take him to Tesco.

I was walking past the freezer section when I had an epiphany. I didn't want to be with the Boy's Dad anymore. It hit me just like that.

There are two pieces of advice I've been given in life that I always remember. One was from Donna, who said when you have a baby you need to get them into a routine. The other was from Shouty Husband, who eighteen months earlier had asked if I could imagine life without the Boys' Dad in it, and to imagine what that would be like. Well, I did, and I decided I could cope. I was prepared to give up my security and a guaranteed income to be a single mum.

So, on that Sunday night in November, I sat the Boy's Dad down and told him I'd had enough. I wanted out of the marriage. I don't think it came as a great shock to him, and we agreed he'd stay until after Christmas - then he'd leave.

Love Her Madly - The Doors

Life carried on as normal until New Year's Eve. The Boys' Dad knew Shouty Husband, and I were together, but I lied whenever he asked me about it.

The Boys' Dad's favourite uncle came to visit and learned what was happening. He wasn't impressed, to say the least. Shouty Husband was invited round to meet him, but it didn't go well – both are alpha males determined to prove their balls are the biggest.

After surviving the New Year, Jodie and Jon – the neighbours – invited us to a birthday party, along with Mick and Shouty Husband. The boys were packed off for a sleepover at my parents' house and Mick and I went to get Shouty Husband. His stomach was playing up and he wasn't in a party mood, so we stayed at his for a couple of hours first, listening to music.

The Boys' Dad had gone ahead to the party, and by the time we arrived he'd been drinking super-strength lager and had smoked a spliff. He was drunk and belligerent, and Mick and I decided to go to my house – we didn't want to be around him in that state.

He came home soon after. He locked the door behind him, removed the keys and then went into the kitchen and started throwing glasses around. When I went to see what was happening, he lunged at me, screaming. Mick told me to go back next door, where I blurted out what had happened. Jon went to check on them and reported back that all was okay – Mick and the Boys' Dad were hugging.

Actually, it more a case of Mick trying to stop the Boys' Dad following me next door, as he was hellbent on getting to me.

I told Mick not to hurt the Boys' Dad, and he didn't – until the Boys' Dad spat in his face and sank his teeth into Mick's shoulder. His eyes were red, and he was beyond reason at that stage. Mick pinned him down and broke two of his ribs in the process – but at least it finally calmed him down a bit. Later, the Boys' Dad announced he was going round to have it out with Shouty Husband, but Mick managed to stop him and bring him home before he got there. Instead, the Boys' Dad went back to the party where he decided to have a go and Jodie's brother and ended up getting a punch on the nose.

He came home feeling very sorry for himself. Mick sent me to bed and the two of them stayed up and got drunk. The Boys' Dad ended up passing out in the bath.

The following morning, I packed a case for the Boys' Dad, and he moved in with his mum and stepdad. The boys were upset, and I admit I was terrified of being on my own – but I was also glad it was finally over.

It felt as though a weight had been lifted and I could finally breathe again. I had no job and a mortgage to pay, but I was free!

I was lucky, really. I had an amazing support network of family and friends. And there was also Shouty Husband…

I will say here and now – I did not leave the Boys' Dad for Shouty Husband. I left the Boys' Dad because we were both unhappy. Honestly, we both knew we'd made a mistake twenty-four hours after we got married. Kids are resilient and divorce doesn't mean screwing them up for life – staying in a bad marriage is worse for them.

Today, my boys are grounded, rounded, and have their own lives and mortgages. Their dad is still part of their world and if we have to share the same space then he and I have learned to play nicely.

Livin' Thing - ELO

My parents came to babysit so I could have some time out, and I went to fill in Shouty Husband on what had happened.

Now I was on my own I wasn't sure what would mean for us, and as always, I couldn't read him. So, as he walked me home, I decided to bite the bullet. I looked him in the eye and told him I was now the one thing he said he didn't want – a single mum. I said I understood if he wanted to end things, but we'd always been good friends – and I could do with one of those right now. If he decided he wanted to stay, then great – but he had to understand we were a package deal, me and the boys, and that they came first, second, third and right down to last on my list of priorities. He wasn't even on it at the moment. And with that, I held my head high and walked away. I didn't look back.

Generally, ultimatums didn't work with Shouty Husband – but this time, mine did. He told me that putting my kids first was the right thing to do; his mum had put his stepdad first, and Karen left her children. He respected me for putting my boys ahead of everything and everyone else, and he admired my spirit. He also always said anyone he got involved with long term would have to be a friend first – and I'd always been that to him.

Six months later, I went with Shouty Husband and my mum to see what would happen to the lodger and his brother-in-law. They'd both pleaded not guilty to causing actual bodily harm, and the case had been sent to the Crown Court.

Shouty Husband didn't really have any 'court' clothes, but he made an effort with a clean pair of jeans, shirt, tie and suit jacket.

The judge kept looking across at my mum and me in the gallery and asked about us. Shouty Husband said we were his support network and had helped with his recovery.

Ultimately, both the lodger and the brother-in-law were found guilty. However, their sentence was community service, which displeased Shouty Husband.

While the case was waiting to be heard, his cousin Charlie had looked on the notice board which carried a list of cases, along with the defendants and their names and addresses. You can guess what's coming, can't you?

A dark night and a trip with a crowbar saw retribution meted out. The cousins started it and passed on the address to Shouty Husband, who finished it.

He had a violent streak. I always knew it, but my rose-tinted spectacles stopped me seeing it. These days, happily, they are broken beyond repair.

So Macho - Sinitta

Shouty Husband was actually very insecure, but he hid it really well and came across as having more front than Blackpool. One of his tactics – aside from fighting – was to dominate every other man who came into his orbit.

It didn't matter if they were friends, relatives, or friends of friends -he'd go overboard on the 'tough guy' crap. He loved to play macho games, either with his cousins whenever they visited or any other friends who were stupid enough to be bullied into it. He rarely lost at arm-wrestling, no matter which hand he used – he could lock his elbows. 'Knuckles' was all about hand speed – you had to clench your fists and try to rap your opponent's knuckles with yours.

Then there was 'fingers', where you locked fingers with your opponent over your heads and then tried to get each other's hands down to waist level.

Everybody who came to party was told not to play with Shouty Husband, but he'd goad them and call them chicken until they gave in. Then, of course, he'd win, and they'd get hurt.

On one Friday night, we visited his cousin, Charlie. I was the designated driver, which meant Shouty Husband could drink and toke to his heart's content.

I didn't know Charlie or his partner, Angie, well. That night, after they played the usual silly games and fuelled by super-strength lager and dope, they decided to up the ante with 'hot knives.

This involves heating a carving knife until it's white hot, usually in the gas flame on the cooker. Then you put the knife on your skin and try not to flinch as it burns.

Needless to say, Shouty Husband was good at this, too. In fact, to this day he has two big burn marks down his shoulder blades and a couple of lighter ones on the top of his chest.

Charlie only played once, so Shouty Husband won. I was terrified he'd want me to have a go too, but he had another plan.

He said that if I wanted to be part of his life and his family, then I had to take a blood oath. This involved making a small cut on my forearm, and one on Angie's, and then we rubbed the cuts over each other so the blood mixed. I was still in Shouty Husband's thrall and desperate to be part of his family, so I did it. I still have the scar to remind me.

On the way home, Shouty Husband had to stay away to guide me around the maze that was the ring road, as I didn't know the way back from Charlie's well and it was dark. Well, he lasted all of five minutes before he fell asleep, and I got well and truly lost. In the end I followed the signs for the motorway; I knew I could get us home from there.

When we got back to the house, I tried to get him inside, but he fell on the driveway and wouldn't move. I knew I couldn't leave him outside so in the end I told him I'd get the neighbour to help me if he didn't shift himself. That worked. He crawled inside on his hands and knees and fell into the hall with his legs still sticking out through the door. I managed to shuffle him in from there so I could close it, then I put a cushion on his head, covered him with a blanket, and left him on the floor while I went to bed.he managed to crawl upstairs after about half an hour; I got his boots and trousers off and he snored and slept.

Shouty Husband rarely suffered from hangovers, but he did this time and I was glad. I hate driving in the dark when I'm unsure where I'm going!

We're Not Right - David Grey

Mick had a caravan which he used as a bolthole when things got a bit too much. He loved living in a caravan – it was always more than a holiday home – and on one occasion Shouty Husband and I were invited to the camp site where he and Joy were staying to see his new one.

As usual, I drove; Shouty Husband was pissed and stoned long before we got there. We went to meet Ally, Mick's brother, in a pub; I'd known him for thirty years but he and Shouty Husband had never met.

It was a beautiful summer day and Shouty Husband, who loved to walk barefoot, had taken his boots off. He handed them to the barmaid to keep safe while I got the drinks in. (Like the Queen, he never carried money.) Shouty Husband started talking to Ally and began by offending him when he said he 'messed around with horses'; Ally trained racehorses for a crust. However, they got on like a house on fire after that.

Then an acquaintance of Mick and Ally's appeared and happened to drop his hand on Shouty Husband's shoulder. I think I've said before that nobody, but nobody, touches him without permission. He jumped up and the pub went quiet as Shouty Husband got loud and tore strips off the guy. We left after one drink; I poured him into the car and we went home. Yet again, a Saturday night alone as he slept off a session.

Babylon - David Gray

Bromance isn't a word I tend to use, but it certainly describes the relationship between Mick and Shouty Husband.

It started after Shouty Husband was attacked with the crowbar and it's lasted twenty-three years.

One day, I was driving past the pub Mick went to when I saw him sitting outside. I missed him, so I decided to stop. I was with my boyfriend of the time, Kevin; Shouty Husband and I were on one of our breaks. Kevin was perfect – a wet lettuce with good conversation who didn't give me any grief. He was the polar opposite to Shouty Husband.

The boys were with their dad for the day and Kevin, who didn't drive, fancied going out for Sunday lunch. Mick took the piss out of him and made him buy a round of drinks. He told me I should be with Shouty Husband, not some dickhead.

Then he told me he planned to marry Joy, which was a real bolt from the blue. We all know someone we can never see settled down – Mick was that person and then some. While I was still reeling from that news, he followed up with the sucker punch: Joy had a problem with me, so I couldn't be at the wedding. While I could understand it, it still hurt.

Joy hated me before we even met. Mick had told her I was the perfect mum, that my boys were doing well in school and my house was always clean. And when he talked about me, he got a certain look in his eye.

Any friendship I might have had with Joy never stood a chance.

Bad Company - Bad Company

The stag do rolled round and Shouty Husband was concerned about Mick's colleagues; he was a bin man for some years before he went back to his first love, farming.

Shouty Husband called them 'a sub-species of Darwin' and was determined to keep an eye on Mick and stop them doing anything stupid. He brought out Super Shouty Husband as a deterrent – otherwise they would have done.

The plan was for them all to go the pub on their pushbikes, hang out in the back alcove, and then go home to the bride and crash for the night. Well, they certainly did that...

Riding a pushbike when you're pissed isn't easy – not even for Mick and Shouty Husband, who can handle their beer. Shouty Husband was determined to go faster than Mick and rode at speed into a wall. Mick thought he was unconscious, so he started slapping him around the face, then when Shouty Husband came to he slapped Mick right back.

Mick never saw it coming and had a handprint on his face for about three days afterwards.

He did marry Joy and took on her five kids into the bargain. For someone who really wasn't stepdad material, that was never going to go well.

Sometimes I Feel Like Screaming - Deep Purple

Next weekend saw the gang in the pub. One of them had been barred from the building, but he could sit outside in the beer garden, so the rest of them could buy him beer and chat through the window.

In the corner was a group of young men, aged around eighteen to twenty-one. They were acting up and being noisy – boys being boys, you might say, but this was a family pub. The gang had the unofficial role of keeping the riff raff in order.

All the windows were open as it was a hot night, but one of the lads decided to close one near Shouty Husband. He opened it right back up again and one of the lads decided to square up to him.

Here's a top tip: Never say 'What are you going to do about it? 'to Shouty Husband. On this occasion, he roared in the face of the upstart, frightening him almost to death, followed by his King Kong act. He didn't quite beat his chest and snatch an aeroplane from the sky, but you get the gist.

The landlord jumped over the bar to intervene, the lads retreated hastily from the pub, and Shouty Husband got free drinks for the rest of the night.

A couple of days later he went to visit Mick. The teenage stepson had his mate's round, and they were playing music at a level that could burst your eardrums.

Shouty Husband strode into the front room and turned it down with his 'don't mess with me' look. One of the lads looked at him, then held his hands up and said, 'I don't want any trouble. ' Turns out he was one of the rowdy group from the pub and Shouty Husband had clearly made an impression...

Unsurprisingly, Mick and Joy didn't make it. Mick came to me to lick his wounds, and when she and Shouty Husband heard we were spending time together, they put two and two together and came up with about sixteen.

For the record, nothing happened. Mick and I were just friends. He'd get drunk and sleep on my sofa a lot.

Meanwhile, Shouty Husband went to see if Joy was ok and, after a boozy night of talking about how much they hated me and Mick, they ended up having revenge sex.

He came back to me not long after this, but it was some years before he told me about it. He said it was because he was jealous of the closeness Mick and I had, and the shared memories he couldn't understand.

At the time, I was touched. Now I realise it was because he viewed me as his property and even if he didn't want me, nobody else could either.

Mick still loves his now ex-wife; he likens her to Everest and says she had to climbed to the summit. She's 'the one', as far as he's concerned, even though he knows it could never have worked out between them.

For this reason, and because I know he needs Shouty Husband's friendship, I have never told him what happened between the two of them – and I never will.

Doctor My Eyes - Jackson Browne

After Mick and Joy broke up, the job and the caravan that went it also disappeared. Shouty Husband offered Mick his spare room for as long as he wanted to stay there. The bromance was as strong as ever.

Mick was in a bad place. He was on anti-depressants that mostly turned him into a zombie.

One Sunday evening he sat on the stairs and cried like a baby while Shouty Husband sat with him, one arm around his shoulders. The pills went in the bin after that. Mick had a safe space while he worked through what had happened and, if he felt sociable, he had Shouty Husband too.

Now You're Gone - Whitesnake

One night in June, a chain reaction started that is one of my favourite memories.

Kevin and I were doing whatever it was we did. If I'm honest, that was a lot of jack rabbit sex and conversation of sorts, but in my heart, I wanted to be back in Shouty Husband's spotlight.

Mick had moved out by now and Shouty Husband's new lodger, Wayne, had a girlfriend who would shag a table if you asked her to, according to local opinions. Mary – or Maz, as she was known – had no boundaries. Shouty Husband didn't like her, but it amused him to take the piss. One Saturday night, while I was enjoying a radio programme about Bob Marley, the phone rang. It was Shouty Husband, inviting us over as he was having people round. Did we want to come? Yes, please! Kevin wasn't happy about it, but wild horses couldn't have stopped me.

It's funny what sticks in your mind. I can clearly remember I was wearing Levi 501s and a lilac cotton jumper over a Wonderbra that uplifted the downtrodden. There was quite the crowd at Shouty Husband's when we arrived – Wayne and Maz, Steve, Lottie, Gary Lottie's brother and Sue, who was a friend of mine and Karen's. The drink flowed, the spliffs got passed round and we were all having fun except for Kevin, who was teetotal and strictly no drugs.

Maz was being very loud and spoiling Shouty Husband's buzz. He started a conversation with her about what she'd do for a dare, and she dared him to walk around his street dressed in women's clothes. Well, he was never one to back down. He worked out that Maz's bra would fit him, and he also took the short jersey skirt she had on, leaving her in her knickers and a long t-shirt. He stuffed socks into the bra and then told me he wanted my sweater – lilac was his colour; it went with his long blond hair. Sue gave up her sandals – he only has small feet – and, with a touch of my very expensive lipstick, Shouty Husband was ready for his close up!

He and Maz went for a walk, and I stood there in my bra and jeans while Kevin tutted. Well, if you can't beat them – join them. I got Wayne to give me a piggyback and off we went. Soon after, Maz went back to the house with Wayne. Shouty Husband and I ended up sitting on the wall at the top of the S-bend on his street, and he uttered the words I was so desperate to hear. 'I want you back, ' he said, and then kissed me!

I felt like I was floating on air. He was mine again, and I basked in his glow. We held hands and got a bit touchy-feely as a bike came around the S-bend. The rider nearly crashed when he suddenly encountered what looked like two half-dressed women having a snog!

Kevin really had the hump by the time we got back, but by that point I didn't care. The only low point was when Shouty Husband ran his hand over Sue's foot and smiled at her – something about the way he did it gave me a lightbulb moment, and I realised he was sleeping with her. But I had to be sure, so I took a leaf out of his book and played with her head. I said I was going to put the moves on Shouty Husband, and did she mind? She couldn't really say she did – she already had a husband and a boyfriend and had no claim on him.

I knew she did, though. She'd tasted the forbidden fruit, and if he'd snapped his fingers she'd have gone back for more. I never really forgave Shouty Husband for sleeping with one of my few female friends, either.

The next morning, Kevin went home, and I went to my mums for Sunday lunch. By the afternoon, I was back in Shouty Husband's bed, and all was good in the world once more – in fact, summer 1999 lives in my memory as the best time he and I ever had.

My White Bicycle - Nazareth

Are you ready to come on holiday with Shouty Husband and me? It's a treat, I promise. We had fun and, twenty-two years later, the memories still make me smile.

This was before we were back together, and he'd temporarily disappeared again. It was coming up to his forty-second birthday; I always got him a present, even if he wasn't around, and this year was no exception. He was a huge motorbike fan, so I got him two tickets to a round of the British Superbike Championship. Even if he didn't want to take me, I thought his brother-in-law, Bill, could go with him.

One Friday night, I got back from dropping the boys at their dad's for the weekend to find a message on my answer-machine saying I'd won a holiday to Turkey. I thought twice about returning the call – I assumed it was some kind of timeshare thing.

But no! I'd paid for the Superbike tickets on my credit card, and it turned out I'd been automatically entered into a prize draw – and won first prize! A week in Turkey, bed and breakfast – flights and accommodation paid for, all I needed was spending money.

The travel company wanted me to collect my prize on the day of the bike races and have some publicity photos taken. At the time I was still seeing Kevin – he didn't fancy the bike races but was up for the holiday, so he came with

me to Oulton Park. We had an amazing day, actually –
afternoon tea in the VIP area and everything.

I was also introduced to a lovely elderly Italian gentlemen
called Giacomo Agostini; I had no clue who he was, as I
wasn't a motorbike racing fan, but those of you who will
recognise the name! He's one of the greatest motorbike
racers ever, winning no fewer than fifteen world titles in
the 1960s and 1970s. (My dad was really impressed I met
him.)

The trip to Turkey was planned for the end of September,
as it cools off a little then and I don't cope well with
extreme heat. As far as Kevin was concerned, we were
going as a couple. But that was before the Evening of
Cross-Dressing – and then Shouty Husband was back on
the scene.

Summer Holiday - Cliff Richard

Aside from a trip to Northern Ireland, Shouty Husband had never been overseas – and you can't really count that, as it's still the UK. Anyway, he didn't have a passport, so we had to sort that out.

Doing the application for the first time is a nightmare, so I got three forms to be on the safe side. What fun we had. It states clearly that you must sign in the box and not to go over the lines. Shouty Husband hates being told what to do and insisted I send the form even though his signature went out of the box.

It got rejected, of course, and it took him to more attempts to get it right. By now we were running out of time, so I spent a day on the phone to the passport office trying to find out if it had been processed.

His passport finally arrived just a week before we were due to fly. The holiday firm let me change the name on the ticket. The Boys' Dad agreed to come and look after them in my house and – bonus – even said he'd do some decorating for me to stop himself getting bored.

Win, win. We were good to go. Turkey – brace yourself!

Kiss You All Over - Exile

We were flying from Manchester, so I organised a taxi and we got to the airport at around 7am. The flight was four and a half hours, and we weren't sitting together. I spent most of it worrying the holiday would make or break us — there was nowhere for Shouty Husband to escape too if things went wrong. He wasn't keen on the flight and then we had a two-hour coach journey from the airport to the hotel. We arrived in Marmaris at 9.30pm; allowing for the time difference, that meant we'd been on the go for over twelve hours.

I knew we were going to hate Marmaris as soon as we got there. It was Blackpool on a bad day — all neon lights and too much noise. Remember, at the time the internet wasn't as much of a 'thing' so we hadn't been able to do lots of research — all we had to go on was a photo of the hotel and an atlas!

We sat on the coach while it dropped people off at their hotels in turn. I was praying for a miracle, and it seems I was heard — ours looked amazing, built into the cliff face and away from the noisy centre. The only downside was having to drag our luggage up the bloody steep hillside...but then our adventure began!

As soon as we'd checked in, found our room and dumped the luggage, Shouty Husband went in search of the bar. Tuborg lager and raki were his drinks of choice.

The barman was called William Shakespeare, apparently – easier for English people to pronounce – and his brothers, Jesus and Moses, also worked for the hotel.

This was before the Turkish currency had been devalued and you got millions of lira for a few quid. Shouty Husband couldn't his head around all the noughts but, feeling generous, he got the drinks in for the Turks. The hotel owner's son came over and barked at Jesus and Moses, and you didn't need to understand Turkish to know he was annoyed. He was muscular, walked like an orang-utan and thought he was somebody - prey for Shouty husband!

By now it was half past two in the morning, and I was dead on my feet. Shouty Husband and the lads were having fun – it turned out they all liked the same music, he was regaling them with stories about his bouncer days, and he was showing off tricks he'd learned from the police, like being able to put somebody on the floor without hurting them. I knew he was going to square up to the owner's son. He eyed up the owner's son, found out he acted pretty much as the hotel's bouncer, and asked him how he stopped any trouble. When he mimicked hitting someone, Shouty Husband told him that wouldn't be allowed in England, so he had other methods. He offered to show him how it was done, cleverly choosing to demonstrate on Jesus first. The lad was six feet tall and reed-thin, but he went down straight away. Shouty Husband stopped him before he hit the floor. The owner's son laughed; he wouldn't go down so easily.

Fatal error. Shouty Husband took him right to the floor before he caught him, and the look on his face was priceless.

It's ironic that Shouty Husband, who is such a bully, would never stand by and watch someone be bullied by anyone else. He told Moses, who was only a kid of about twenty and got the worst of the son's temper, that he could teach him the move he'd just used.

The owner's son laughed and sneered, but Moses learned quickly and did put Shouty Husband down (although he always had complete control). He told Moses he'd done well and said he'd get him work on the doors if he ever came to England. The owner's son never came within six feet of Shouty Husband for the rest of the holiday.

Meanwhile, I gave up at 3am and left them to it. Shouty Husband rolled in at 5am; apparently, he'd asked when the bar closed and was told it was when the last customer left. William Shakespeare, the barman, had to be back on duty again at 8am.

I let Shouty Husband sleep in while I went for breakfast – sweet rolls, boiled eggs and dubious-looking cooked meat. There wasn't anything else. When I told Shouty Husband he said we'd go out and have breakfast in style on our own. So off we went into Marmaris. He held my hand, the sun shone, and I was happy.

We've Only Just Begun - Carpenters

The café owners all try and entice you in, but Shouty Husband just said hello and kept walking. We found a market with the 'genuine fakes' that Turkey is so famous for. Shouty Husband loves a good market and even though the jeans clearly weren't really Armani, he could tell the denim was decent quality.

He haggled successfully and ended up with four 'Ralph Lauren' polo shirts, two pairs of black 'Armani' jeans and a dress for me for the equivalent of £20. Then, for an exorbitant £3.50, he bought a fake Rolex watch and a Turkish stamped silver ring with an unusual design. He wore it as his wedding ring for years and it was the only personal thing he wanted back when we split up; I sent it.

Next, we found a supermarket - Turkeys' version of Asda. The first thing on the list was a travel kettle, as there were no tea or coffee-making facilities in our room and Shouty Husband really needed his coffee. That was joined by a jar of Nescafé and brown sugar lumps shaped like playing card suits – aces, diamonds, clubs and hearts. Coffee Mate, as there was no mini fridge for milk, then with plastic cups and some minestrone Cup-a-Soup sachets, we were sorted. We got bread and the makings of sandwiches too, but sadly no bacon. Shouty Husband loves a bacon sandwich, but in a country where the majority of people are Muslim, it wasn't widely available.

Another market stall yielded a small penknife that could be used for prep and then we discovered one of my favourite places - Attila's the greengrocers. It was piled high with strange fruits and vegetables – we hadn't got a clue what they were but went in anyway. Attila himself came rushing over. It wasn't a touristy place at all, and he spoke no English, while our Turkish was limited to 'please' and 'thank you'. Shouty Husband mimed Bugs Bunny because we wanted lettuce – though what we got looked more like dandelion leaves – and he also bought me a big pear, as I love them. It was getting hot now, but we carried on to the indoor market where we discovered the stallholders love to get you in for a chat in the hope, you'll spend money.

Well, Shouty Husband was game. We sat down and were given proper Turkish tea in little glasses, and I listened to him talk with the traders. Eventually he bought some fake Calvin Klein underwear and then off we went.

Jet lag, too much beer and the heat were getting the better of Shouty Husband by now, though, so we caught a dolmuş – the public minibus – back to the hotel. It was time to sleep.

Shouty Husband had bought a big bottle of Jack Daniels on the plane, so we had alcohol, but he decided he fancied beer. Our hotel room was rustic but comfortable, and it had air conditioning. So, after a shower and a sleep, we had some food and then we were ready to hit the night life in downtown Marmaris.

Little did I know this night out would change the course of our relationship for ever!

Shouty Husband always liked to go off the main drag to find the real, non-touristy places – but doing this in Marmaris wasn't one of his better ideas.

Finding a café, he decided we should go inside – and knew immediately it was a mistake. It was full of Turkish men, playing cards and drinking tea, and we were the only tourists in there. The place went silent and then a young man came up and spoke German to him. We got that everywhere – Shouty Husband had long, blond hair so people assumed he was German. They looked very puzzled when he said he was Irish and spoke English!

Still, making the best of it we sat down and had tea and a good chat with the young man, all the while being stared at by the rest of the men. He wanted to know all about us and asked if we had children. Shouty Husband told him I had sons and showed him a photo of the boys. Then the man asked if Shouty Husband had been to the doctors –

after all, if he didn't have children, it must be because there was a problem. They didn't understand that Shouty Husband never wanted children of his own, but they did look at me differently for having sons.

After three cups of tea, I was desperate for the toilet. I sat there quietly while Shouty Husband asked for me; I knew this wasn't going to be a comfortable experience. Sure enough, there was no lock on the door and the nice young man had to hold it shut while I used the facilities. That remains my quickest comfort break ever!

Shouty Husband told the young man we should go as we needed to eat, so a plate of pistachio nuts appeared. Then it all got a bit surreal.

The young man asked whether Shouty Husband was prepared to sell me and, if so, for how much? I knew then we were out of our depth and that his reply would determine if we could leave the café easily.

There was a brand-new Mercedes Benz outside, a beautiful big car. Shouty Husband pointed at it and said loudly he'd trade me for the car, but only for one night.

The young man looked me up and down and told Shouty Husband he must love me very much.

While he was on a roll, Shouty Husband got up, took my hand and said 'Çok teşekkür ederim '(Turkish for 'thank you very much'). Then we walked out of the café and, as soon as we were outside the door, we ran back towards the lights of the main strip.

She Wears My Ring - Elvis

The first restaurant we came to looked clean and wasn't too busy, so we went in to eat. Shouty Husband being Shouty Husband wanted to sit at a table that was not laid up so he could see everything that was going on, and if it all kicked off, he could protect me. So, the staff laid the table while we read the menu.

I'd always wanted to try sea bass, so Shouty Husband told me to go ahead and order it. He decided to have a lamb kebab with all the trimmings but no chips, as he doesn't eat them.

The food was amazing, and then the bill came – nine million lira. This was before the Turkish currency was devalued, so it wasn't even the equivalent of a tenner, but Shouty Husband hadn't got his head around all those noughts, and it turned out we didn't have enough money on us to pay the bill.

Shouty Husband said we'd go back to the hotel to get some cash and then come back. The staff were brilliant and agreed, so that's what we did. It was midnight by this time, but the main drag was still busy. We decided to walk along the harbour and found a boat offering a moonlight cruise around the bay with cabaret. Since it was a beautiful night and Shouty Husband was in a good mood, he booked us on it – it would be fun, something to look forward to.

Then came the moment that changed everything. I don't wear jewellery, but I stopped to look in a jewellery shop window as the display was just incredible. A very neat ring caught my eye – beautiful and unusual, with a blue stone. I wasn't going to buy it; I just thought it was pretty.

Shouty Husband saw me looking and asked if I'd like it. Then, before I had time to answer, he'd pulled me into the shop and had me trying it on. It was too big, but the jeweller said they'd resize it and it would be ready the next day.

It cost thirty million lira – a princely £28 – and I loved it. The only finger it fitted was the ring finger on my left hand, so that's where Shouty Husband said I should wear it.

Shouty Husband had bought me a Ceylonese water sapphire set in 14 carat Turkish gold, and I loved it. I wore that ring for twenty years, and now it's in my ring box with all the other jewellery he bought me.

We left the jewellers for a slow walk back to the hotel, where we sat on our balcony and had a drink. I don't ever remember feeling so much in love and being so happy as I was that night.

Fernando - Abba

The following morning, Shouty Husband decided to go and sit round the pool before it got too hot. He also fancied a proper wet shave, as the hotel had a proper Turkish barber. I was quite safe, with a good book and the joy of Abba blasting out at 9am, and he arranged for the hotel lads to keep an eye out in case anyone bothered me.

Once he was done, it was time to go for supplies.

It wasn't long before we found an opticians. As both Shouty Husband and I both have bad eyesight, glasses at home cost stupid money. But Turkey is famous for its eye care, so in we went... He was sent over the road to the health centre for an eye test, and I was left in the shop with Vouge.

At this time I smoked, and there was no problem smoking in the shops – except this one. So, I took myself outside to have a ciggie and was quietly minding my own business when an English lady shouted at me to ask if I spoke English. When I smiled and said yes, she said she looked a bit taken aback as she'd thought I looked Turkish. Anyway, they wanted to know where the bus stop was, so that was easy – there wasn't one! Instead, you just stuck your hand out when it came along, and the driver would let you get on.

Shouty Husband came back eventually and said he'd had the eye test to end all eye tests. He ordered his glasses, which would be ready in three days – that wasn't a problem, but we knew we'd need to be a bit careful with money for the rest of the holiday. We were okay, but not flush. however, for Shouty Husband, money equalled pleasure tokens and our next stop was at a leather shop. Because he'd treated himself, he now wanted to treat me.

The shop was owned by Osman, who wanted to tell us he was Kurdish. It was important to him, but we didn't think anything of it at the time. (More on that later.)

I must have tried on twenty leather jackets before Shouty Husband said yes to one. Then he sat down to do business, which meant drinking apple tea for two hours while he and Osman chatted and haggled. I have no idea how much my jacket cost in the end, but they came to an agreement.

We were down to a budget of £20 a day now, which actually wasn't too bad at the time. Shouty Husband had worked out to feed us on a pittance and he'd still have enough for his beer – he did love Efes Extra.

Listen to Your Heart - Roxette

As both Shouty Husband and I have fair skin and burn easily, for the next two days we were like vampires we mostly came out at night. We'd nip out around three o'clock in the afternoon for food, but then we'd wait until it got cooler at around 8pm.

Time to explain the carat about the ring now - please excuse the pun!you remember the moonlight cruise around the bay we booked? Well, we went along as planned and boarded a small cruise ship. The moon was shining on the water, and it was a beautiful night.

Shouty Husband and I were both wearing our new clothes and felt great.

We decided to sit at the front of the boat and look at the moon, and a young Dutch couple offered to take our photo. Shouty Husband looked at me and said, 'You'd better call that your engagement ring. ' I looked back at him and asked, 'Are you sure? '

That moment of us gazing at each other was captured on film for posterity. (No digital cameras in those days!)

It was the perfect romantic moment. Right then, I truly believed Shouty Husband loved me and we did the Kate and Leonardo thing from the Titanic movie, standing at the front of the boat with our arms out. Even now, twenty-two years later, I still get a warm and squishy feeling when I think about it.

Big Balls – AC/DC

Then all hell broke loose. Bet that got your attention. Are you sitting comfortably? Then I'll begin.

The moonlight cruise round the bay with cabaret turned out to be a disco ship. Shouty Husband stuck it for about half an hour before he braved going inside to get a beer, and that's when he found they were charging silly money for drinks. To say he was unhappy is an understatement. It got worse.

He'd had enough, but it was only 10.30pm and the ship wasn't due to dock until 2am. It was too far for him to swim back, so Shouty Husband was trapped – which always makes him dangerous.

There was a lifeline – a water taxi that would take you back to shore. We were the last ones to get on it, and everyone else on board was English too. (That's important to remember later.) Everybody was complaining, saying they'd been sold a pup, and they all said they wouldn't pay the water taxi captain. However, when a young lad – he couldn't have been more than fifteen years old – came round to collect fares, they all coughed up. It was a million lira each, which was about 70p.

We were nearly back at the shore by the time the lad got to us, and Shouty Husband told him 'No '. He has a terrifying voice when he's in that mood, you can hear the ice in his tone. The young lad backed away quickly with his hands up, no mean feat on a small boat, and said he was just doing his job. Enter the boat owner, a small, squat guy with swarthy skin and a hairy body, wearing a dirty white vest. He wanted his fare and got up in Shouty Husband's face to demand it. There was a crowd watching and Shouty Husband played to it, getting very loud and waving his arms about. He said he'd been ripped off on the boat, ripped off to get back to shore, and how he'd had enough.

He told the boat owner he had no money left and asked me if I had any. My purse had two pockets, so I opened the side with the coins in and offered them to the boat owner, who shook his head in disgust and walked away.

All the wives of the husbands that were on the boat with us clapped Shouty Husband for having the guts to do what their husbands had only talked about.

When we got to the main road, Shouty Husband said he did have money really, and I laughed and showed him the notes I had in my purse.

I'll never forget that night on the boat and watching Shouty Husband in action on the quay was amazing. I asked why he'd shouted, and he said Turkish men carried knives so if he was loud, everybody would watch, and he'd be safe – nobody would risk upsetting the tourists!

When we got back to our hotel, Jesus, Moses and the owner's son already heard about our exploits – everyone was talking about the Irish guy with the long blond hair!

Show Me Heaven - Maria McKee

One thing we did notice was the lack of Turkish women around. There were the teenage girls working on the supermarket checkout, who looked about eighteen, but that was all.

The other thing we found was that Turkish men are tactile. Shouty Husband, however, not. One time, we were walking along the main road and a gorgeous, gorgeous man was walking towards us. He looked me up and down twice and I felt like the cat that got the cream! Except...turned out, he wasn't giving me the glad eye – he was giving it to Shouty Husband! I looked over my shoulder after he'd passed by and realised it was Shouty Husband's bum he was looking at!

Men also always wanted to touch Shouty Husband's hair. It had gone really blond in the sun, fell halfway down his back with curls at the ends, and he always carried a small brush to make sure it looked amazing.

My 'get away, don't touch me' Shouty Husband liked to be worshipped and he was proud of his hair, so there he was – quite happy to let them stroke it! We were midway through our holiday now. Money was running short, and we were tired, so we had a rest day – we slept, went out for food, and enjoyed book and us time. Shouty Husband went down the hill to buy an Efes Extra from a hole-in-the-wall shop, and I had Jack Daniels with a splash of lemonade.

At 3am, Shouty Husband fancied another beer, so off we went down the hill to the shop. Thing was, it was still really hot outside so by the time we got back to the hotel, the Efes was warm – and there was no way he was drinking warm beer!

Always inventive, though, he worked out that the paper bands that came with his polo shirts would fit through the grille in the air conditioning and the beer would hang inside the bands Hey presto – ten minutes on full cold, and the beer was cold enough for him to drink!

In the meantime, while the air conditioning was doing its thing to the Efes, Shouty Husband suggested a swim in the pool. So, at half past three in the morning, with my costume under my dress, I followed Shouty Husband under a moonlit sky to the pool. It was being cleaned, so we waited till they had gone – and they left what my mum would call a witch's broom behind on the floor. Shouty Husband looked at me and asked if I trusted him. Well, right then, I'd have died for him if he'd asked – so I said yes. He was a Catholic and I knew he followed pagan ways a lot. He took my hand beneath the full moon and asked me to jump the broom with him. I had no idea what it meant, but I was caught up in the moment, so I did. Then he told me that under the old religion, we were now married. We jumped into the water and kissed, and I knew that in Shouty Husband's eyes, we were now man and wife.

Something's Gotten Hold of My Heart - Marc Almond & Gene Pitney

Marmaris was a haven for English tourists who liked lots of noise and flashy lights, but Shouty Husband wanted something quieter and more laid back. Jesus and Moses had a solution – they told us to get the big bus and go to İçmeler, which was just two miles away.

So that's what we did, the day before we due to fly home.

When we got on the bus at four in the afternoon, it was hot. I mean, it always was, but it felt even hotter than usual. We sat at the front on the right-hand side and, on the left was a Turkish lady aged around 30 wearing a jersey skirt and tights. Her skirt covered her knees as the bus pulled away, but after we'd been around some very windy roads it was up round her thighs. She just kept right on smiling at Shouty Husband as it happened – we did laugh about it when we got off the bus.

We'd planned to spend a few hours in İçmeler; the buses ran back to Marmaris until 11pm so we had plenty of time. First stop was the beach, where we had a paddle and Shouty Husband said it would be a good place to sleep if we stayed there. After a lovely afternoon, we decided it was time to head back.

I needed the loo first, but there was a lack of public toilets. My options were either a hotel or to pay for a strange coin-operated one. I got my coins ready, and a little old lady opened the door after I paid her about 100,000 lira – around 20p at the time.

While I was in the loo, Shouty Husband was having a nosy at a beautiful old BMW bike he'd found and made a new friend out of the owner.

After half an hour of talking bikes together, we were invited to meet the guy's other friends. There were six of them and I never really got their names, but Arman, who owned the jewellery shop, was the main man. When a German couple turned up, he went to work. The wife spoke English to some degree and her husband had Mr Magoo glasses, so Shouty Husband gave her the card for the optician he'd used. (He loved those glasses – they were the best pair he ever had.)

While the German woman shopped for jewellery, we sat outside. The bikers bought beer for Shouty husband and Pepsi for me; it was more expensive than beer, so I drank slowly. Shouty Husband told them we had enough to get home and went on to buy a round, so I realised we'd be walking back to Marmaris later.

The German couple spent a lot of money, and it was very clear Arman was someone who had power – after being around Shouty Husband, I knew an alpha when I saw one. The two of them got on like a house on fire, while I did my best wallflower impression.

I know that might upset some women – that I was such a doormat, but it was a very male-oriented culture and that's how I fitted in. I had my say from time to time and

Shouty Husband did include me, but yes – most of the time I sat there and listened.

By now I needed the toilet again, but we had no money left to pay. When Shouty Husband explained this, I was escorted to the bathroom above the jeweller's shop. Having a bodyguard threw me a bit, but I was desperate, so I didn't argue!

I'd noticed most Turkish men hug when they meet, but this group had a funny handshake and then touched heads. So, when a new guy arrived, Shouty Husband did the same thing – and it went down very well, as they all thought he was one of them. Turned out we'd managed to link up with the local branch of the Turkish fascists. Trust Shouty Husband to find fascist bikers...

At 2am, we were still there. Arman shut the shop and invited us to eat with them. Shouty Husband pointed out we had no money, but they insisted; we had to be fed.

The first course was soup. Well, I say soup... It was more like greasy washing up water with bits of rubber band floating in it. It smelt revolting and there was no way I could eat it without being sick. Apparently, it was lamb's intestine soup and was a real delicacy. I'm sorry, Turkey, but it was disgusting. Shouty Husband – drunk, while I was still sober – at mine as well as his own, and Arman ordered me a lamb kebab instead. It looked and smelt amazing, and the only bad bit was when Shouty Husband told me the chilli that came with it wasn't hot, so I took a big bite. He lied. I was choking and red in the face, and drinking water wasn't helping. Everyone in the restaurant was looking at me.

Shouty Husband told me to eat some sugar – and what do you know, it worked. Good tip there – a spoonful of sugar takes the chilli burn away.

As it was now 3.30am, Arman offered us a bed for the night. Neither of us wanted to walk back to Marmaris in the dark, so we accepted; it was in a storeroom over the shop and the lad who usually slept in it had to give it up for us and sleep on the floor. Shouty Husband told me he would stay awake and protect me; he managed five minutes before he started snoring.

We got up after four hours sleep and went for a walk on the beach. The water was so clear we could see the fish swimming around our feet.

The German lady from the night before was there with her friend and said hello. I told her today was our last day and we were going to walk back to Marmaris as we had no money left on us. I showed her my beautiful ring, too, and told her we'd just got engaged.

She declared I wasn't going to walk, pulled out a roll of money thick enough to choke a donkey, and peeled off a million lira note which she handed me for bus fare. It was far too much money, but she was insistent.

Shouty Husband said we had money back at the hotel, so if they were going to be around in a couple of hours we'd come back and return it, but she laughed and said it was ok. For romance, she told us.

Well, after we'd returned to the hotel and packed our stuff ready to go home, we did get the bus back to İçmeler, and we did pay the lovely German lady back. She was very surprised to see us. And then? Well, it was back to the hotel to wait for the coach that would take us to the airport. It was due at 1am and the transfer would take two hours; our flight wasn't until 8am. We settled in for a long night.

Baby I Don't Care - Transvision Vamp

As we said goodbye to Jesus and Moses and the owner's son, Osman – the guy from the leather shop – appeared. He wanted to take Shouty Husband for a farewell drink, but the lads weren't happy as Osman was Kurdish. (If you know your history, you'll understand why.)

Shouty Husband didn't care, though. He took the last of our money, asked the lads to look after me, and off he went. I got to spend my last night in Turkey in the hotel's security hut. At least I felt safe. Turned out Osman wanted to offer Shouty Husband a job for the next season, as he'd bring in more English tourists. Honestly, I thought he might accept the offer and even stay there and then for the end of the season and over winter. But Shouty Husband is a home bird at heart, so he said no. He'd miss his English beer and rain. We were both exhausted by the time the coach came, having had virtually no sleep for the best part of two days and not much food; our last meal, hours earlier, had been a minestrone Cup-a-Soup.

At the airport we couldn't even afford a bag of crisps, but a lovely assistant took pity on us and gave us a bag of crisps for what small change we had left. Then we went to the departure lounge, which was full of Liverpudlian ladies of a certain age.

No word of a lie, when Shouty Husband walked across the departure area – which was quiet at 6am – they all stopped to watch him strut his stuff. He was wearing his fake designer gear and he'd taken the bobble out of his hair, which shone like gold as it tumbled down his back. He was drop-dead gorgeous in that moment, and he was with me, whose default style setting is 'dragged through a hedge backwards'. Pretty sure they wondered what I had that was so special! We had seats together on the plane home, but we were right at the back and the seats were cramped. Shouty Husband has bad hips and can't sit squashed up, and the little old lady in the aisle seat wouldn't swap, so once we were in the air he went to sit on the 'trolley dolly' seats where he could stretch his legs .All the Liverpool ladies went to talk to him on the pretext of going to the loo. He pointed to me, curled up in one corner fast asleep, drooling from my open mouth, and told them all we'd just got engaged on holiday in Turkey.

Honestly, it one of the great weeks of my life and it gave me memories I'll carry in my heart forever. Life with Shouty Husband wasn't all bad.

With a good education, you can rule the world. Shouty Husband knew this, and I agreed with him. So, when the time came to look at secondary schools for Jordan, there was only one choice.

We are lucky that we had a non-fee-paying school nearby that produced impressive results every year. This was the school I wanted Jordan to go to. The problem was that the Boys' Dad objected to it. It was too posh, he said. Jordan would struggle, what was wrong with the local schools? The thing is, Jordan was a bright lad. He needed pushing, and Thomas Telford School would do that.

Shouty Husband agreed Jordan should have the chance and encouraged him to aim to get in. When he was offered a place after passing the entrance exam and the interview, I don't know which of us was prouder.

Jordan did well and made some great friends, but his school report showed he was getting Bs in his classwork when he was capable of As. He wanted to fit in with his friends, who were also B-grade students. Shouty Husband gave Jordan the 'friends are important but getting a great education is more so' talk and told him if he got his grades up to As, he'd treat him and his brother to a new video game. These were expensive, so it was a huge carrot – and it worked. I only ever got the stick!

When exam season came round, Shouty Husband promised a new, top-of-the-range games console as a reward for good results. The proviso was that both boys had to do well. It meant Jordan had to tutor Luke, but it worked – and they agreed it was worth it.

Star Spangled Banner - Jimi Hendrix

We didn't with New Year's Eve. Most years, the only way Shouty Husband and I knew it had happened was when we heard fireworks going off – and then we rolled over and went back to sleep .

But in 1999 – for the new millenium – he decided we'd do something special. That turned out to be going to Shrewsbury to buy a record deck for him; it's a good job he knew the area as the traffic was horrendous .

I still have the handwritten receipt for that deck – it cose £100. Shouty Husband spent the next five hours setting it all up and I had to listen to the opening five minutes of Bat Out of Hell over and over again while he fiddled.

The perfect music to welcome in such a momentous year was, according to Shouty Husband, Woodstock 'album on vinyl – hence the new record deck.

This was accompanied by lots of cans of Kestrel Supers – they'll be important later – and a whole load of dope.

At quarter to midnight, Shouty Husband put on the Star Spangled Banner as by Jimi Hendrix. It's not my favourite Hendrix track, I must say, Shouty Husband's. My abiding memory of that night is that, as Big Ben chimed twelve to welcome in the year 2000, Shouty Husband was running to the downstairs loo to be sick. What a way to mark not just a new century but a new millenium!

Bat Out of Hell - Meatloaf

So – New Year's Day, in the year 2000. Shouty Husband spent it recovering from the night before and then, when Mick appeared, he decided we should see it in all over again in style.I drove us all to Shouty Husband's home town and we started in one of his favourite pubs, which had great beer and was frequented by the local Hell's Angels.Shouty Husband and Mick went off to play pool, leaving me safe in the company of Gorgeous George, a tall, thin black man in his 50s. He was wearing a sharp suit and a trilby hat, which he raised when we were introduced. He had a famous brother who carved intricate scenes on match heads. He showed me a newspaper article about him, and I said I'd seen him once on Blue Peter.

I had fun chatting to George – Mick came to check on me, but Shouty Husband was too busy arm wrestling. When it was time to go, Gorgeous George thanked me for an good time and said if I ever needed a job, I should come back and find him.

Shouty Husband laughed till he was red in the face and, once we were outside and he'd got his breath back, he told me Gorgeous George was a well-known pimp. He was a safe bet if I was interested though, said Shouty Husband – he treated his girls well and they didn't have to work the streets.

I did see the funny side, and thank you, Gorgeous George – that encounter still makes me smile twenty two years later.

Next we moved on to a rough pub that Shouty Husband wouldn't have taken me to without someone else – Mick, in this case – to keep an eye on me.

Shouty Husband was well-known in this pub and he was spoiling for a fight. The turn of the millenium had brought his mortality home to him and he dealt with it by walking in like he owned the place.

It was the most uncomfortable half hour I'd spent in a very long time . Shouty Husband was loud and obnoxious and he upset the barmaid. It annoyed her husband, too, who was something of a man mountain and invited Shouty Husband to step outside to resolve matters.

Out we all went, and Shouty Husband told Mick to put me in the car, which was parked just up the road. I did as I was told and panicked as I tried to see what was going on. The man mountain and Shouty Husband were arguing, with Mick trying to calm things down.Then Shouty Husband pointed out the CCTV, which was wired to the police station five minutes away. There was no point in a fight, but if the man mountain wanted to... They went their separate ways. The man mountain saved face, Shouty Husband felt like a man again, and we went home and had amazing sex .

A strange way to start a new century – but a memorable one!

As all boys do, Jordan found his feet when he became a teenager. He came in one day at the age of thirteen while Shouty Husband and I were talking and laid down the law as he saw it.

When Shouty Husband told him off for disrespecting me, Jordan uttered the time-honoured words of so many stepchildren: 'You're not my dad so you can't tell me off. 'As you can imagine, that was a red rag to a bull.

Shouty Husband and Jordan squared up to each other, the young blood trying his luck against the old man. Shouty Husband wagged a finger and told Jordan nobody spoke to 'his woman' like that, and Jordan looked at me to back him up.

My next actions defined the future of my relationships with the man and the child I loved. Shouty Husband was right, so I backed him. It meant I didn't have the horrible teenage years with my boys as they knew I wasn't a pushover and Shouty Husband would have my back. But he had theirs, too. When they were being bullied and told to stay away from the local play park, Shouty Husband went and had a quiet word with the head bully's dad. Word got around that my boys were under Shouty Husband's protection, and they were never bothered again.

Happy Birthday - Altered Images

The first time I had the pleasure – I use the term loosely – of meeting Shouty Husband's sister, Sarah, was on her fortieth birthday.

On a rainy Friday night, Shouty Husband decided to drive the two hours to surprise her. He checked with Ed, her husband, that she'd be in and off we went. It was 10pm by the time we arrived, and it was clear by the look on her face that she wasn't pleased to see him. Me – well, she looked at me like a snake looks at its prey. She terrified me, but I knew it was important that I meet her. (Ed was lovely to me, incidentally.)

At one stage, I was left alone with them while Shouty Husband went to say hello to his nephews. I got the third degree – was I with Shouty Husband for his income, did I want his house, was I after a father for my kids?

I'd say it felt like the iron fist in the velvet glove – but without the velvet glove! I felt like they'd put me in the spotlight and my answers would affect any future I had with Shouty Husband.

I knew she'd be able to tell if I lied to her, so I was honest. I said I provided for my boys myself, my house was paid for, and they already had one dad and didn't need another. This seemed to satisfy Sarah and I breathed a sigh of relief. Four hours travelling just to stay an hour, drink a cup of coffee and annoy his sister while I got a grilling!

Let's Talk About Sex - Salt-N-Pepa

Shouty Husband had been around the block and even described himself as a tart. He loved being in control when he had sex and wanted to be the best of the best. (And he was amazing, until his health stopped him.) He's done it all – one girl, two guys, and vice versa. He even slept with one woman while her husband watched, which he said was a huge power trip.

He and I had the same mentality to sex - we were 'try sexual' and would try anything once. If we liked it, we'd do it again. If not, then at least it was something crossed off the bucket list.

He was never into pain, though. Things never went further than light bondage, and he'd stop in a heartbeat when I said 'enough'. I trusted him completely.

He was as competitive about sex as he was in life. He needed whoever he was to award him Olympic Gold for stamina and adventure; they had to have at least one orgasm. He was a dedicated giver of pleasure and sometimes it was like having a banquet when all you really wanted was egg and chips.

Shouty Husband had trained himself to last as long as possible, which was great, but alas – eventually that caused problems and he got to the point where he was unable to ejaculate. It's a form of male impotence.

Honestly, you might think having a man who can go for hours is a blessing, but not always. Add in the booze, dope and breathing issues, and finally it added up to not being able to maintain an erection or even perform at all.

Shouty Husband was very adventurous, though. He loved foreplay in strange places where he might get caught, and I had great fun going along for the ride. He took a good girl and turned me bad, and I loved it.

One that really sticks in the memory and still makes me smile (and blush) was the Saturday night shop in Tesco. He dared me to go out wearing nothing but hold-ups, high heels and a cream raincoat.

I've mentioned before that Shouty Husband hated red, and how I was never allowed to wear the colour around him. Except for one dress, it was from C&A, a red and white summer frock that always made him rise to the occasion. I still have it. I don't wear it, it's tatty now, but it holds so many good memories of Shouty husband and the amazing sex I had while wearing it.

In those days, before you could order anything you desired at the click of a mouse, buying sex toys meant a trip to the sex shop with its sleazy, blacked out windows. While I was still with the Boys' Dad and Shouty Husband was still with Karen, Karen needed a new vibrator. I'd never been in a sex shop, so Shouty husband offered to take us both to Broad Street in Wolverhampton, which is full of them.

Shouty Husband was wearing a suit and a black fake Burberry mac. His hair was loose, and he had Karen on one arm and me on the other. He walked down the street liked he owned it, and it was great fun. We went into all the shops and Shouty Husband haggled the price down. Karen got a new toy, and I got some great memories.

About twenty years ago, Shouty Husband rediscovered the joy of amyl nitrate. Sex with Shouty Husband on poppers was mind blowing but – and it's a big but – the headache you get is horrendous and really disrupts your ability to breathe.

So, we dabbled, we loved and boy, we enjoyed, wow, just wow. But then we agreed we both liked breathing, and the high wasn't worth the low. If he ever suggested it again, I reminded him how bad he felt when he had a three-day headache and couldn't breathe properly.

Of course, when someone has rules for everything else in their life then of course there are rules for sex too.

You had to be clean, first off. Whenever Shouty Husband asked me if I fancied a bath, I knew it meant I was on a promise. When he drove the bin wagon, he was paranoid about being clean and would bath or shower with Dettol as soon as he got home. It became a standing joke that I had to be disinfected before he'd touch me. I still love the smell of Dettol, though.

Because he smoked cigarettes and a lot of dope, and drank a lot too, Shouty Husband's lungs deteriorated over the years. Today, he has asthma, COPD and diverticulitis. He needs an inhaler that has bromide as one of the main ingredients, so his already limited sex drive has now disappeared.

Being a good boy, he told his GP and was prescribed generic Viagra. We had to pay for it privately, though – it wasn't covered by the NHS – and he was only allowed four tablets each month. So, we worked out we could have sex once a week for a fiver.

Of course, there's always a downside. Shouty Husband got all the side effects - banging head, stomach cramps, a face as red as a baboon's bum. He did try, but the pills proved to be a nightmare so that was the end of that.

Since sex was Shouty Husband's way of being tactile, once Boris Becker the Bionic Pecker – don't laugh - stopped working, any form of affection disappeared too. I had just turned fifty, and if I wanted a hug I had to ask.

Our relationship went from 'wow' to 'woe'. He refused to talk about it and stonewalled me whenever I tried to raise the subject. As far as he was concerned, sex was all or nothing; as he couldn't breathe properly, he decided on nothing.

He still looked at porn, but I was demoted from wife to housekeeper. I went from living with my soul mate to sharing space with a friend – and one you'd rather just left, but you're too scared to tell them that.

Stand By Me - Oasis

'Shouty husband doesn't have a bucket of sand to put his head in, he has the bloody Sahara!' My mum

Mum first met Shouty Husband twenty-six years ago when she was babysitting for Karen. He came home from a late shift, got changed and met us in the pub. Half an hour later he was back at the house, throwing up in the loo, after having a bad pint. He always said he knew how to make an impression!

Shouty Husband always said my mum was the nearest thing he had to one of his own, because she was really caring.

She could tell there was something seriously wrong with his mental health, but because both I and my boys loved him, and he was brilliant with them, she kept her thoughts to herself.

After one break-up early in our relationship, she did what she called 'This is interfering, but... ' and wrote to him. Ok, I admit I asked her to, because I knew he'd listen to her.

She told him that if he didn't want to be with me that was ok, but I needed a friend and we'd been friends for a long time. Shouty Husband came back to me because he could dictate how our relationship would be, and he kept the letter for years until it got lost in a house move.

My mum was really the only person Shouty Husband came close to trusting. He was useless with money, regarding it as pleasure tokens, and was hopeless when it came to paying bills. He refused to have direct debits, apart from the mortgage.

So, my mum took overpaying his bills for him. He'd give me money to give to her every week and, when we weren't together, he'd post it through her letterbox. He liked knowing his bills were paid on time and he didn't have to worry.

Mum kept excellent records and he was always welcome to look at her bookkeeping and have it explained. He never wanted to, but he did nickname her 'Al Capone's accountant'; he said if she'd been looking after his money, the Mafia boss would never have been done for tax evasion.

Shouty Husband really respected my mum, but she knew was something not right about him. She just couldn't put her finger on it.

Whenever we visited my parents' house, he'd always ask if the kettle was broken. He'd walk around the garden having a ciggie, and then add cold water to his cup of tea and make me leave before I'd finished mine. It was all about him being in control and everybody knowing it, but it never worked with my mum. She knew he was a bully. Sometimes he'd hug her, something she hates. He'd hug her too hard and hurt her – it was his way of showing he had power over her. That sounds terrible now it's written down. My mum says that it sometimes takes a while for the penny to drop. Well, it's well and truly clanged now, and the echo is still deafening me!

Take It to the Limit - The Eagles

Shouty Husband is happiest when he has wheels beneath him. He went from motorbike couriering to driving a van and then moved up to a seven-tonne lorry – that was as much as his licence would allow.

However, with it being agency work, it was all a bit hit and miss and Shouty Husband had a mortgage to pay. He worked out that if he took his HGV Class 2 licence, he'd be laughing – the industry was crying out for Class 2 drivers!

I've got a knack for finding the right courses and had the time to do the Google and make phone calls. I found out that there was a government grant available towards the cost of the tuition, but even so Shouty Husband would need to find about £1000.

As he was on great terms with my mum – as far as he was concerned, anyway – Shouty Husband went to her cap in hand to ask if she would lend him the money. When he passed the course and had plenty of work, he could pay it back easily – he reckoned he could make three times more money once he got the licence.

Mum agreed for the sake of me and my boys, so it was all systems go. Shouty Husband went off for his week's course and passed with flying colours, as I knew he would.

The first job he got was driving an eight-leg tipper wagon with a sixteen-gear split box. The gearbox defeated him, so back to the drawing board. Next, he worked for a slightly dodgy haulage firm that gave him a good grounding in how to drive a big wagon.

He was right, though. The money was fantastic, and he paid back the money he borrowed from my mum within three months.

Then a friendship came into my life that didn't last anywhere near long enough. Through no fault of their own, Tracey and her husband ended up losing their home, so the council put them into temporary housing. This was at the back of me, and we had great fun. Tracey and Shouty Husband always thought of each other as brother and sister, so there was lots of teasing and lots of affection.

I was looking at taking the boys on holiday to Spain. Tracey had taken her son, Matty, to one particular resort twice and said there was lots to keep them happy, so off I went with my two for a week.

I topped up an old mobile with enough credit for roaming charges and called him every day to check in. I even managed to find the elusive green fairy – absinthe, which he'd always wanted to try but which was banned in many countries. It cost me £15 for a bottle the size of a Coke, but I knew it would make him happy.

Every evening before dinner I'd go down to the bar for happy hour – me-time with a drink and a good book. The boys were aged fourteen and twelve at the time, so they were quite happy to lock themselves in the room and play on their Gameboys.

I always called Shouty Husband from the bar, so I was surprised when my phone rang while I was in the lift, and it turned out to be him. He was calling to tell me Graham was dead. I remember it so well – 6.30pm on a Saturday, and I sat down on a sofa feeling numb. Shouty Husband had gone to visit him at the flat and a neighbour told him – turned out Graham had had a heart attack. He couldn't tell me anymore until he had spoken to Trev.

I offered to get on the next plane home, but Shouty Husband said no. He needed time to process, and it would be good for him if I was away until the Tuesday as planned. I went to the bar and ordered a Ballantine's whisky – Graham's tipple of choice, he said it was a nice, blended drink. The boys and I bought a candle and went to the beach, where we lit it and remembered Graham.

So many memories.

Flying kites together while Shouty Husband was cooking lunch, just so Graham could check he was ok. Sitting in the armchair in his flat, drinking Vimto and reading his Far Side cartoon books while he chatted to Shouty Husband.

Graham could talk the hind leg off a donkey – when he called us, we'd be on the phone for at least four hours.

The New Year's Eve when Shouty Husband was recovering from flu. Graham and I had a quick chat and when I told him I'd been looking after Shouty Husband, and said I deserved the Bilston and Thanet medal for bravery beyond the call of duty.

Watching the last-ever episode of Inspector Morse while Shouty Husband had Graham time for two hours until Big Ben rang out for midnight.

When I got home from Spain, my answer machine was full of calls from the same number, but no message had been left. Turns out my number was in Graham's computer, so one of Grahams friends had been trying to reach me.

Trev came up trumps and found out all the details for Shouty Husband and, on the day of the funeral, sweet Williams were in full flower, so Shouty Husband cut them, tied them with a ribbon, and added a card from us

. Graham would have approved of that – home-grown flowers for a coffin rather than shop-bought that would just be left to die.

Shouty Husband lost more than a friend that day – he lost the closest thing to a dad he'd ever had.

Absinthe - The Damned

Shouty Husband got to try the green fairy three times. All were memorable, but you know what they say – you never forget your first time!

He was over the moon with the bottle I gave him and allowed me a small taste. That was enough, thanks – it was disgusting and tasted like mouthwash. However, he sipped a wine glass full and had his normal Friday night beer and dope on top – he loved it!

He told Charlie he'd got his hands on some, so he came over to party with us. All was going well until Charlie had a wine glass of the green stuff...Instead of sipping the absinthe, Charlie necked it in one go. He'd already consumed a lot of super-strength lager so twenty minutes later there he was, collapsed on the floor in a heap. We left him there – in fact, I went to bed.

A couple of hours later my bedroom door opened, and there was Charlie – stark naked and with no clue where he was or where he should be. Shouty Husband came and took him to the other bedroom and, the next day, Charlie had no memory of what had happened and was mortified when we told him. He asked us not to say anything to his missus, Angie, but then told her himself when she happened to call. She was more annoyed that I had seen Charlie naked than she was about him getting drunk – but as I told her, while he was worth the once-over, he was too skinny for my taste!

Car Wash - Rose Royce

When he first passed his HGV test, Shouty Husband himself would admit he knew nothing. His first proper job was delivering plants all over the south of England for a local nursery; it meant he was away four nights a week, so our relationship was half an hour on the phone every night.

One Friday his truck broke down and he was stuck in a compound until the right part arrived. He ran up a huge bill on his company phone, calling everyone on his contacts list. His boss had known the clutch was on its way out but she still sent him out on deliveries, so he thought to hell with it. He was there for two nights and didn't get home until the Sunday.

Still, he loved the job. Even though it was just for the summer, he was getting valuable HGV driving experience. Then it all went to hell.

Shouty Husband always read the road well. But it's much easier to react when you're on a motorbike; lorries aren't as easy to manoeuvre, and they don't stop quickly. A transit van in front of him decided to turn right without indicating at a known accident blackspot. Shouty Husband's truck was fully loaded and heavy, so it didn't respond right away even though he immediately rammed on his brakes.

He hit the van and squashed it.

The artic behind him had better brakes, but just touched the truck and pushed Shouty Husband more into the van. Then a lady in a car behind that swerved and clipped the artic.

The van driver was shaken up and had an injured wrist. Shouty Husband ended up with cuts and bruises from the shattered windscreen.

The police came and closed the road, and everybody involved ended up being charged with driving without due care and attention.

Shouty Husband's truck was totalled. He got six points on his licence and lost his job, and the bad memories contributed to his depression.

On top of that, he already had three points on his licence for jumping a red traffic light. He decided it was time to come off the road until some of those points were removed – a whole year later.

Give Me All Your Love - Whitesnake

When Jordan started school, Shouty Husband promised him he'd be there on the day he got his exam results because he was so proud.

When the time came, Shouty Husband and I had split up for the umpteenth time – no doubt I'd done something wrong again – but he still intended to be there. He was doing temp work and, when he said he needed the day off, his bosses refused. Shouty Husband told them they could sack him if they wanted to, but he'd promised to be there so he was going – he wouldn't let Jordan down.

It was uncomfortable for me, but Jordan was so happy Shouty Husband was there. It was the icing on the cake for him – he did brilliantly and got As in everything except drama, which was a C.

Silly Games - Janet Kay

My brother-in-law, Bill, had two children from his second marriage.

His eldest son, Ben, got into lots of trouble. He'd been living in a flat with his girlfriend but messed it up, so he moved in with Shouty Husband. However, the girlfriend's family wanted their pound of flesh; Bill couldn't sort it out on his own, so he asked Shouty Husband to go to the flat with him.

Shouty Husband stayed by the door listening in. The family wanted Bill to contribute towards the rent and various other things, but Bill refused. Then they turned to Shouty Husband so he could put his twopence in.

He said Bill would give them £50 – a lot of money then – and that would the end of it. It was two kids playing at house and it hadn't worked out – no big drama, it happened.

Bill was relieved to have it sorted out, but said he'd expected Shouty Husband to threaten them. But Shouty Husband was only using violence as a last resort by now – he'd realised there's usually a way to compromise and, in this family's case, they needed a carrot – money – rather than a big stick.

Milk and Alcohol - Dr Feelgood

Ben's mum didn't want him back home, but he needed work and to get out of his hometown, so he came to live with Shouty Husband. I got on well with him and enjoyed his company, and he also introduced me to the joy of Baileys in coffee.

Mum was asked to deal with the money side of things for him as he was even worse than Shouty Husband. He owed money to his nan and his dad, with no way of paying it back.

Every week I received two envelopes full of cash, one from Shouty Husband and one from Ben, to give to my mum. When Ben moved out nine months later, he was debt free and had a savings account with enough money for a deposit on a flat with some left over.

Ben came back into my life again later. Shouty Husband had fallen out with me so when the doorbell rang one night, I thought it would be him. But no - standing there with a suitcase was Ben.

He asked if he could stay as he had nowhere to go and, never one to kick anyone when they were down, I said yes.

The boys weren't very happy as Ben needed a good wash. I put all his dirty clothes in the washing machine and the boys took him upstairs for a shower.

Afterwards, I made him a bacon sandwich and told him he had to ring his dad. He didn't want to, but he did it. Then he slept on my sofa for a week before his mum let him go back.

I saw him on and off at Paula and Bill's house over the years, and Bill made a point of taking me aside to thank me for looking after him. I didn't have to do anything, as Shouty Husband and I weren't together when Ben rocked up, but he was very happy I'd been the bigger person and taken his son in.

Grantchester Meadows - Pink Floyd

Among my great memories of life with Shouty Husband are our trips up the Long Mynd – part of the Shropshire Hills with amazing views. It was a safe place, somewhere we went when the world got too much.

One warm summer's night Shouty Husband decided we were going out for a ride on Rocky – you remember, the bike with hit-and-miss brakes that handled really badly. So off we went – up the Burway to the top of the Long Mynd on the bike from hell. We made it three miles down the road before Rocky spluttered and died. Shouty Husband told me to hunt for a ring pull on the verge. (Do you remember those days – when drinks cans had ring pulls that came off, rather than staying attached?) Anyway, I was puzzled but did as I was told.

I couldn't tell you what he did, but somehow, he fixed Rocky with a ring pull, and we were on our way again. We spent a great hour on top of the Long Mynd with some really nice dope before we had to come back down the Burway. It's a very steep hill, quite narrow, with a sheer drop of around 200 feet on one side and we were riding along on a dodgy bike while Shouty Husband was off his face.

At the bottom, he told me the urge to drive over the edge to see if we could fly had been really strong, so he decided he needed to straighten up before he tried to ride home.

We stopped at a small village pub. Everyone went silent when we walked in – to be fair, we looked like the kind of scruffy bikers you'd cross the road to avoid. It did feel like everyone was watching us. I ordered two Cokes and two Twix's, and we went to sit in the sunshine in the field at the back of the pub.

After that he was okay, and we got home safely. I still remember that night with great fondness - it was the start of our love affair with the Stretton Hills.

Slow Ride - Foghat

Shouty Husband is a typical Taurus, a real homebody, and he always liked to come home to his own bed.

Whenever I was on holiday, if he wasn't just driving up and down the motorway, he'd take me along with him in his big truck for a day out. If it was long-term agency work, he always asked them if it was okay, but for the odd day here and there he'd just hope we weren't caught. One particular time, he was going to Lancashire. It was the only drop of the day, so we had plenty of time.

When we got to the industrial estate at Pocklington, Shouty Husband gave me some money and dropped me by the food van. I couldn't go in with him while he did the drop as I wasn't supposed to be there, so he told me to get a coffee and wait. My sense of humour has evolved over the years to become a bit strange and dark, so I told the husband-and-wife team who ran the butty van that it was a council initiative – 'Take Your Wife to Work Day', because most women had no idea what their husbands did. (They made an excellent cup of coffee, incidentally.)

Shouty Husband played along with me when he came back, and we had the default truckers' fare of a bacon and egg sandwich before driving home.

Happy days.

London Calling - The Clash

It was rare for Shouty Husband to work overnight, but when he got offered a night run on double time he jumped at the chance. As he was working full time for a company at the time, I was allowed to go with him.

It was a dark and rainy Friday night that started with a delivery of CDs to Stoke. That didn't go so well – the stacker truck driver was on his tea break, so Shouty Husband had to handball the load, which nearly killed him.

Our next stop was at a crisp factory in London, and by now I needed the toilet. I thought I'd be able to go when we arrived, but no – it would have meant me going through the factory so they wouldn't allow it. I had to hang on and hope the next drop was more reasonable.

This was a bonded customs warehouse and by now I was desperate. Shouty husband asked very nicely, and the security guards took pity on me. There was fancy soap, soft towels and even perfume – I'd never been in such posh loos before! Even better, the guards then made me a great cup of coffee in a bone china mug, and I sat in the truck watching the sun come up over the flight path into Heathrow airport. A plane would begin its descent every ten minutes, so low I felt I could just pluck them out of the sky.

I even enjoyed the journey back, when I got to experience the Hanger Lane gyratory – Shouty Husband always complained about it, but at 6.30am it was really quiet.

Get Outta My Dreams, Get into My Car - Billy Ocean

When he wasn't employed by haulage firms, Shouty Husband did agency work. It could be a bit hit and miss, so when he was offered a night's work, he jumped at the chance – after all, he had a mortgage to pay.

We drove twenty miles to pick up the truck and Shouty Husband said the run would be a pain, as it was to a regional distribution centre.

Off we went at 8pm, the truck full of Jersey Royal potatoes, headed for the outskirts of Bristol. We made good time and got there before shift change – no waiting for the new shift to start and get ready for us. Shouty Husband hoped it would be a quick in and out, but once we got to the loading bay and he opened the back, he knew there was a problem.

The potatoes were bagged, but poorly wrapped in cling film and the load had slipped. He tried to put them back so there'd be no problem for the forklift, but then the shift supervisor said they should have been in a refrigerated lorry and rejected the load. Shouty Husband did his best to persuade them to accept it, but to no avail. He decided to wait for the shift change in the hope the new supervisor would be more amenable.

We waited another hour and Shouty Husband tried again, but the load was still refused. So, he rang the boss to explain what had happened and ask what he should do and got an earful for his trouble as though it was all his fault.

Shouty Husband explained he'd done his best for the past two hours, but there was no way that load was being accepted. The boss got very abusive then, so Shouty Husband told him the load was coming back to the yard.

And that's what we did. We drove back to the yard, left the truck there, posted the keys through the office door and went home.

He never got any work from that particular company again, but as he said – if his best wasn't good enough, bugger them!

Every day is a Winding Road - Sheryl Crow

Shouty Husband might not have done holidays, but he did days out and they were always fun.

On one occasion, we went to Chester and found the parking charges were horrendous - £5 just for an hour. Shouty Husband wasn't paying that, so he decided we'd go to the seaside instead, as it was a beautiful day.

We ended up in Rhyl, in Wales, which was one of the nearest resorts to us. We had a walk on the beach, but no paddling as Shouty Husband didn't like the look of the sea foam. Then he decided he fancied fish 'n' chips for lunch.

This was a rarity as too much fat upset his stomach, and he could only tolerate haddock – not cod. So off we went for a wander around the charity shops in town and get some food.

Well, there are more chip shops in Rhyl than you can shake a stick at – but none of them offered the elusive haddock. We finally gave up when the heavens opened – it was time to go home, and we ended up with KFC instead.

For me, the bit of the day was finding a copy of The Small World of Don Camillo for David. He loved the books but finding them was nigh on impossible. But here was one, in paperback for only 50p, and it made him very happy.

Rock 'n' Roll Outlaw - Rose Tattoo

After five years together, Steve and Lottie got married. The wedding was a chance for Shouty Husband to show off in front of a bigger audience.

Lottie was only twenty-one and nervous as hell. As she stood at the front of the register office, slowly shredding her bouquet, Shouty Husband went up to her and, in a very loud whisper, asked whether now the right time for his blow job was.

Lottie went bright red and got very indignant and everybody laughed at his theatrical bow as she went to hit him with her flowers.

Nobody knew he was flying on a combination of ecstasy and dope. Weddings were an opportunity to make mischief, something he loved.

Steve's mum and stepdad had arranged an after-ceremony do at a nearby pub, and I sat in the corner while Shouty Husband kept everyone entertained. The day was all about him, after all — at least that's how he saw it. After a while, the party moved back to Steve's place and, once the parents had left, things really got going. It was the first time Shouty Husband showed the world we were together. He hated having his photo taken, but let Steve take two — I'm cuddling Shouty Husband from behind and he's sticking his tongue out. I framed them both and treasured them for years.

It was a big deal for me, us going so public, and I'd have done anything he asked – in this instance, it was upskirt shots. Lottie and I were the only women at the party so we both got snapped. I was halfway decent as I was wearing tights; Lottie just lapped up the attention Shouty Husband was paying her. Then he decided to spice things up a bit and play his macho games with some of the other men there and, after a while, he upped the ante to 'hot knives'. You might remember he'd got a bad burn on his arm from a workplace accident some time earlier and all the nerve endings were destroyed.

Putting a white-hot knife on his arm caused him no pain but – in his eyes – was a great way of showing how macho he was.

Everybody watched but nobody wanted to play. Job done. Shouty Husband's ego was boosted sky-high – he was the king. I kept out of the way and wondered why he would do something so stupid.

Blaze of Glory - Jon Bon Jovi

Once Shouty Husband discovered the joys of throwaway barbecues, there was no looking back. They meant he could cook outside and be the centre of attention, both of which he loved. Having friends' round for weekend barbecues was the way to go.

We bought a gazebo so Shouty Husband could barbecue in both heat and rain. In the summer he'd go to Bilston market every week to buy meat and salad, and we'd have open house. If there were any leftovers, Lottie would take them home – she could eat for England.

Unfortunately, whenever Shouty Husband decided to up and leave me – which happened fairly frequently – it meant I couldn't visit Steve and Lottie in turn in case he was there. Instead, Lottie would come to see me and fill me in on all Shouty Husband was up to and who he was seeing. During these times he'd spent more time at their house, which meant Lottie could play up to him and enjoy the attention. I think she rather enjoyed hurting me by telling me how nice he was to her.

Driving Home for Christmas - Chris Rea

On Christmas Eve twenty-two years ago, Shouty Husband and I, along with the boys and Lucie, drove all the way to Cambridgeshire in our Mini so his sister Sarah could meet my sons.

If you've ever had a female puppy, you'll know one of the joys is that they wet themselves with excitement. We'd just got back in the car after a loo break when we found Lucie had piddled all over Shouty Husband's seat. Of course, the boys thought this was hilarious.

Anyway, after a two-hour-plus drive on the busy Christmas Eve roads, we arrived and had a lovely two hours at Sarah's. Just as we were leaving, Jordan – who was holding her – dropped Lucie on the floor and yelled, 'Lucie has fleas! '

Sarah had a dog herself, so she wasn't impressed, and we left under a cloud. On Christmas Day, while I drove the boys to their dad's, Shouty Husband put Lucie on a towel in the bath and smothered her in conditioner because she was too young for flea shampoo. We'd only had her for a week, but she was infested – luckily, the conditioner worked and suffocated the fleas.

Build Me Up Buttercup - The Foundations

My favourite car was the white Mini, Tree Bee. We got it when Jordan was thirteen and it was the one, we went visiting in.

Shouty Husband decided it would be a good idea to teach Jordan to drive, because you're never too young to learn.

Every Sunday afternoon, for as long as Jordan wanted to, Shouty husband taught him how to drive around two car parks on an industrial estate. He drove me around to show me how well he was doing, and he could only just see over the steering wheel.

Jordan is a very good driver and that's thanks to Shouty Husband. We'd taken a video of him driving Luke, which I had transferred to DVD. Sadly, when Shouty Husband left he took it with him. I'd love to get a copy, but that'll never happen.

Shoot to Thrill - AC/DC

Lottie's brother, Garry decided to move to Scotland to be with a girl he met. He didn't drive, so asked Shouty Husband if he'd help.

We hired a big van and piled Garry, all his stuff, his budgie and our dog into it, and off we went.

The weather was good, and we made great time up to Grangemouth, where the girlfriend lived. It turned out she lived in a tenement flat up six flights of stairs, so Shouty Husband said he'd stay in the van – he couldn't manage that many steps and we'd be robbed blind if the van was unattended.

So, it was left to me and Garry to lug the bin bags that contained his whole life upstairs. A bunch of local kids watched us intently from the stairs, prompting me to yell on the umpteenth trip, 'Have you never seen mad people on tour before? '

Finally, we left Garry to his new life. (We didn't go in – I didn't even want a glass of water after seeing the state of the kitchen.) Garry had covered the cost of hiring the van and the fuel and gave us some money for a drink – £150 in total, which wasn't bad for a move all the way up to Scotland.

We ended up in Bigga and found a great chippie that had the elusive haddock, so we ate well that evening. Then we found a road that went nowhere beside a wood, so we stayed there for the night.

I walked Lucie while Shouty Husband got drunk and listened to The Hitch Hiker's Guide to the Galaxy on tape. We had a reasonable night's sleep and started for home at 5am. After a bacon butty and coffee from a food van we found, we were raring to go. It had been a fun trip.

When I sent Garry the bill from the hire company, he started arguing about the cost. Shouty Husband told him in no uncertain terms that he'd moved on the cheap and he should be grateful; we did get an apology eventually when he came back to visit.

Benny and the Jets - Elton John

Shouty Husband had a habit of collecting people he thought might be useful and who he could dominate.

Benny – the biker who once thought Shouty Husband and I were women kissing on the street, barely dressed – was one of them. One night when Shouty Husband was drinking the super-strength lager, he told everyone not to try and keep up with him – they'd lose. But nobody gave Benny the memo. We watched Benny drink two cans of the stuff, then he got belligerent and started mouthing off. Shouty Husband was pissed, stoned and not going to stand for someone challenging his masculinity in his own home. He told Benny that if he fancied his chances, they could go outside and sort it out.

Out they went into the garden. Steve pushed the sofa to the wall and told Lottie and I to stand behind it, then he went to the patio door so he could make sure any fight stayed where it was.

Steve gave a running commentary of events, taking the piss out of the two of them. Benny ended up flat on his back in the dog poo patch with Shouty Husband kneeling on his chest. He sobered up pretty quickly when he realised there was nothing he could do, so off he went home – covered in dog muck and with his tail between his legs.

Shouty Husband was pumped. He kept going on about how Benny was a waste of a brain cell, and it took hours for him to come down from the high. For him, the best bit of the whole thing had been dominating another man in front of friends.

The Quiet Room - Alice Cooper

Not only does Shouty Husband sleepwalk, something he's done for years, but he sleep cooks. He's never been tidy, but he did always clean up the kitchen before bed. He also rarely cooked a full meal after work.

So, when he started getting up on a regular basis to find pots and plates and mess lying around, it was a surprise. (It was mostly mash, peas and parsley sauce but sometimes it was pie and mash with gravy. How he never burnt the house down is beyond me.) Shouty Husband sleepwalked when he was stressed and when he was very drunk.

He rarely stayed at mine when the boys were at home, or at any other time in fact; he hated my bed and my bedroom was much smaller than his, and he said he could never fully relax as it didn't feel like home.

But on this occasion, he was there. The boys knew he was staying and, as he loudly fell up the stairs, Luke came out of his room to see if I needed a hand.

Shouty Husband asked Luke what he wanted and he replied to a fiver, so Shouty Husband gave him a tenner and told him to keep the change. Then he managed to get his clothes off and get into bed, and before long he started snoring.

In the wee small hours while I was asleep, he got up to go to the loo. And now he's sleep walking and, of course, as it wasn't his house it was a different layout. Jordan woke up to find a naked Shouty Husband about to pee on him. Shouty Husband stopped and fell on him, so Jordan went into Luke who, in turn, decided to come into bed with me.

A couple of hours later Shouty Husband woke up in a bit of a panic and came back to bed – except it was Luke he ended up hugging.

There we were, at 6.30am, with a cross and naked Shouty Husband shouting, 'What the fuck? ' It was a real French farce, but it still makes me smile. Luke got to keep his tenner – he did offer to give it back – and Shouty Husband never slept at mine again when the boys were there.

Jack-knife Johnny - Alice Cooper

Do you remember the story about Shouty Husband, Charlie and the 'Green Fairy'? Well, here's part two.

I found some absinthe in Tesco for a reasonable price, so I bought it for Shouty Husband's birthday. We just had friends' round, a barbecue, booze and dope; Shouty Husband drank Kestrel Super at the time, so he was flying. And decided the absinthe was a good idea on top of it all.

After he'd hit the stratosphere, I got him into bed. He did his best impression of a starfish across the middle of it and started to snore. He proceeded to fidget, thump and shout, 'Fuck off, I ain't doing that, you can't make me ' over and over, all while he was asleep.

At 2am he shot bolt upright, got out of bed, walked over to the wardrobes, pulled open a drawer, lifted out the jumpers and put them neatly on the floor, and then pissed in the now-empty drawer. He followed that up with a loud fart, gave a satisfied 'Aah ', then shut the drawer and fell over backwards. He didn't try to stop himself and it gave his head a right crack, but he just started snoring again. I checked him over, but he seemed fine, and ten minutes later he crawled back into bed on his hands and knees and carried on snoring. I put a towel in the drawer and spent the rest of the night dozing. He felt rough for the next three days, and the Green Fairy went into retirement – until the next and last time!

'Till I Collapse - Eminem

If you hadn't guessed it yet, Shouty Husband is neither a tolerant nor a patient man. His temper has got him into trouble over the years, but he has only been found guilty of any criminal offence twice; the rest were only driving offences.

One Friday, he was doing agency work and had a drop at a B&Q distribution centre. It was very windy and just starting to rain.

According to Shouty Husband, he was just standing in the entrance to the loading dock trying to sort out his paperwork. Then a young lad started to get into his face about it, because he wasn't supposed to be there.

He did try to explain he was just sheltering from the bad weather while he got himself straight, but in the way that only he could. The lad then poked him in the chest and told him he was the boss here, not Shouty Husband. You can guess how well that went... Shouty Husband got the lad in a head lock over the railings outside the loading dock and told the lad how it was, and the whole thing was captured on CCTV.

He got home and had a beer and a few spliffs to make himself feel better, but he was still in a foul mood when there was a knock at the door. It was a policeman wanting Shouty Husband's version of events, as B&Q wanted to press charges.

Shouty Husband always made a point of knowing his rights according to the letter of the law, so he said that as he was under the influence of alcohol, he couldn't make a statement; he was mentally impaired so anything he said could not be used. He did agree to go to the police station the following day, though. He was subsequently given a police caution.

It was a real debacle but listening to Shouty Husband's voice on tape was fun. He looked horrified and said he didn't sound like that at all in real life, but he did to me.

Fast Car - Tracy Chapman

It's time to introduce you to the last of the cousins, Billy. He was fun and I liked him. Billy loved fast cars and, as he always had money thanks to driving a big lorry all over Europe, he'd lease whichever one he fancied and keep it for a few months. Rinse and repeat.

Whenever Billy had a new car, he would visit and take me out in it. My favourite was the Porsche Boxster, and one time Billy came over I asked if he'd take my dad out in it as it was his birthday, and he'd always wanted to ride in a Porsche.

At this time, I had a Ford Ka called Jinty Bug. It wasn't quick, but I loved it. Shouty Husband took the boys, Luke's best friend Michael, Lucie and me to Wolverhampton and we stopped off to visit Charlie. Billy was there and decided he was coming back to ours as the Porsche needed a good run out.

Billy was fine in a straight line, but he couldn't go round corners at speed to save his life. He left us for dead at first, but when we hit the windy country roads Shouty Husband came into his own.

He was really chuffed to that a small car containing two adults, three teenagers and a dog beat Billy in his Porsche back to our house.

Billy, not happy at all, suggested they go out on their bikes. His was much more powerful than Shouty Husband's – but again, he was great on the straights and useless on the bends. Shouty Husband wiped the floor with Billy again. I did feel sorry for him.

Skinhead Girl - Symarip

A road trip was a joy for Shouty Husband, as long as it was on a motorbike. We had the Honda CX500 when he decided we'd run down to the market in Swindon, then on to the charity shops in Marlborough.

We had a fun day, and then the heavens opened. We were soggy even in our waterproofs. The only place open in Marlborough at 5pm was an Indian restaurant. They were happy for us to eat there, even given the state we were in, so we stripped off our wet gear and sat down.

The food was amazing, and they were very nice people. As we were leaving, the waiter gave me a carnation 'for a beautiful lady'. It made me smile, even though I knew I looked like I had been dragged through a hedge backwards. Shouty Husband left a good tip and then we went back out into the rain for the long ride home.

When a rare Honda Seeley came into the local bike dealership, Shouty Husband had to have it. It was very expensive for an old bike - £2,500 - but it was a rare one.

Of course, old bikes tend to go wrong – and the Seeley did, big time. It was one of a very long line of lemons Shouty Husband spent a fortune on.

He fancied a camping trip on his new toy so off we went to camp for the night at Stonehenge. We actually only looked at it from the road – even twenty years ago, you had to pay silly money to go in.

As a child I'd played there with my brother and touched the stones, something which Shouty Husband envied as it was no longer possible. I had to put my waterproof trousers on when the Seeley started to spray oil all over me, so we headed off to a campsite where we set up the tent and sat in the sunshine with a beer (and a spliff for Shouty Husband). He got in with some Spanish lads who were also toking, and they had a bottle of a very strong liqueur from Venezuela. They were diluting it with plenty of Coke, but Shouty Husband poured a measure and necked it neat.

By 7.30pm he was in the tent snoring like a warthog, and I sat in the late evening sunshine and enjoyed some quiet time.

We went to Bournemouth for a paddle the next morning before riding towards home. We had to stop at a country garage for more oil, and it turned out the owner was a biker; he admired the Seeley, and he and Shouty Husband had a good chat about all things biking.

I loved riding pillion with Shouty Husband, but that time I ached for about a week afterwards – not to mention my waterproofs being covered in oil.

Cool For Cats - Squeeze

Out of all of the bikes Shouty Husband had, I only really felt unsafe on two. The first was Rocky, the one he fixed at the roadside with a ring pull.

The second was the Yamaha RD250 LC. It was a hooligan of a bike, and Shouty Husband loved it – and killed it very quickly. That bike was the biggest money pit in Shouty Husband's bad bike history. It cost a fortune - to buy, to keep on the road, and then some (as you'll see).

I called it the Elsie, and Shouty Husband took me out on it twice before we worked out it wasn't a bike where he wanted me as pillion. I was glad – the bike scared me, and so did the way he rode it. The first trip was to the Stretton Hills, which was fun. Then we went to visit my great aunts, Percy and Barbara. Both in their 90s, both as sharp as tacks. We had tea in bone china cups, with cake and a dash of finesse.

Great Aunt Percy really took to Shouty Husband. He turned on the charm and she played up to him. (As for her name – she was really called Gwendoline, but she used to be a nanny and the children couldn't say that. They called her Percy and it stuck.)

If it hadn't been for her, I wouldn't have been sitting at my dining table on a Friday night writing this. More of her to come.

Night Boat to Cairo - Madness

Shouty husband had no work so fancied a ride out, it was overcast but not too bad an afternoon.

He rode that bike like he stole it with me on the back country lanes until the lug nut that holds the oil in came out.

So, we are at the side of a country road, and I have my fingers stuck in the bike trying to stop us losing all the oil.

It was bloody hot even with gloves on and it was not working. There was a garage a mile away, so Shouty husband decided to free wheel the bike as much as possible and I had to walk.

Then it started to rain, and I am walking down the road in full bike leathers with my helmet getting very wet. Being on the back of the Elsie scared me because it did not scare Shouty husband, and he always told me he was still alive as bikes scared him.

Burning Love - Elvis

Elsie had another problem, aside from spending more time broken than on the road. A design fault meant the fuel pipe ran very close to the spark plugs.

One time, as Shouty Husband was trying to fix her for the umpteenth time, she decided to bite back. The fuel pipe came off as Shouty Husband turned the bike over. There was a spark and then whoosh! The bike went up in flames and so did Shouty Husband!

His hands were on fire, and he was burnt yet again. He called me to say he thought he'd broken his hand, and could I take him to hospital, so I was surprised to arrive at his place and find Elsie a burnt mess. The neighbours had called the fire brigade, so all else was well at least. He had his hands in a bowl of cold water and I got him in the car, driving slowly so not to spill it. We refilled it three times and Shouty Husband's hands were bandaged like a prize fighter wearing boxing gloves.

To take his mind off the pain, we had a laugh thinking up suitable songs for the occasion – all with Shouty Husband's special touch. Like...

(Hunk-a-hunk of) Burning Bike

(Burn baby burn), Elsie Inferno

Wheels on Fire

Putting our own words to songs became one of our 'things' – and I still do it now.

House of Fire - Alice Cooper

Shortly after Shouty Husband's close encounter with Elsie's retaliation, an officious little man from the council knocked on the door.

He got up into Shouty Husband's face, telling him he had to move the heap of blackened metal off the drive.

That didn't go well.

Shouty Husband was still in pain. His prize possession had gone up in smoke and the insurance company was playing silly buggers. It wasn't the time to press his buttons.

Shouty Husband went outside, looked at what was left of Elsie and said he'd clear it away when he was good and ready. He held up his hands and pointed out he couldn't do much with his hands in bandages. He also pointed out that, as the bike was on his own land, if he wanted to leave it there as a modern art sculpture, he would – and there was nothing the man could do about it.

He was being quite loud by now and the neighbours had come out to see what was going on.

The little man backpedalled quickly. He said the council was cleaning up the estate, so they'd remove the bike for him if Shouty Husband wanted them to. Well, that would be handy – so Shouty Husband calmed down and agreed.

Fracas averted. The neighbours went inside and that was that - until the next time, and the time after that.

And So It Went - The Pretty Reckless

The whole time when I was with the Boys' Dad and also with Shouty Husband, I worked. I'm very proud that I've always supported myself.

For a couple of months, I even worked with Shouty Husband, while he was a courier with Securicor Pony Express and I got a temporary job working in the office.

They sent him to Aberdeen regularly, which he loved as it was very lucrative. One job that still makes me smile is when he took a box to Grimsby, and it was transferred to a big boat by a smaller one. The little boat was swamped by high waves and the parcel was ruined – but Shouty Husband still got paid as he'd delivered it and got it signed for.

Another time, he got the chance to go to Aylesbury, cash in hand, and took me. It would be a quick drop and then we could go and look round the charity shops.

Shouty Husband had had his long hair chopped off and shaved down at this time; he looked like a thug and his attitude became more aggressive.

As we were walking, Shouty Husband was approached by someone selling the Socialist Worker. The guy didn't want to take no for an answer and got into Shouty Husband's face; I don't know what was said, but he went a funny shade of white and backed off quickly.

Shouty Husband without hair was even harder work than normal so I was glad when he grew it again.

It was a great few months – we were both happy and I was making good money. But while Shouty Husband was earning a small fortune on paper, by the time he'd paid for the van hire and all the incidentals it only worked out at about £50 a week. He lasted as long as he could, but the mortgage needed paying. My contract ended and Shouty Husband went back to the agency.

Southern Man - Neil Young

When it came to cars, Shouty Husband had a soft spot for Minis. He knew what to look for, what the bad bits might be, and could weld whatever he needed to. He had four Minis while I was with him, though only three of them were driveable.

The first one was Hubert, which lasted three months. After he bought it, I was with him when he decided to go through the car wash. Turns out the door seal on the passenger side leaked, and I got drenched.

Then we got Mother, a Mini Clubman that was great fun. The petrol gauge never worked so filling her up was a bit hit and miss; we used to put a broom stave in the tank and see how wet it got.

One night, we went camping in Wiltshire. We ended up on Hackpin Hill and had to drive down a badly rutted track to a clearing in some woods. When we got up, we found it had rained hard overnight, and the ruts were all full of water. Shouty Husband had to try hard not to get us stuck as we drove back up the track, but the exhaust didn't like being bashed about and fell off while we were in Cirencester.

It was a Sunday, and the only open shop we could find was a bike shop. We bought a jubilee clip to hold the exhaust on for the journey home and it sounded like a bomb going off.

Mother eventually got too bad to fix so off she went to the great scrap yard in the sky.

The Mini that never ran was an old 1960s' model that Shouty Husband bought as a restoration project. It sat on the drive and rotted and, when the neighbours complained, he put a tarp over it. It stayed there for two years before he decided to scrap it – what a waste of £250!

My favourite was Tree-Bee, which was white. This was the car we went to visit Sarah in, and the one in which Jordan learnt to drive. Still, in the end she went the way of all the others and ended up in the scrap yard.

Last One Out Turn Off the Lights - Thunder

The road Shouty Husband was a quiet cul-de-sac. It had just one council house, which was next door to him and lived in by a widower called Len. Everyone knew Len – he'd been there for ever. Len went to the local pub every night, and Shouty Husband was used to hearing him come and go – always at pretty much the same times. Shouty Husband was settled by regular noise, and once he knew Len was home, he could sleep.

One night, I was visiting Shouty Husband – who was in bed with a bad cold and a chest infection – when we heard shouting from Len's place. That wasn't usual – we sometimes heard the television if it was on loudly, but that's all.

Shouty Husband dragged himself out of bed and went round. It turned out his sons had gone round to watch the football with him, and they were celebrating a goal. So Shouty Husband dragged himself back again to resume his 'dying swan' routine.

Len died very quietly one morning, which prompted a worrying time for Shouty Husband – who would move into the council house now? And would he get on with them?

Empty Rooms - Gary Moore

If Shouty Husband just wanted a lump of solid dope he went to the local dealer, Druggie Deedee, rather than his usual supplier over in Wolverhampton. She was a fearsome woman – I'd see her on the school run, and she terrified me.

On one occasion when he went to see her, she offered Shouty Husband crumbs, rather than a lump. He told her where to stick it and went off on one; there was a house full of men who'd have ripped him apart if she'd clicked her fingers, but instead she gave him what he wanted.

As he left, he wedged the lump between the inside of his mouth and his gum. Someone asked him why, and he told them that if the police pulled him as he left, he'd swallow it.

He knew the law – it was illegal to be caught in possession of the dope, but not to be under its influence. The police would have nothing on him – though he would be ill later.

I'll See You in My Dreams - Giant

When the new neighbours moved in Shouty Husband went to say hello – mostly so he could lay down the law on what life would be like next door to him.

They were a lovely family – Kelvin, Beth and their three young children. Kelvin and Shouty Husband hit it off, and Kelvin was sure he recognised him.

Then the penny dropped. Shouty Husband was the 'crumbles' man who'd kicked up a fuss with Deedee. When Shouty Husband checked Kelvin out he found he had a reputation too – there'd be no trouble on the cul-de-sac with him there. That was proved when Kelvin got burgled, and twenty-four hours later his stuff was returned!

He liked Beth too, and they used to chat over the garden fence. All in all, he was happy with his new neighbours.

Down Down - Status Quo

You know by now that Shouty Husband loved his music. His Tannoy Legacy Eaton speakers certainly kicked out the bass, but he didn't crank them up too often – he was aware of the kids' bedtime next door. One evening at 6pm though he did turn up the volume – and the sound vibrated through the walls, causing Beth's ornaments to bounce around on their shelves and pictures to rock on the walls.

She shouted over the fence, called Shouty Husband's landline, even banged on the kitchen window. He was oblivious. Eventually she called me, and I went round and let myself in.

I explained what had happened and he went round to Kelvin and Beth's to apologise. They were fine with it – they loved his taste in music, just not at that level.

Good neighbours are worth their weight in gold, and they were brilliant. You'll see why later.

This Ole House - Shakin' Stevens

The first silly thing I did, according to Shouty Husband (though his words were stronger) was to get his gas boiler condemned.

I went to pick up Lucie, as I was looking after her while Shouty Husband was out on deliveries, and when I walked into his house I could smell gas. Being sensible, I rang the gas company who said the boiler was dangerous.

The house needed a lot of work doing, from roof to floor, and a lot of money spending on it. It was so cold you needed to wear a coat to use the downstairs toilet in winter. The bathroom tiles were tatty and orange, the bath was old and had dodgy taps. There was far too much wrong with it for me to go into here.

But it wasn't a council house, so Shouty Husband got away with spending as little on it as possible – a bit of cheap paint and carpet from time to time, and job done.

The front porch was rotten, but he didn't want to spend the mortgage money on getting that repaired. Then one day, the council came to fix next door's porch. The workmen made a mess and when Shouty Husband came home to find his side trashed, he went ballistic.

The workmen ended up calling their boss, and two senior council officials came to see what the problem was. Shouty Husband's bit of the porch needed all the wood and felt replacing, and the workmen had just tried to patch the two sides together.

Shouty Husband said he wanted the council to fix his side properly, even though it wasn't theirs. The boss tried to argue, but Shouty Husband was getting louder. All the neighbours had come to watch, and he wasn't backing down.

The council guy gave in and told the workmen to get on with it in the end. Shouty Husband won – his porch was watertight, repaired and looked better than it had in ages.

Eagle - Abba

On the day Shouty Husband decided to stop drinking, we were invited to a party.

He never went these things early doors, so on the same day he decided the dining room carpet needed tacking down. It was sticking up and looked a mess.

We didn't know that the council built the house they'd put the water pipes just under a skim of concrete on the floor. So, when Shouty Husband hit a nail, a thin but highly pressurised stream of water shot up and out. There was no way he was going to rip up the concrete floor to replace the pipe, so he bodged it in true Shouty Husband style. He dug up enough of the floor to get to the pipe and wrapped it in white plumber's tape with a jubilee clip to hold it in place. Job done. (It held for the rest of the time we were in the house, though the new owners weren't so lucky.)

Later on, we went to the party, but Shouty Husband was in a foul mood. When he saw the friend's dogs pinch food off the table, he walked out and left me behind. I stayed an hour to be polite and went home to find him drinking beer with music blaring out. So much for abstinence – he'd lasted nine hours!

Werewolves of London - Warren Zevon

The rubble pile at the bottom of Shouty Husband's Garden had been there for years. Bees nested in it every summer and he also used it as a compost heap.

Then I got a job at a recycling centre, where one of the perks was free access to a builder's skip that held ten tonnes. Shouty Husband told the boys he'd give them £20 each if they'd transport the rubble pile from his garden to the skip. They were aged sixteen and fourteen at the time, so that was decent spending money.

We went out for the morning and left them to it. Later, one of the neighbours told us Luke had done all the hard work while Jordan supervised.

The skip was full, the rubble pile was gone, and Shouty Husband gave the boys £20 each as he'd promised – then he gave Luke another £20 for his extra effort.

Southern Cross - Crosby, Stills, Nash & Young

Here's a good memory about Luke, Jordan and Shouty Husband. Luke went to college to do a course in engineering and functional skills; at that time, the local school wasn't the right place for him with his autism.

Twice a year, I went to his parents' evening but on one occasion I had a heavy cold and really couldn't do it. I'd been to work even though I'd felt rough, and now had no energy left.

So Shouty Husband and Jordan went instead. They saw three tutors who said that, overall, they were pleased with Luke's progress. However, one said Luke would never make it as an engineer as he wasn't the sharpest tool in the box – and this was in front of Luke. Before Shouty Husband could react, Jordan got there first and ripped into the guy, with Shouty Husband giving a death glare behind him.

We all knew Luke wasn't cut out for engineering, but he needed to get his maths and English qualifications and he wanted to try it. College was good for him, and so was seeing Jordan and Shouty Husband fight his corner.

The whole thing brought him closer to the boys. He'd tell everyone how proud he was of them both. He never wanted children of his own, but he loved my two and they're where they are today because he was there for them, supported their dreams and, yes, kicked them up the bum when they needed it.

For all the things that were – and are – wrong with Shouty Husband, for all the bad things in our relationship, I can say hand on heart that he's a big part of why Jordan and Luke have done so well, and for that I will be forever grateful.

Landslide — Fleetwood Mac

When he was sixteen, Jordan got a girlfriend. She was called Poppy and she stayed over a lot, so I got to know her well.

When Jordan was seventeen, the two of them decided to go on holiday to Cornwall. He booked a flat over the internet, but Shouty Husband insisted on making sure it was up to scratch. So, we ended up driving them the seven hours to Cornwall, and the flat was wonderful.

We took the tent and stayed overnight in Indian Queens — just us and a solitary caravan in a huge field. I ended up locking my car, putting the keys in my handbag and then, because I was paranoid someone would come and steal it, I put my handbag in the boot. And shut it. With my car keys inside...

Shouty Husband pointed this out to me in between fits of laughter and told me I needed to sort it out. I honestly thought he'd find a way, or would at least help — but no.

Luckily, I had breakdown cover. Off I went to find a phone and a short time later a man from Green Flag rocked up and broke into the car to retrieve my bag. Shouty Husband laughed at nearly the whole time and dined out on that story for years.

Luke's college tutors really encouraged him, and when he was offered a job working away from home at a residential outward-bound centre, we thought it was a great idea.

It was only half an hour away and we would go and bring him home for lunch when he had a Sunday off.

Then, with fewer than 24 hours' notice, he learned he was being moved to Norfolk.

It threw him completely, but Shouty Husband told him if he hated it, he'd drive down and bring him home with no questions asked. Luke went, Luke loved it, Luke stayed, and his confidence went through the roof.

Durham Town - Roger Whittaker

I'd always wanted to see Hadrian's Wall and Durham Cathedral, so when Shouty Husband agreed to pack up the tent and go away for a couple of nights, that's where I suggested.

We drove for the best part of eight hours to Northumberland, where we found a campsite and Shouty Husband got cooking on the throwaway barbecue. He loves cooking in the great outdoors and our set-up was quite civilised – we had a table and folding chairs!

The next day we went off to find Hadrian's Wall but decided not to pay the ridiculous amount of money required for parking. Instead, we parked in front of a farm gate, and I went to stand on the wall. It was well worth it.

Then we headed into Durham, where Shouty Husband said in the sun while I looked round as he doesn't do churches. It meant I didn't stay as long as I'd have liked, as I felt I had to get back to him. He fancied the seaside next, so off we went to Scarborough.

The sea mist had rolled in by the time we got there, so we found another campsite and had another barbecue.

The site was nice enough, but it had a clubhouse. The guy opposite, who was there with his two daughters, spent the evening in the bar and then proceeded to snore like a water buffalo all night. I generally sleep through most things, but it even kept me awake. As for Shouty Husband, who sleeps badly at the best of times, he was in a foul mood by the time morning came.

I had a very grumpy chauffeur on the drive home!

All the Young Dudes - Mott the Hoople

Mick is a huge fan of the rock band Mott the Hoople and its lead singer, Ian Hunter. While I lived with him, I heard it all, so I love the music too.

Mick promised that if Ian Hunter toured locally, he'd take me to the concert. I didn't realise it would be 18 years before he made good on his promise.

Shouty Husband didn't fancy it, so Mick and I went together. We had a great time, and Mick said he'd get Shouty Husband to come next time. As luck would have it, Ian Hunter announced a date in Shrewsbury, which was just up the road. Shouty Husband agreed to come with me and Mick, so we piled into the car and off we went to the gig.

Mick was already pissed when we picked him up, and then Shouty Husband gave him some dope to eat. (He doesn't smoke it.)

We managed to get a table and I was sent to get a round in. Two pints, a Red Bull and a Coke came to £10, and I only had £20 on me. No fun at the merchandise stalls for me, then.

Mick lasted till halfway through the support act then put his head on the table and tripped out.

Shouty Husband spent the whole night watching Mick and keeping the bouncers away.

But me, I had a great time, singing along to all the songs –
even if I ended up spending my last tenner on Shouty
Husband's drinks and had to make do with the one Coke
all night

Even though Max, Sharon and the kids moved around a lot over the years, Shouty Husband always kept in touch with them.

I really thought Max and I were friends. I knew most of Shouty Husband's friends liked to mess with people's heads for fun, but I never thought anyone would try it with me. But Max decided it would be fun and decided to do so for no reason other than he could.

Max didn't believe in monogamy. He'd slept with Karen (something I was unaware of at that time), even though she and Sharon were best friends. And how his sights were set on me.

Friday nights were the nights I could drink, so when Max rang to say Sharon was having an Ann Summers lingerie party, I wasn't capable of driving. No problem – Max said he'd come and pick me up and take me home again afterwards. So I went and, although I didn't know anybody else there, I sat quietly in a corner and enjoyed the evening.

When Max took me home later, he told me about Karen. He then said he'd always fancied me and asked I wanted to sleep with him. I assumed he was kidding and laughed it off.

I told Shouty Husband, who said Max was just playing games and he'd sort it out. Not with violence – he didn't always go that route. He was also very good at finding people's weak spots and exploiting them.

Max might play around like he was cock of the walk, but the truth was adored Sharon and would never leave her.

However, she, like most women, found Shouty Husband fascinating. She'd not had much life experience and a compliment from him would brighten her day. Shouty Husband always reckoned he could take her away from Max if he wanted to. And that's what he told him – if Max didn't back off and accept I was off limits, Shouty Huband would go after Sharon.

Max knew he meant it, and that he'd more than likely succeed. We didn't see much of Max and Sharon after that.

Bad Medicine - Bon Jovi

'No one is more arrogant toward women, more aggressive or scornful, than the man who is anxious about his virility.' The Second Sex, Simone de Beauvoir

Gender fluidity might be accepted now, but it wasn't a 'thing' in the world when Shouty Husband was growing up. He'd explored pretty much all that interested him sexually, but the one thing that stayed on his mind was sleeping with a man.

As we'd say today, he was bi-curious. He'd never do anything about it, though – or, if he did, he always said he'd 'be the postman, never the post box '.

Nigel, who you may remember was an expert on all things pharmaceutical, was bisexual. He was a true hedonist, with neither conscience nor soul. He came to stay, bringing with him some Brazilian hallucinogenic mushrooms. Shouty Husband was up for anything that would be a new trip, but Charlie didn't mention he'd starved the mushrooms to make them more potent.

We tried them on a Saturday afternoon. I was having a fun trip until I looked over at Nigel, sitting on the floor with the sun behind him. He was all lit up and looked like he was on fire, and, in that drug-induced moment, I saw his true character. It felt like I was in the presence of the devil; I went cold all over and wanted to run and hide.

I felt better after going to bed for a couple of hours, but I was still very wary of Nigel. I went home in the morning, but he stayed on, as Shouty Husband didn't have work to go to.

After a heady mix of dope, beer and toxic mushrooms, Shouty Husband was high for three days and decided it was time to explore his sexuality. It would be ok with Nigel – he was an old friend, and it would be fun in the haze of a bad mushroom trip.

If he'd stuck to his normal chemical romance, it would never have happened. But it did, and it had a huge effect on the way he viewed the world and my place in it.

Sebastian - Steve Harley & Cockney Rebel

It's funny how life can change so completely sometimes without you even realising it at the time. We'd enjoyed a barbecue one Friday night – a regular thing. Friends round, we always ate well.

I'd no need to think this one was any different. But then Shouty Husband proceeded to ignore me all weekend, even when we went to his sisters for Sunday lunch.

Afterwards I went home as normal – and that was the last I saw of Shouty Husband for six months. He just cut me out of his life completely – I guess today it would be described as 'ghosting'. He did keep in touch with the boys, though, and as he was good for them, I wanted him to stay in their lives. But I was a wreck. I didn't eat. I couldn't sleep. I was going through all the stages of grief.

Then I lost my job at the waste station. The company got fined for dumping waste and made redundancies as a result – and I was last in, so first out.

To make ends meet I got a job though an agency, packing brackets for TVs, but it was terrible, and I hated it. Lottie worked there too, so I'd give her a lift to work and back each day and she'd keep me updated on Shouty Husband.

Then my mother-in-law died, and I had to deal with the fallout. I got into an argument with my line manager when

I asked for some time off, so I knew my days were numbered.

It was a month before the shit hit the fan, though – the agency rang to tell me the firm didn't want me back on the day of my mother-in-law's funeral!

I didn't care, it was nearly Christmas. I signed on for the dole and determined to enjoy it.

River of Pain - Thunder

Then, one day, I woke up and my first thoughts were not of Shouty Husband. I was finally free of him - or so I thought.

I got a fill-in job as a cleaner and I met a new man, Martin. Life was normal and I was happy.

It was January and I was doing my usual Sunday morning thing, ironing, and singing along (badly) to the radio.

Then the phone rang – and it was a call that caused my world to spin on its axis once again.

Family Affair – Sly & the Family Stone

Shouty Husband would take me to visit Bill and Paula on a regular basis, and sometimes we'd stay for Sunday lunch.

When Paula was coming up to forty, she decided to have a bit of a do. Sarah and Ed were coming up, so it would be a family affair. This was a huge deal! Shouty Husband going to take me to a family party where I'd be introduced as his other half, his girlfriend, partner, missus, whatever. I'd be acknowledged as an important part of his life. I was so happy!

I've never been a party person and I'm certainly not a social animal, so even then my selection of party clothes was pretty much non-existent. I couldn't afford a new dress, so I went through my wardrobe and found a long skirt and a blouse. They made me look like a secretary rather than a party goer, but it was the best I could do.

Shouty Husband hated my outfit and made me swap the skirt for jeans. All the other ladies were in their best party dresses, so I stuck out like a sore thumb.

I didn't know many people, so I did my usual trick of hiding in the corner and pretending to be wallpaper. It meant I got to see everyone interacting and it was fun watching Shouty Husband and Sarah snipe at each other.

Shouty Husband was on good form, the life and soul of the party. I was driving, so not drinking, and I was sitting quietly on the stairs when Little Ed, Sarah's eldest son, came to talk to me. He wanted to pick my brains about his memories of his nan.

I knew something of the relationship between Sarah and her mother at that time, but it was more than my life was worth to repeat anything Shouty Husband had told me, so I suggested Little Ed go and talk to him instead. He was in a good mood – maybe he'd open up. Well, when Sarah heard Shouty Husband talking to her son about their mother and the relationship between them, she went bat-shit crazy. In a subdued way, though – after all, it wouldn't do to make a scene in somebody else's home.

Big Ed disagreed with her. He said Little Ed needed to know and Shouty Husband was on Sarah's side. Shouty Husband told his nephew it was all down to his nan that the family didn't see her.

The party carried on, but there was an issue between Shouty Husband and Patrick, one of Bill's friends. Two alphas in the same room never works out well. Patrick's wife got on well with Shouty Husband and decided to flirt with him to wind up her husband. He played along, of course, and Patrick seethed quietly.

By 11pm the party was beginning to break up. Shouty Husband was happy drunk and stoned, and Patrick was spoiling for an argument. So he told Shouty Husband he wasn't a very good motorcyclist to try and put him in his place.

The whole room went quiet, waiting for Shouty Husband to go bang. Which he did, but not in the way Patrick expected.

Instead of exploding, he laughed and said loudly that when Patrick had covered as many miles and ridden through as many winters as he had, then he'd have the right to comment.

He also pointed out how much Patrick's wife liked a real biker, so he might want to be careful he didn't lose her. The party ended abruptly after that, and Shouty Husband had to apologise for ruining Paula's party. To be honest, Bill was more annoyed than Paula was – she thought it was great as she didn't like Patrick much.

It wasn't my fight and I wasn't involved, but it was fun to watch.

Ashes to Ashes - David Bowie

A couple of years after the mind game incident, Shouty Husband bumped into Max again. He'd missed him, so he decided we'd visit one Friday night.

By the time we got there, Shouty Husband was well on the way to being fall-over full - very pissed and stoned.

Max had moved into a three-storey house with an odd layout. The kitchen was on the ground floor and the hall was only just big enough to stand in – if you stretched out your arms, you could touch the walls. Three steps led up into the living room, with a full flights of stairs going up to the bedrooms.

Shouty Husband and Max were in the kitchen talking and I was shunted into the living room with a friend of Sharon's, Monica, and her son. He was still a baby really – about twelve months old. I tried to make conversation, but she ignored me and walked out, leaving him with me.

Sharon appeared soon after. I told her Monica had walked away and left the baby. Sharon admitted she was scared of Monica and didn't really want her there as she was hard work, but she was afraid to say no to her. Now, Sharon's family was a bunch of tough nuts who could soon have turned Monica into a stain on the pavement. Whatever this woman had over Sharon must have been huge, but I never found out what it was.

Monica came back soon after, so I escaped to the kitchen, when Shouty Husband decided he needed the toilet. Monica happened to be coming down the stairs towards the hall at the time and he, drunk and high as he was, decided to block her way. Monica looked at him, narrowed her eyes and said, 'Move. ' The rest of us held our breath waiting for his reaction. Shouty Husband smiled at her and said, 'Please. 'She glared at him and repeated herself. 'Move. 'Instead, he stretched out an arm and leaned on the wall. He wasn't going anywhere.

Then Monica took us all by surprise – she sank her teeth into Shouty Husband's arm and raked her nails across his face!

He yelped in pain and, in retaliation, put two fingers around her throat and lifted her off her feet. It was very rare for him to use force against a woman, and even though she was sturdily built it was as though she was light as a feather.

Monica stopped biting, but by now she was going red in the face and struggling to breathe. Max was hitting Shouty Husband on the back, trying to get him to let go, and I was blocking the way into the kitchen as the baby was there in his buggy.

Shouty Husband was in a world of his own until Sharon did the 'mum' voice and told him to let go of Monica in no uncertain terms. He did, and Monica fell to the ground, clutching her throat as she tried to breathe.

 Sharon told Shouty Husband he was no longer welcome in her house, so we left, him livid and me trying to keep up and wondering what he'd do next. It turned out to be a trip to the local shop for more beer, then on to Steve and Lottie's.

He ranted on about how Max and Monica were in for a world of pain and how dare Max disrespect him by jumping on his back. I daren't point out Max was just trying to stop him suffocating Monica.

Shouty Husband knew he needed to come down from the high of his anger, so he asked Steve to slap him. There was a loud crack and his head whipped round – he had the handprint across his face for days afterwards.

It sort of worked, as he did calm down, but the anger resurfaced after some more beer and dope. Shouty Husband challenged Steve to see if his punch was as good as his slap and told him to give him a dig in the ribs. Before he had time to blink or tense up, Steve punched him hard. Lottie and I had stayed in the living room and winced as we heard the crack. A few days later, Shouty Husband went to hospital where X-rays confirmed he had a broken rib. He ended up being unable to work for six weeks.

And all for some macho bullshit!

My hair may have been boring brown in those days, but the purple-haired warrior with knobs came out sometimes – especially if anyone fucked with my family.

When the estate where Shouty Husband lived was built, loads of trees were planted as part of the development. It was sited over an underground spring, so the water table was in heavy clay; doing anything that would upset it was a bad idea.

However, when Kelvin decided he needed the garden for the children to play in, he cut down five mature trees and even ripped out the stumps, even though Shouty Husband had warned him this would cause massive problems.

And, in time, he was proved right. First, Kelvin and Beth couldn't close their back door or the upstairs bedroom window. Cracks big enough to put your finger in then appeared all down the side of the house.

The council was called in and a video made that showed the whole corner of the property was slipping. It would need underpinning to make it safe.

The council decided it wasn't worth fixing, so they moved Kelvin and Beth to another house. That wasn't the end of it, though.

Big cracks appeared over the living room lintel in Shouty Husband's house and spread all over the back of the house. The last house on the row, attached to Kelvin and Beth's on the other side, had a similar problem with his damp course.

It was time for us – well, me – to go to war.

War - Edwin Starr

Shouty Husband was annoyed with the problems next door, but he viewed it as cheap rent. He'd worked out that the doors wouldn't shut properly and the house was on the move six months after he'd moved in. It would sort itself out, even if the house fell down around his ears.

First, I contacted his house insurance company, as they should help. After all, he paid enough for the policy. No joy there, though. So next I went to the council, but they gave me the run-around.

So, then I started a campaign. Next door was likely to fall down and take our house and the house on the other side with it, so the council should do something.

I kept copious notes of every conversation I had about it and we even had a survey done to prove the council was liable for the damage.

Next door stood empty for six months and the local kids got in, so I got the council to board up the doors and windows. Then the kids kicked down the fence between the houses, and Shouty Husband put up a tarp.

One night the noise drove him past the point of no return, and he lost it big time. He went out, ripped the tarp down and got mad. When one gobby girl got in his face and asked him what he was going to do about it, he turned the hose pipe on the whole bunch of them full blast.

Then he called the police, so the council had to do something. They replaced the fence – only with something cheap and cheerful, but at least it was secure. Word got around and the youths stayed away.

The council was never going to play ball – even our MP couldn't help – and the house was sold at auction.

The new owner was a doctor who got a builder in to repair the damage. We found out what was happening when the builder came to say hello and told us about the new owner's plans to fix up the house.

Luke was on summer holidays at the time, so he was offered some labouring work. He ended up building a small wall between next door and the end house; he'd never done anything like it before, but that wall is still there.

The builder and his labourers dug a six-foot trench around the back of next door and the corner that had slipped. Luke told us they'd dug up the dining room and living room floors inside, right down to the foundations. The ceilings and the corner were held up by six acrows, big metal poles.

Shouty Husband was very concerned about what was happening, so he asked his friend Normal to take a look. (He'll pop up again later, he was my neighbour for twenty years and knew Shouty Husband for over thirty.)

Norman knew something about building work after his house burnt down one Christmas Eve while he was at work, and it took him two years to rebuild it.

The builder had left the kitchen window open so Norman, who was skinny, let himself in and took some photos. I took the film to Boots to get them printed as big as I could – no digital cameras then. Shouty Husband told me I was wasting my time – neither the insurance company nor the new owner wanted to help us.

I was determined though and went to the council offices to see the building inspector. We knew the builder had broken the foundations in the living room and, as the ground was heavy clay, any rain would fill the trench and the water would ingress under the foundations – which were also Shouty Husband's foundations, as they were built on one platform.

The council made me stay in reception and wasn't inclined to be helpful, so I made a scene. Everybody could hear as I slapped down the photos showing dangerous building work and a severe breach of health and safety rules. Then I threatened to go to the local paper.

By 2pm, the building inspector had been out to look round and condemned the work as dangerous. The trenches were filled in and so were the living room and dining room floors, but they weren't tamped down which meant everything was still on the move.

I'd won, kind of, but we still had a house that could fall down and there was nothing I could do about it.

Shouty Husband did say he was proud of me, though. He didn't think I'd achieve anything, but I did. His praise made all the hassle worthwhile. That was the beginning of the end for all the houses in the row, and it also made Shouty

Husband realise I'm unstoppable once I get the bit between my teeth.

Afro Celt Sound System

Norman had been around Shouty Husband for ever, right back to the Jinx days, but he only played a small part in our joint history. He lived at the back of me, and I knew him to say hi to.

Time to put some flesh on the bones. Norman was only 5ft 7ins tall, but always seemed taller as he walked perpendicular to the ground. He was rake thin and had long, white hair. He was the eternal hippie; life was about having fun.

Norman was a committed veggie. He liked his uppers and heroin was his thing, but he had been clean for years. So now, speed was his poison, with dope to smooth out the edges.

He was our go-to for dope when we were between regular dealers.

I first heard about him when I got home from work one Christmas Eve and saw his house having a quiet smoke by itself. Mum and Dad were babysitting for me; I ran in and told them what I'd seen, and they called the fire brigade.

The inside of the house was destroyed, but luckily it was fine structurally, so it could be restored.

When I told Shouty Husband, he said he knew Norman and it was possible he'd caused the fire himself. But Norman always denied it, and it was never proved .Anyway, it meant the two of them reconnected – and Norman became a key part of the saga that is Shouty Husband and me.

I'm a Man - Chicago Transit Authority

The porch door at Shouty Husbands was stiff, hard to open and close, and I hated it. Then one day, it came off the hinges and hung there limply. It certainly wasn't secure.

I got a real telling off from Shouty Husband for that one, even though it wasn't my fault. I'm surprised that door lasted as long as it did!

Norman was very handy, so Shouty Husband got him to replace the frame and fit a new door. I made the mistake of paying Norman up front so he vanished for a few days, and I got shouted at for that as well.

Still, finally the house was secure again. One less thing to worry about - or so I thought.

Smoke on the Water - Deep Purple

Shouty Husband always wanted to play a musical instrument. He bought a penny whistle from a car boot sale – well, he is Irish. I learned the recorder in junior school and can still play Three Blind Mice, which both impressed him and pissed him off.

Norman offered to teach Shouty Husband to play guitar, but he didn't want to learn chords – that was boring. What he really wanted was to learn how to play Smoke on the Water by Deep Purple, but that wasn't going to happen.

Then Norman got out his bodhrán, which is a hand-held Irish drum you play with a beater. Norman was very good at it, which displeased Shouty Husband.

I bought him a cheap bodhrán and a beater and Shouty Husband bashed it to his heart's content, but he could never get it to make the same kinds of sounds Norman's did. Norman wound Shouty Husband up and we ended up going to the Custard Factory in Birmingham so he could buy a tuneable bodhrán.

It cost £200, including the fancy beater, but Shouty Husband still couldn't get the hang of it.

Then Luke had a go and was amazing. When Shouty Husband asked how he did it, he was told, 'You just need a limp wrist and a spazzy hand. '

Luke showed him and that was it; Shouty Husband practised like it was going out of style.

He had a favourite band to play along to, so now Rodrigo and Gabriela got played to death and it drove me mad. The constant bashing sent me to hell and back, but Shouty husband loved that bodhrán.

It ended up living on the wall of his chill room and I don't think he's touched it for years. But by the end he was better than Norman, so he'd won – and that was all that mattered.

 The last instrument Shouty Husband decided to try – again, Norman had one - was an African drum. We found one at yet another car boot sale for a tenner, and it was a five-minute wonder.

Ring of Fire - Johnny Cash

For Christmas 2005, Shouty Husband decided he'd do a family Christmas. No tree, but a full lunch.

My favourite friend, David, was braving the train to come visit, so it was going to be fun!

Two weeks before Christmas, Shouty Husband went into hospital for day surgery to sort his piles out. (He'd been suffering for years; the joys of riding a motorbike!)

He was in agony afterwards, and I have no idea if it was normal or not. Usually he's got a high pain tolerance, but this really knocked him off his feet. He took massive amounts of pain killers, booze and dope but they didn't touch the sides. The only relief he got was sitting in the bath in four inches of boiling hot water.

Everybody offered to cancel Christmas lunch, but he insisted on carrying on. He was determined to cook a roast beef dinner with all the trimmings. Not turkey – he didn't eat it the rest of the year, so why at Christmas?

We'd bought a camcorder so we could video my dad, something to watch when he'd gone. (Ironic that he's still here but Uncle David, who only had a minor role, isn't.)

So Jordan played Spielberg and recorded Christmas Day. My boys look so young! There are cameos by Lucie and our cat, Teeny Puss, who are no longer with us.

I got the tape transferred onto DVD. I watch it when I miss Uncle David, and I watch it when I miss Shouty Husband. Ten minutes in, he shouts at me to hurry up with the presents as dinner will be ruined. He even had to control Christmas – and at that point, I don't miss him anymore.

He was in pain from the piles until March, and then he went back to work.

Upside Down - Diana Ross

On the same day we were going to see the registrar, Shouty Husband signed up for an agency. He'd been getting no work and they were advertising for drivers. However, it turned out to be a complete waste of time – he was in a lousy mood on the way back so I really through he wouldn't want to organise the wedding.

The people at the registrar's office were brilliant, and they could marry us at noon on my fortieth birthday. That seemed like a good omen to me.

Next stop was my parents' place so he could ask my dad's permission. Dad was doing a jigsaw and asked Shouty Husband if he was sure, as I could be a bit of a handful. He wasn't worried about me, but he was concerned about my boys.

So, I had a month to plan a wedding on the tightest budget possible. I got the flowers ordered and the invites were freebies taken off the internet. Since it was going to be a small affair, Shouty Husband said he'd do the catering and the reception could be at his house.

I roped in Sue and my mum to help me hunt down a dress. There were some beautiful long ones in Debenhams that would do; in fact, it took me longer to pay than it did to pick one, try it on and love it.

It was strapless, a beautiful ivory colour, and it looked fantastic on me. I don't wear heels and struggle to walk in them, but as the dress was slightly too long, I needed a lift. I added the lowest heels possible, got some good, pull-me-in undergarments, and I was done.

Sue organised my hen do - an Anne Summers party – and Shouty Husband's aunt made the cake with handmade icing flowers on it. My ex-father-in-law offered to do the photos as he was a bit of a whizz with a camera.

Shouty Husband didn't go cheap for my wedding ring; I had an 18-carat white and rose gold ring, which is still kept safe in my china cabinet.

David was coming up from Hampshire to see me get married and Shouty Husband lined up his friend Trev as best man. My Auntie Jean gave us a wedding present of £150 which paid for the reception, and everybody said they'd bring something for the buffet.

The stress was unbelievable, but I did it – I arranged the whole wedding in a month.

I Do, I Do, I Do, I Do, I Do - Abba

And so, to the big event on a rainy day in March. Shouty Husband was going to the register office with the boys, and I'd go with Sue and her husband, Col.

When we got to the register office, in time to do the official bits before the actual ceremony, there was no sign of Shouty Husband. Sue was panicking in case he'd jilted me at the altar, but I knew he'd come; he'd never have been that cruel.

It turned out he'd left in plenty of time but realised halfway there he'd left the ring at home. Jordan was still a new driver, so he was sticking to all the speed limits, though he had a narrow miss at one junction when he pulled out in front of another car.

When they arrived, there was a huge cheer. Shouty Husband threw the ring box to Trev amid whoops and shouts from our guests and then he came into the office and saw me. Everyone said I looked beautiful, but he just looked me up and down, made me twirl, and then told me I'd 'pass'.

Pass! I looked and felt incredible, but he always was one to build you up and put you down at the same time.

At noon, with my hand on my heart, I married Shouty Husband. I didn't get to walk down the aisle, there was no music, but I finally got what I wanted.

What is it they say? Be careful what you wish for...

Twilight Zone - Golden Earring

We'd just got married so we had to have photos - Shouty Husband couldn't get away from that one. We took lots.

Then we went home in separate cars so he could put the finishing touches to the buffet. I was just married but on my own – as usual!

The reception was brilliant and by 5pm everybody had gone, so it was just us. My birthday had been forgotten about, but I didn't care. I was Mrs Shouty Husband at last, I'd got him to do the one thing people said he never would. He loved me, trusted me enough to marry me, and I was head over heels in love and feeling powerful.

I look back on that day now and remember it so well, and all the hopes and dreams I had. Most of them have come true – except for the one about living happily ever after with Shouty Husband.

Still, it's not so bad. I like being the purple-haired warrior with knobs on much more.

Suicide Blonde – INXS

As we'd got married on my fortieth, my birthday party was the day after. We had a few friends over to celebrate and Lottie was among those who turned up.

She'd started visiting Shouty Husband's house on her own once she knew we were getting married, and he'd stopped answering the door.

I let her in, showed her the wedding cards and explained that Shouty Husband and I had done the deed. She didn't take it well and began to play up to him, really throwing herself at him so everyone noticed.

He played along until she was lying on the dining room table pulling her skirt up, offering him sex there and then in front of everybody. I finally told her enough was enough – he was my husband, and she was behaving like a tart.

She took umbrage at this and decided to leave, but not before she'd filled two carrier bags with leftovers, we'd said she could have.

Off she flounced, weighed down with food, and that was the last time I ever saw her. She'd crossed a line, so Shouty Husband cut Steve out of our lives, too.

I never saw Lottie again.

Honeymoon – Johnny Stimson

Are you sitting comfortably? This is something that changed Shouty Husband's life, and not for the better. There's a story within a story first, though.

You might remember Sarah, Shouty Husband's sister. Well, she decided it was time to find their dad, the man who hadn't seen his kids for forty-eight years.

The last time Shouty Husband saw this man was when he was turning five. His dad turned up and promised him a bike for his birthday, and then got a bit too close to his mum and raised his hand. Shouty Husband kicked him hard in the shin and that was that – he never got his bike and never saw his dad again, either.

A couple of weeks before our wedding, Sarah dropped the bombshell that she'd found their dad who was now back in Ireland and retired. He wanted to get to know his children and be part of their lives, she said.

Sarah had been talking to him for a couple of months already and passed on our phone number. Shouty Husband was prepared to give him a chance - he wanted to fit the pieces of his childhood jigsaw together – so when his dad rang, he invited him to the wedding. However, his dad didn't think that was the best way to appear in his children's and grandchildren's lives, so instead he offered us a honeymoon in Ireland to meet the extended family and sent us £50 as a wedding present.

Forever Young - Joan Baez

Shouty Husband was curious about Ireland and wanted to fill in the gaps in his memories of life there, so off to Ireland we went.

As a gesture of goodwill, we had a beautiful album made of our wedding pictures so his dad could see us all, the family.

Flying would be easier than taking the car, and Finbarr, Shouty husband's dad, said he'd be our chauffer for the week.

I got some Valium from my doctor and Shouty Husband did the same; he hates flying as it is and meeting his dad for the first time in so long was a big deal. The boys were staying at home with my parents on speed-dial. The Valium, plus a joint in the car park, meant Shouty Husband was flying before we even got on the plane. The security guards were very suspicious and searched him even after I explained why he was doing a great impression of a space cadet; luckily, he was too bombed to argue with them.

The plane was very small, but the flight was only an hour, and once there we recognised Shouty Husband's dad from a photo he'd sent.

Shouty Husband walked up to him, and they hugged, which surprised me; he's not a hugger.

We got into his dad's big 4x4 and drove the hour to Ardglass in County Down, his dad's hometown and where he'd retired. As the whole family lived within a twenty-mile radius, he had a good support network.

My first impression was of how similar Shouty Husband looked to this man. Even though he was blond, and his dad was what was called 'Black Irish' – dark and eyes – you could see they were related. He had a booming voice and a larger-than-life personality.

Finbarr lived in a bungalow with a field to one side where cows grazed peacefully. 'Rural' wasn't the word; Ardglass was a fishing village with a church and a pub and nothing else. It was wonderful.

Our room was lovely but small, with a double bed pushed against the wall, and I had to go around taking all the push-up air fresheners out of the house as Shouty Husband would never have been able to breathe. I unpacked while he talked with his dad, and then we went out for a pub lunch.

We had roast beef and all the trimmings, which was delicious, and then we went into Ardglass to buy beer and some bits and pieces.

Next was a trip to meet Auntie Nuala We ate so much cake while visiting various family members, I was sure they must have a secret supply of it somewhere. We also drank our own body weight and then some in alcohol.

Auntie Nuala was formidable but made us feel very welcome.

Shouty Husband was a little perplexed as he had a memory of her voice but couldn't place it. It turned out she and Shouty Husband's Aunt Grasta Aine had lived with Finbarr and Shouty Husband's mum when he was little. They took him to Mass every week and fed him sweets to keep him quiet. The ice was broken, and Shouty Husband could fit some of his jigsaw puzzle together.

We were told about all the aunts and uncles who lived locally and who we'd visit, not to mention the cousins. There were so many of them, and a lot of the names were similar, so we didn't even try to remember them all; we just smiled.

Our first evening was spent in a pub in the wilds of nowhere and, as the licensing laws are different there, and we rolled out at around 1am.

Our first night in Ireland ended on a high note. It had gone very well, I thought – I hoped that would continue.

Dirty White Boy - Foreigner

The next day, Finbarr took us for a drive to get fuel. Since he lived on the north-south border, he took us on a tour of the coast road. We crossed the border into the south to buy jerry cans of diesel as it was cheaper. We had lunch out and did some shopping as Shouty Husband decided to cook for us all.

Finbarr's choice of television viewing wasn't mine, but I'd come prepared with my body weight in books. He was very impressed that I read, but I just wanted to stay out of the way as I felt like a gooseberry.

Finbarr had bad legs and was supposed to apply cream daily, but he was a very large man and hadn't been doing it. He had Type 2 diabetes, and his diet was horrendous; the cupboard was full of goodies which were bad for him, something I did point out. I offered to cream his legs while I was there to help prevent him getting another ulcer. It became a chore, but I wanted to be a good daughter-in-law.

I went to bed early so Shouty Husband and his dad could drink whiskey and talk. Shouty Husband was smiling the next day so I hoped all was good.

Bernadette - Four Tops

Finbarr wanted to show off his son to his ten brothers and sisters and he wanted to show off his son, I went along for the ride. Shouty Husband got to meet aunts, uncles, cousins, their children – so many family members! Among them was Finbarr's brother, Frank, and his wife Bernadette. Frank was the hard man of the family who wanted to check out Shouty husband

They had a beautiful home, but that was all show for the priest; they lived in the tatty bit at the back. There was a huge garden with a dead lawn and a massive kitchen which Shouty Husband loved.

We all went to a pub in Lurgan for lunch, and the waitress ignored Shouty Husband when he asked what cask beer they had. Finbarr shouted her back and told her off; nobody ignored his son, except him for the previous forty-eight years.

Shouty Husband thought it was because he was English, but it was more likely the way he asked her. Anyway, they had no beer he'd drink so he had Coke.

The waitress happened to walk behind Shouty Husband's chair, and he shoved it out backwards, hard, and caught her on the ankle. She nearly went down. Never piss off Shouty Husband, especially when he's trying to make a good impression on his newly rediscovered family.

We stopped to buy beer on the way back as Bernadette had none in and, back at theirs, Finbarr and Frank watched snooker while Bernadette and Shouty Husband flirted with each other. I was okay with that; it was a fun afternoon and I liked Bernadette.

In Your Easter Bonnet - Judy Garland

Finbarr didn't go to Mass on Easter Sunday, but we did do the biggest family thing we could - lunch with Aunt Nuala, uncle Gearalt, their children and grandchildren. I can't for the life of me remember the names of everyone who was there.

Nuala cooked lunch for fifteen people – melon, roast turkey and all the trimmings, and fruit salad with cream.

Well, Shouty Husband doesn't eat melon (and it was hard). He doesn't eat turkey either, so he made do with mash and veg. And guess what? He didn't eat the pudding either.

At least I earned brownie points as I wiped up after lunch. I think if someone takes the time to cook for you, the least you can do is help with the washing up.everybody wanted to talk to Shouty Husband, find out about his life and tell him how proud his dad was.

He was a prize animal to be poked and prodded – they all wanted to see what Finbarr had sired and whether he was worthy of the name.

Oxygene - Jean Michele Jarre

Another road trip to visit yet more relatives.

First the home of Finbarr's youngest brother Dominic. The only home that was not welcoming at all. Dominic refused to acknowledge that we existed and grunted at Finbarr, so it was a very quick visit.

Then a two-hour car ride to visit the black sheep of the family, Shouty husbands, Aunt Grasta Aine. She married an Englishman which was bad enough, but he was also Protestant, and this was the 1950s so not good. She had three sons and then her husband died so she came home to Ireland, then she remarried another Englishman but this time he was catholic, then she fostered troubled boys and ended up adopting two more boys.

Aunt Grasta Aine was an 80 a day smoker and had the voice to go with it. As soon as she said hello to Shouty husband he knew the voice. He did not remember her, but the voice took him back to a small boy and he was happy.

We sat in the kitchen so Grasta Aine could smoke, her husband was in the living room on oxygen and the room was filled with pop up air fresheners that would have turned Shouty husband blue within a couple of minutes.

Finbarr left us to it and Shouty husband found out all the family history that nobody else would tell him. We had a great time, Shouty husband got beer and I got over sweetened builders tea and cake.

Grasta Aine had a big hardbacked red leather sofa and chairs that she wanted to change, Finbarr loved it as he could sit upright so a deal was done. That left Finbarr to get rid of his comfy green leather sofa and chairs. Shouty husband loved Finbarr's sofa and his was cheap and nasty so a cunning plan was hatched, more on that later. It all fits honest!

As we were leaving Shouty husband was looking at one of the son's flash car and since Shouty husband was sensible he had been dope free for a week. On the dashboard was a ripped rizla packet, a sign of a toker.

Shouty husband had a chat with the son and enough dope for a three skin was provided. That evening we went for a walk around the village so Shouty husband could have a smoke.

My Man, a Sweet Man - Millie Jackson

We had our honeymoon, a whole two hours of it. Finbarr was sleeping in so at 8am we left a note and went for a walk.

We got lost and ended up in a yard with a big Hereford bull hanging over a gate. I love bulls; I know not to go into a field with one, but I went and rubbed his nose and talked to him like a small child. The farmer came out and Shouty Husband pointed at me and said, ' English. ' He apologised for being in his yard and asked for directions.

We ended up at Sheep Land Cove, which was heavily pebbled, and built a cairn with stones and seaweed.

Then, while Shouty Husband was trying to find the perfect stones to take home, he found a piece of granite with a tiny strip of quartz running through it. The sea had worn it into a perfect heart over the years, so that was my present from Ireland.

When we got home, Shouty Husband glued a ring to it, and I wore it around my neck on a chain for years. It's in my ring box with all the jewellery Shouty Husband gave me.

We found a well, fed by a natural spring. There was a Madonna by it, so the water was blessed. Not drinkable, but a great photo opportunity.

When we got home, Finbarr was waiting for us as he needed to go into Downpatrick to do some shopping.

Shouty Husband's Uncle Gearalt had a shop, so Finbarr told us to go and have a wander while he had a cuppa.

Shouty Husband hadn't found a wedding ring he liked before our wedding, so he looked in jewellers' windows and there was an 18-carat white gold ring he loved, so that was that sorted.

We had a trip to what Finbarr called 'the God shop', a little place up some steep stairs that sold all thing Catholic. It was run by two lovely little old ladies; they gave us tea and Shouty Husband bought mass candles for home and a couple of prayer cards.

He bought a beautiful bunch of flowers for his Aunt Nuala, and we visited her for lunch. I didn't really want to drink but there was no stopping her, and she gave me a wine glass three-quarters full of Bacardi with a drop of Coke. I dumped half of it when she wasn't looking. It was a sunny day and Shouty Husband fell asleep in the chair. I got a tour of Nuala's house while he snoozed; it was on three levels and built into the side of a hill - beautiful but the stairs were a killer, curved and very steep.

It was our last evening, so we spent it in the pub and a good time was had by all.

Fear of the Dark - Iron Maiden

The following morning Finbarr drove us back to Belfast for our flight home after what had been a great trip. Shouty Husband didn't have enough Valium to get him into a happy state on the way home, so he freaked out when we were coming in to land as the blinds on the window had to be up. Being a good wife, I held up a magazine so he couldn't see out. That was the last time he ever went on a plane.

Living After Midnight - Judas Priest

Soon after the honeymoon, Shouty Husband planned our return trip to pick up Finbarr's sofa. He was having a new one so we could have his, it was a big green leather one and in great condition.

The easiest - but longest - way was to get the ferry from Stranraer, which was an eight-hour drive from home. I found out the ferry times and hired a van. We used a one-man band – we didn't want to say where we were going as the price would have gone up – so it was a bit of a heap.

The ferry was due to leave at 11pm and it was a two-hour crossing. We drove up in the day, stopping Northumberland to have coffee and remember my Great Aunt Percy who was being cremated that day. I stood and looked at the beautiful countryside and thought of her.

We got to Stranraer at 7pm and parked up. Because we had time to kill and Shouty Husband didn't fancy the sandwiches he'd made, we went on the hunt for food.

Stranraer's claim to fame is its port – it's certainly not a gastronomic delight. On a Friday night, with the locals out in force, it was a busy town. We found two chip shops - but of course Shouty Husband doesn't eat chips. But then – hurrah! An Indian restaurant! We went in and sat down.

I was thirsty so Shouty Husband ordered me a Coke while he checked the menu. All was going well until he moved a side plate and saw the tablecloth was dirty. Then he gave the cutlery a good once-over and found that was also dirty, with dried food on the fork.

Shouty Husband got up and told the waiter that if they couldn't get something as basic as washing tablecloths and cutlery right, then he couldn't trust their kitchen hygiene and had no intention of eating there. I had to leave my Coke to trail behind him as he flounced out.

We walked all around the town but there was nowhere Shouty Husband would eat, so we ended up back at the van with three hours to kill before we could board the ferry. We sat in the dark, listening to Radio 2 and eating our sandwiches.

The ferry was quite busy, and we had to look for somewhere to sit. All the lounges had televisions blaring out whatever rubbish was on at that time of night. Shouty Husband wanted a nap, but it was too noisy, then two women who'd taken a shine to him came to sit next to us. They literally took his breath away – because they seemed to have taken a bath in cheap perfume.

We got up and moved to another lounge, where I got to watch Halloween 20, and we docked in Belfast at around 1am. We made it to Downpatrick but then, with no satnav, Shouty Husband got lost. There we were at 3am, driving along unlit country roads and struggling to find any signposts. Then we came across two teenage girls walking home, so Shouty Husband stopped the van, and I asked them for directions. They were brilliant, and we finally made it to Finbarr's at 4am after being on the road for sixteen hours.

I woke at 9am to find a note saying Shouty Husband and Finbarr had gone to get new tyres for Finbarr's 4x4. I made tea and toast and decided to run the vacuum around while I waited for them, and in the meantime, I took a call from Sarah who was shocked to find out we were there.

When they returned, Finbarr got Shouty Husband to mow his lawns and then the sofa arrived. No peace for the wicked! We had the fun job of moving Finbarr's old sofa and chairs into the van and putting the new ones into their place. After tea – cooked by Shouty Husband – we went to bed to get some rest before the long drive home.

On the way back to Belfast, Finbarr told me to travel with him and keep him company. As we came to a bridge leading into the city, there was a mural on the wall of a red circle with a line through it, and the words 'No Protestants'. Finbarr joked that meant I wasn't allowed to cross, but I laughed and pointed out there was Methodist chapel next to the house with the mural, and they liked me. That was the first time Finbarr ever commented on me not being Catholic. It wasn't the last.

. The return crossing was horrible; the weather was bad, the sea was rough, and the ferry rolled. Luckily, we discovered we both had good sea legs.

We finally got home at 11pm, knackered but with a beautiful, new (to us) comfy sofa and chairs. The following day, with a bit of help from our friends, we got the sofa over the back fence and into the living room and the old suite was in turn recycled to some of Shouty Husband's friends.

Watching the Wheels - John Lennon

By now, Shouty Husband had got regular work driving a bin wagon. He really wanted to get to know his dad, so he decided to invite him over to stay with us for a week in the summer holidays. He even booked time off work for it, which was unheard of.

As well as his grandchildren, Finbarr would be meeting my boys for the first time. Shouty Husband was looking forward to showing them off, as he was extremely proud of them.

We arranged to meet Finbarr just outside Stoke as he didn't know the way to our house, so it was an early start. When we pulled up at the house – well, I've said before it wasn't the best. Finbarr clearly wasn't impressed, even though we gave up our bedroom for him and had to sleep on a mattress in the spare room.

After breakfast, Finbarr went to have a nap and Shouty Husband worried that inviting his dad to stay was a bad idea. It was.

Rose Garden - Lynn Anderson

Finbarr wanted to go clothes shopping, so we had a trip out to a huge discount shop that did clothes for big men.

After that, we learned Shouty Husband had an uncle who lived near Paula, so off we went for a visit.

His uncle and aunt were lovely to us, but Shouty Husband wasn't happy as Finbarr was being loud and rude. We went to see Paula after that, and Finbarr was in heaven because the house was lovely. He had to get his two penn'orth in about how Shouty Husband hadn't done as well for himself.

I realised it was going to be a hard few days.

I Want to Be Free - Toyah

Shouty Husband wasn't coping with his dad being around, so he arranged to go back to work. That left me babysitting Finbarr. He wanted to do a good market and then see his friend John, so we ended up in Walsall. We sat in the sun and had a bacon sandwich, and I realised I was thoroughly fed up with 'the world according to Finbarr.' He slagged off Shouty Husband's mum and went on about how his son should have made more of his life.

Then came a moment that was unforgivable. A well-dressed black man walked past, clearly a very proud dad as he pushed a new born along in a buggy. Finbarr pointed at him and said very loudly, 'You don't see that very often, a coon pushing a pushchair.' The man stopped and looked at us, and I mouthed an apology. I told Finbarr he couldn't say things like that, but he just waved his hand and ignored me, and then we went to see his friend, John, and then on to Paula's.

Finbarr was in his element, going on to Paula about Shouty Husband's shortcomings, and I reached the point of no return. I would never normally lose my temper in someone else's house, but I couldn't help it. I told Finbarr that Shouty Husband had lost one home and was doing his best to improve his new one, but money was tight, and it couldn't all happen overnight. I apologised to Paula afterwards, but she said I'd done the right thing.

That evening I ended up going out for dinner with Finbarr and John, as Finbarr didn't want to drive on his own. I spent the whole evening being ignored and decided I couldn't wait until this visit was over. Little did I know it was going to get a whole lot worse.

Make It Real - Scorpions

I was left with Finbarr on the Saturday as Shouty Husband had gone to work, so I took him to meet the boys.

He was impressed with my home, but even though Luke told him I was a great mum and had paid off the mortgage on my house, Finbarr still thought I was after Shouty Husband's money. I realised he'd never accept me or my boys, but why should I care? I had Shouty Husband.

Then the tension that had been building up to came to a head.

When Shouty Husband got back from work, Finbarr was watching the horse racing – which Shouty Husband hates – with the volume turned right up. He wouldn't turn it off or down. Not a good start.

We were going for a family Sunday lunch the next day, and Shouty Husband mentioned Finbarr would get to meet his grandchildren, all six of them. Finbarr waved his hand dismissively and said he only had four grandchildren – my boys didn't count.

Shouty Husband was tired, not in the mood, and this was all that was needed to set him off. All the pain from his childhood rushed to the surface and Finbarr got both barrels. Finbarr was scared, I could see that, and decided he was going to stay at his friends for the night. It was the best thing he could have done.

Shouty Husband could deal with his dad hating his house, his life, his hair, beer and everything else, but he wasn't going to let him diss the boys he was so proud of. They were going places. They'd have all the chances to make a good life that had been denied to him.

Standing up for us like that was one of the best things Shouty Husband ever did for us. He'd put us first. He'd proved he loved us and how important we were to him. And that meant the world.

In the Name of Love - U2

After speaking to Paula, and because Sarah was coming up, it was decided the family lunch should go ahead. His sisters did wonder if it was just a case of Shouty Husband being difficult and, after all, they had their inheritance to think about.

We all went to Paula's house first and naturally the hot topic of conversation was Finbarr. It turned out we all felt the same way about him, and Sarah admitted she'd made a mistake in tracking him down.

Still, it was rare for us all to be together and the sisters wanted to give Finbarr a final chance. They also wanted to see if Shouty Husband was being unreasonable; they hadn't experienced Finbarr's vitriol in the way we had.

When we got to the pub, we found Finbarr was already there with John, his friend. That meant thirteen of us for dinner, one of whom wasn't family. Shouty Husband was seething and on the verge of leaving, but Luke managed to talk him down; he always was good with him. Shouty Husband said he wouldn't eat, but he did agree to stay. We were seated at a long table with one chair at the end of it, and John said Finbarr should sit there as he was head of the family.

The whole pub heard Shouty Husband roar that as he was the one who'd been around for his sisters, nieces and nephews their whole lives, that made him head of family.

Then he sat his niece at the head of the table and Finbarr sat at the other end, well away from us, with his daughters and sons-in-law to talk to. We had fun with the younger family down our end and enjoyed our food.

Shouty Husband and I never saw Finbarr again, though that wasn't the end of him. Sarah and Paula, smelling money, kept in touch and visited until he died ten years later. They got their inheritance in the end, though the rest of the family contested it and it took them two years.

Shouty Husband didn't care. We didn't go to the funeral and he was never interested in the money. He'd just wanted a dad. And just like in his childhood, he had one for a while and then he was gone.

Don't Stand So Close to Me - The Police

After Shouty Husband and I got married, we decided we'd live apart until the boys were sorted. Jordan was going to university so would be home on and off, and Luke would be off to college. I didn't want to move until I had a plan.

We'd reached an impasse. Shouty Husband didn't want to move, and I refused to disrupt my boys.

As it was the summer holidays, I cleared all the clutter out of my house so that it was nearly empty; after all, I was planning to move in with Shouty Husband. But I still had my home – a bolthole if I ever needed one. Not that I thought I ever would, back then.

Girl, You'll Be a Woman Soon - Urge Overkill

With Jordan due to go to university soon, I was staying at Shouty Husband's at weekends and Poppy, Jordan's girlfriend was staying with Jordan and Luke.

After a while, though, Luke asked if he could stay with us. We assumed he wanted to get used to his new home; his autism meant he needed time to accept change. After the third weekend, though, he told Shouty Husband that Poppy was bullying him, making him do all the housework and generally picking at him.

She had to be told, and I'd be the one to tell her. Not Shouty Husband - this was my fight.

At 10am on Sunday, Luke, Shouty Husband and I went to my home to clean up.

We cranked up the stereo to blast out the Red-Hot Chili Peppers' greatest hits and after three tracks Poppy stuck her head out of the door and shouted down the stairs. She asked me to turn down the music as they were trying to sleep.

I told her I was here to clean up and she should come and help. Jordan appeared, took one look at me, and left her to it. I gave her both barrels – I knew what she'd been doing to Luke, I wasn't having it, and she was no longer welcome in my house. Jordan was off to uni soon, so she'd be history soon anyway - no great loss.

Shouty husband and Luke just watched as I made my wrath felt. Nobody hurts my boys. Nobody.

Smack My Bitch Up - The Prodigy

When Jordan went to university, I moved my bed to Shouty Husband's place as it was more comfortable. I was still trying to come up with a plan, so if I stayed at my house during the week, I slept in Jordan's bed.

Luke was quite happy for me to go home, feed him, then leave to sleep at Shouty Husband's place. He knew I was always on the end of the phone and only a two-minute walk away if he needed me. The neighbours kept an eye on him, too.

So, six months after our wedding, my house was stripped out and I was almost living with Shouty Husband full time. and then it all went to hell.

Shouty Husband was many things, but he wasn't a wife-beater – until he was.

The very first time he raised a hand to me was my own fault. I know all domestic abuse victims say that, but it's true. It was when I was still with the Boys' Dad, and while we were at his house one Saturday evening I hid under the stairs and jumped out at him as a joke when he went to the loo. He wasn't expecting it and lashed out with the flat of his hand, sending me down like a sack of spuds. I ended up with double vision and one hell of a headache.

The next time was an accident. We were having a picnic in a field, play-fighting and messing about, and he caught me across the cheekbone. The sick feeling set in when I got home, and I knew I was concussed.

Then the third time...

After his dad's visit, Shouty Husband became deeply depressed and was very hard to live with. Everyone he loved - and who should have loved him – had let him down. His dad was just the latest in a long line. I was walking on eggshells around him with no clue how to make it better.

Norman's solution was to give him pure base amphetamine sulphate – speed. It always increased Shouty Husband's paranoia and if you add his depression and anger into the mix – well, it was asking for trouble.

But Shouty Husband wanted to get off his face and beer alone wasn't doing the trick.

I remember Alice in Wonderland - the Disney cartoon version - was on the television. I was on the sofa and Shouty Husband in one of the comfy chairs as he raged against the world and his dad.

To this day, I can't remember what I said to make him go off on one, but suddenly something very hard hit me on the side of my face and the world exploded into stars before going black.

Shouty Husband had thrown a heavy wooden African drum at me. I remember curling into a ball and was apparently whimpering as I waited for the next assault. When his head was straight enough for him to realise what he'd done, he tried to see what damage he'd inflicted. I tried to run away but he caught me and hung on. Blood was pouring down my face and out of my mouth, my glasses had ended up on the floor, and that combination meant I was pretty much blind.

Shouty Husband yelled at me to get a grip and then walked away to call Norman. He told him to come and 'deal with me' as I was ruining his trip.

I stayed curled up, waiting; Shouty Husband was manic and it seemed the safest option. When Norman came, he helped me up and found my glasses, then cleaned my face with toilet roll and warm water.

I had the start of a black eye, a cut on my forehead and a badly split lip. I was seeing double and wanted to be sick.

Shouty Husband's gauge had hit 'full' and he'd gone to bed, so Norman offered to take me to my house. The two-minute walk seemed to take forever, and Luke was still up when we got there. Norman told him I'd fallen over at his house, and this was the easiest place to bring me. I went to bed in Jordan's room with a bucket and lay there all night, wondering what I was going to do.

Should I go back, or should I walk away before I got in any deeper? We were newly married and I loved him. I was sure the man who'd thrown the drum and behaved so horribly wasn't some stranger – he wasn't the Shouty Husband I knew and loved.

The next morning, I rang work and told them I'd tripped over the dog and gone face-first into the wardrobe. I couldn't go in that day, and it was the only reason I could think of to explain why I had a black eye and a bruised, swollen face.

Shouty Husband only realised I wasn't there when he got up, so he walked down to my house to see if Luke had had a problem in the night. When he saw my face, he looked horrified. I told him what he'd done, and he couldn't remember doing it.

I've never seen Shouty Husband as upset as he was at that moment. I was so sure he'd only acted that way due to a combination of the drugs, booze and being upset about his dad that I forgave him – fool that I was.

My condition for going back, though, was that he never touched speed again – and he did keep that promise.

My injuries faded in time, but the memory didn't – I never forgot what he'd done that night.

Insomnia - Faithless

Shouty Husband had been paying emergency tax for years so, as I had a talent for sorting things out, I decided to do something about it. I found all his pay slips, put them in date order and sent them off to the tax office. It paid dividends - he got a huge rebate.

Chunks of money tended to get spent on the house, so as I was moving in, he decided to buy new bedroom furniture. The joys of a huge bedroom and being able to fill it with Argos flat pack! There was plenty of space for both of us and, finally I was allowed wardrobe space. It only took ten years and getting married – previously I'd not even been allowed to leave a toothbrush there and lived out of a bag.

I have what's known by my boys as 'the Mum face', which ranges from one to ten depending how angry I am. I've only done number ten twice – but this time, it changed our lives forever. It wasn't easy, trying to make us a family unit after I married Shouty Husband. He was used to living on his own, and of course we had the two houses.

Should I sell my house, which was mortgage free, so Luke and I could move into his place? It would mean giving up my lifeline, my bolthole. It felt like I'd be walking blindly over a cliff, not knowing what would happen. Could I put the boys through that? In the end, Jordan made my mind up for me. Even though he was at university, he came home at weekends.

On one occasion he asked if some friends could stay too, and as Luke was coming with me to Shouty Husband's, I agreed. They arrived on the Friday night, and we left them to it until the Sunday afternoon, when we went to pick Jordan up and take him back to Birmingham. (Shouty Husband was using Jordan's car during the week, so he needed a lift back to uni.)

I'd left my house clean and tidy, so it was nice for Jordan to show it off to his friends. We arrived to find it had been trashed. I smoked then, so there were plenty of ashtrays – but they'd stubbed out their fags on my waxed, wooden coffee table and left white rings all over it. Someone had cooked and used what seemed like every bowl and saucepan, leaving them dirty in the sink. There was food ground into the carpet. I was furious, but I didn't raise my voice. Instead, I rolled out Mum Face Number Ten.

On the way back from Birmingham, I told Shouty Husband I wanted to sell up and move into his house, along with Luke. If my house wasn't respected when I wasn't there, then I'd had enough – it was time to move on and make a home with Shouty Husband full time.

See Me, Feel Me - The Who

My house was valued at £90,000, which was pretty good as I only paid £13,000 for it back in 1986. I sold at the right time, too, while the property market was on a high - it crashed a year later.

My house went up for sale at 9am on a Thursday, and the first viewing was 5pm that evening. The guy offered £5,000 below the asking price, so I said no. There was another on the Saturday, and one on Sunday. Jordan did the last one and said they were tyre kickers; they lived round the corner and were just being nosy, not serious buyers.

I was vacuuming upstairs when Shouty Husband yelled that the estate agents were on the phone. The second couple had offered the full asking price – so of course I accepted. Three days for me to sell my house - I was so pleased.

Luke was happy with his own bedroom at Shouty Husband's house. He painted it the darkest blue he could, put up all his posters, and we bought him new furniture. Best of all, as next door was still empty, he could play his music loudly.

Beds Are Burning - Midnight Oil

Sadly, the empty house wasn't there forever, and we ended up with the neighbours from hell.

I tried to be nice when I saw the van arrive and the furniture being unloaded and went round to welcome them to the neighbourhood. I told them when the bins went out, what times the shop opened – the kind of things it's handy to know. The husband was a tall, thin man and his wife – well, she was obese, with badly bleached hair, and her conversation was peppered with swear words. She said they'd bought the house and shouted me down when I tried to tell them about the problems it had had.

They'd moved from Birmingham and had three boys who'd be attending the local secondary school. I worked there as a teaching assistant, so I said I was more than willing to help if there was anything she needed. She wasn't impressed to have 'a teacher' living next door, though, so I beat a hasty retreat and told Shouty Husband what I'd learned.

He didn't complain about the noise all weekend while they moved in, and kept out of the way, but within a week he was on the warpath. The walls were thin so we could hear teenagers thumping up and down the stairs, rap music blaring out, and her screaming at everybody with foul language. He was very restrained, though. He explained to the husband that he worked strange hours and needed quiet after 9pm so he could sleep. The husband said he'd do his best to keep the noise levels down.

Then the wife appeared – or Swamp Donkey, as Shouty Husband nicknamed her. She gave him a mouth full of abuse, rolled her eyes and asked what he thought he was going to do about it. She didn't know better, of course. Shouty Husband just smiled his evil smile, the one that meant 'you have no idea what you're about to unleash' and walked away.

A week later, they saw Shouty Husband at his worst. He was lying on the drive, painting the underside of the car with something to prevent rust.

The guy opposite was a taxi driver and came out to wash his car. Their drive was flat, but ours sloped, so Shouty Husband asked him nicely if he could wait until he'd finished – otherwise he'd get soaked.

Shouty Husband had had run-ins with this neighbour before, and the man waited until he was back under the car and then started to clean his car. Yes, the water ran down and Shouty Husband got wet. I heard the roar from inside the house and ran out to find him emerging from under the car with his long hair everywhere and his jeans soaked. He ran towards the neighbour who, sensibly, retreated inside. He'd left the hose running, though, so Shouty Husband picked it up, took it to the top of our garden, and ran it on the ground to make thick clay mud. Then he threw handful after handful at the neighbour's car until it was literally dripping.

Shouty Husband always put on a good show, so everyone was out in force to watch what was going on – including Swamp Donkey. You'd think she'd have taken it as a lesson not to mess with Shouty Husband, but no. The noise got worse and Shouty Husband lost sleep, and he'd had enough. Norman had given him some killer bass speakers, but they ended up in the small bedroom as they had bright red cases – the colour Shouty Husband hates. Now, though, he had a use for them.

One Sunday, we were up and out of the door by 7am as we were going to do a car boot sale and then have lunch at Paula's. Shouty Husband set up the spare CD player, which had a multi changer, and hooked it up to the big red speakers. Then he put on three CDs of hardcore trance music. On repeat. We were out nearly all day, so by the time we got back they'd had nearly nine hours of it booming into their house.

Swamp Donkey very sensibly never came round to complain.

Learning to Fly - Pink Floyd

Shouty Husband decided he'd had enough and took my mum's advice. She told him about Mrs Jones, who remarried five years after her husband died suddenly. Her new husband also had a house, but they decided to sell both as they held too many memories and move somewhere else for a fresh start.

So, he got the falling-down house valued – and it was worth more than expected – but we held off putting it on the market as we needed to find somewhere first. As Shouty Husband also still had a mortgage, it meant we were limited as to what we could buy.

Then my mum came up with a solution to our money problems. You remember Aunt Percy? She'd left my mum an inheritance that was intended to help the next generation. Mum decided her grandsons were the generation that needed help, so she agreed to pay off Shouty Husband's mortgage as long as he left his half of the new house to the boys.

I was in my element then, poring over the property pages in the local paper and going around every estate agent's I could find. We found a house on a cul de sac that ticked every box, so we made an offer and the vendors accepted. So far, so good.

Then came the searches. The letter from our solicitor was carefully worded and, reading between the lines, we understood it to mean, 'DO NOT BUY THIS HOUSE! 'To be sure, Shouty Husband showed it to Norman, who had the kind of mind that would spot anything amiss.

We were right. The house had a rear garden that stretched seventy-five feet and backed onto a busy dual carriageway. But the current owners had taken about twenty-five feet of land that didn't belong to them, so it could be claimed back if the road needed to be extended. The garage belonged to the house, but the drive didn't – so any random person could park on it, and we'd have to allow it. The road was also unadopted, which meant we'd be liable – along with everyone else on the street – for any maintenance, for any necessary work as a result of repairs to the gas, electric and water infrastructure, for new bulbs for the streetlights. It was a money pit – we'd need to make sure we had at least £2,000 put away at any time in case it was needed.

I wasn't happy at the money wasted so far, but we had to walk away from the house. It was a lemon – and while Shouty Husband was very good at buying lemons, this one was too sour even for him.

In the Army Now - Status Quo

Whenever he could, Shouty Husband bought cheap baccy from abroad. We always bought in bulk, so when Billy offered us some, we said we'd take fifty quid's worth.

We picked it up from Charlie's in a carrier bag and, as he was family, we didn't check it. Billy said the money was going to his mum, Shouty Husband's aunt, who'd bought it from a friend.

When we got home and Shouty Husband looked at it, he realised it was counterfeit. There was no way he was smoking that – he wanted his money back and got straight on the phone to Billy.

He was still furious when he hung up, but he said we could have our money back – we'd just have to go over and get it in the morning. It was Saturday, and by 8pm Shouty Husband was pissed, stoned and in bed snoring. A knock at the kitchen window made me jump – only people who knew us did that, so I woke up Shouty Husband and he went to see who it was. There was Billy, looking like an angry praying mantis. He accused Shouty Husband of disrespecting his mum by claiming she'd sold us dodgy baccy, and he was there to sort Shouty Husband out.

Shouty Husband was happy to oblige. He said he'd just go and get dressed and they could both go out the front.

That stopped Billy in his tracks, and he went from aggressive to calm in the blink of an eye. Shouty Husband was ready for the confrontation now, though.

Unfortunately, while Billy was jumping up and down with rage, he'd knocked the dog's water bowl and there was a puddle on the floor. That kitchen floor was lethal when it was wet and as Shouty Husband went to get dressed, he slipped and ended up flat on his back, dressing gown open, giving Billy an open view of his crown jewels.

This immediately diffused things. Billy was laughing his head off and he left cackling about how he'd beaten Shouty Husband.

Shouty Husband was of course fuming, so he rang Charlie and demanded to know why he hadn't warned him Billy was coming over. Charlie said it was nothing to do with him and he hadn't known he would.

Shouty Husband cut them both out of his life after that, and I lost a good friend in Charlie's partner.

Brothers in Arms - Dire Straits

Shouty Husband had a passion for sports cars, especially Triumph Spitfires. He always said he'd buy a reconditioned one, but they were about £5,000. For a forty-year-old car! They were also hard to get parts for. Still, it didn't stop him taking me to look at them sitting on garage forecourts. In the meantime, my Ford Ka - Jinty-bug - was getting long in the tooth and needed replacing. I could do that – my house had sold, and the money was coming.

We went to look at cars and Shouty Husband fell in love with a second-hand Ford Ka Sport – it was a beautiful metallic blue, with full leather upholstery and a powerful engine. He really wanted it and, even though it wasn't what I had in mind, her persuaded me I wanted it too.

I rang my dad to ask if he'd lend me the money until my house sale was completed, when I could pay it back. He agreed, so I put down a deposit and we went back the next weekend, along with £7,500 which Shouty Husband had withdrawn from the bank.

It caused a few problems, paying in cash, but two hours later Shouty Husband was the proud owner of a sports car. My dad never did ask for the money back – he gave it to us as a wedding present.

While the Ka was wonderful in many ways, it went through tyres like they were going out of fashion and drank petrol. Shouty Husband loved it, though – he called it Rollo and it effectively became his. (Eventually it got too expensive to run, so Shouty Husband sold it to his niece and bought a bike.)

That left me still needing a car, so back we went to the showroom. I fell in love with another Ka - a gorgeous metallic green this time. The saleswoman wouldn't accept cash this time, so we went back the following week with a cheque, and I became the proud owner of Snotbug who lasted until a student hit me up the rear end at an island and wrote it off.

The hunt was on for another car for me, a cheap one that would be covered by the insurance. After a failed attempt to buy a Nissan Micra, I ended up with a Fiat Panda called Percy. Percy is still going strong today. I can't deny Shouty Husband picked well for me there.

Our House - Crosby, Stills, Nash & Young

We were still looking for our new home, and I'd found four houses that met the long list of criteria Shouty Husband demanded. Three were in the same area, and the other was in an area we loved but thought we'd never be able to afford.

It was a rainy Saturday when we visited the first one. The garden was huge, which Shouty Husband loved, but the house itself was tiny. Among other things, Shouty Husband wanted a big dining table, so it definitely wouldn't do. We cancelled the other two appointments in that area, and off we went to see the fourth house.

The area it was in had always been expensive. I'd lived there thirty-four years earlier as a lodger in an attic room, and Jinx – the first Mrs Shouty Husband – had always aspired to move there one day.

The owners opened the porch door to reveal a very pale green carpet. We were both wowed by the living room, which was open plan and very airy.

The kitchen was small with a built-in cooker and hob, but it was badly laid out – there was no way Shouty Husband could cook in it. That wasn't insurmountable, though. The dining room led off the kitchen and already had a huge table in it, so Shouty Husband was delighted. He told the owners he was in heaven, and they beamed.

It turned out that they'd been left another property by a relative, so they'd moved into that. This had still been their home for forty years, though, so they didn't want to sell it just anybody. Shouty Husband charmed them both with talk of making it a real family home for the two of us and my boys.

I was concerned there was nowhere in the kitchen to put a washing machine, but then it turned out that one end of the garage had been converted into a utility room – there was room for a washing machine, dishwasher, tumble dryer and a big freezer. Hurrah! The garden was huge, forty feet square, all used as a vegetable garden.

Then we went upstairs. All the bedrooms were a good size – okay, they were all magnolia-painted anaglypta, but we could live it until we got round to decorating.

When it came to see the bathroom, I was blocked from seeing while the wife apologised and said her husband had picked the suite. I could see why she wanted to explain – it was salmon paste pink, including the tiles and carpet! Barbie Doll heaven – but there was no way that was staying!

Shouty Husband said we would love to buy the house if they'd sell it to us, and the husband said he'd knock £2,000 off the asking price and take it off the market if he'd shake on it there and then. They understood we needed to sell Shouty Husband's house first, but happily they were prepared to wait.

So Shouty Husband shook the man's hand and...we were buying a house! In an area we loved, with all the things on Shouty Husband's list. Happy days!

Zombie - Bad Wolves

Shouty Husband's house went on the market the following Friday, and on the Saturday, we had our first and only viewing.

It was a landlord looking to improve his portfolio, so we cleaned thoroughly and moved all the crap into the loft. We left all the doors open, too – none of them closed properly. We told ourselves it meant our potential buyers would see the size of the rooms and think of the money they could make through multi-occupancy.

Shouty Husband was asking £85,000, but when the guy offered £82,500, he looked at me and decided it wasn't worth arguing for the sake of a couple of thousand.

The buyers went away happy to put the wheels in motion, so we did the same. Then came the survey...

We knew the roof needed work, possibly replacing entirely. There was a hole that leaked water into our bedroom so, before it went up for sale, Shouty Husband stuffed the hole with newspaper and painted over it.

As we were both at work when the surveyor came, Luke showed her around. The loft was so full of stuff she couldn't see much of the roof, and as she had killer heels on, she wasn't keen on climbing the steps to get right up there. It was a horrible day with heavy rain, and we hadn't poo-picked the garden so there was dog muck all over the patio. As a result, she only stuck her head outside and didn't see the cracks running down the outside wall as a result of next door's subsidence.

She passed the house. Result. We were on our way.

A World of Fantasy - Triumph

The house sales went through without any fuss, and we made one more trip to the new house so Shouty Husband could measure up. Luke came too, and it was great to show him around without being watched. I was so happy!

The only problem was that it had a lot less floor space than we were used to, and our new bedroom furniture was not going to fit. Shouty Husband had an idea, though.

A couple of weeks earlier he'd gone with Carl to drop some stuff off at a friend's place. Helen was a single mum of three who was short of money and rented a house which didn't have much furniture. He'd forgotten his tobacco when he left – a full pack – and, although Helen smoked and could have kept it, she ran after him to give it back.

This had impressed him, so Shouty Husband said she could have the wardrobes if she wanted them – they were only six months old, and he'd even take them apart and get them round to her house.

She came round to ours with her boyfriend to look at them, and we gave her a pad of post-Its. I'd show her what we couldn't take with us, and if she wanted it, she could have it for free – she just needed to claim it with a post-It.

She took some convincing this was a genuine offer, but once she believed us, she was delighted.

The Green Manalishi (With the Two Prong Crown) - Peter Green and Fleetwood Mac

Norman came with us to pick up the keys to the new place. Shouty Husband was still in a lot of pain, so he'd self-medicated with beer and dope. What a picture he was, stinking of beer and with his swollen face.

He insisted on giving me a fireman's lift over the threshold and Norman took a photo, which I still have.

We should have moved on the Friday, as that's when we signed the contracts, but Shouty Husband offered the new owners of his place £50 to hang on a couple of days so we could move over the weekend instead.

It's a Sin - Pet Shop Boys

When moving day arrived, Shouty Husband wasn't up to driving. Little John was helping with the heavy lifting, but he couldn't drive so, after racking our brains, we asked Carl who lived opposite.

Of course, as he was the master of procrastination, nothing had been packed up. So, as well as the house, we had the garage, the shed and a loft full of crap to sort out. I'd ordered a big skip and Shouty Husband sat and looked at everything we brought out, then decreed whether it was 'skip' or 'take'.

Thank the gods for good friends who helped me pack and wrap everything that was going with us. The only thing Shouty Husband dealt with was his stereo – nobody else was allowed to touch that.

For some reason he decided his lifetime's collection of vinyl, some three hundred records, was going in the skip. I never did understand that one – I knew some of them were very rare and worth a lot of money.

He had lots of tools, too – he loved them and bought loads, but then never used them. They were split between Little John and Carl.

The neighbours at the new place watched us move in. The gods know what they must have thought of us – Shouty Husband with his long hair and swollen face; Little John, tall and loud with his badger's mane; then Luke and his best mate, Mike, in their full greebo goth gear with black-painted fingernails and studded collars.

By 5pm, all that was left in the old house was the stuff that was going to Helen's the next day. Even though the new owners had done us a favour, Shouty Husband resented paying for the privilege of being able to stay and move over the weekend. As the gas and electric were on pre-pay meters and had quite a lot of money left on them, he whacked up the heating to Barbados level and lit up the house like Blackpool illuminations. There was no way the meters would have run out of money, but in his eyes, it was a small victory. That, and leaving the garage and the loft full of crap for them to deal with.

Of course, at the new place, my lovely big sofa wouldn't fit through the front door, so we had to carry it up the neighbour's drive, lift it over the garage roof, and take it in through the patio doors.

Those first few nights we had to sleep on a mattress on the floor until our new bed was delivered, but at that point I honestly didn't care. We'd done it – we were in our own place.

Emerald - Thin Lizzy

As we moved just before the Easter holidays, I had two weeks off work. Shouty Husband also took a holiday, which was unheard of, and after finally getting his tooth pulled it meant we could crack on. The house already had good quality carpets and curtains, so we just needed furniture that would fit in it. Apart from the hideous bathroom, which needed dealing with immediately, we planned to live in the house for a while and get a feel for it before making any changes. The only exception was the small bedroom, which Luke wanted – that would be decorated straight away.

Then the built-in cooker wouldn't work. We knew the fuse box needed replacing – it was ancient and one reason why the previous owners dropped the price. We stupidly thought it would be a simple job – but no.

Little John was good with electrics, so he came over with his special screwdriver. He sucked in his breath and shook his head at the fuse box, then checked the rest of the light switches and sockets. When he took the cover off the brass dimmer switch in the front bedroom, he found bare wires; we'd have had a nasty shock if we'd turned it on. In fact, he said, the whole house was dangerous and a fire hazard.

Shouty Husband couldn't do with angle grinders and the dust, so the rewiring would have to be done by hand. Our new house was going to be broken and rebuilt.

It took nine months and was finally finished a week before Christmas. And it nearly broke us.

See Emily Play - Pink Floyd

An old neighbour worked for a company that made electrical equipment, so Shouty Husband asked him if he knew any electricians that wanted to do the house as a cash in hand job., As long as we got the relevant certificate at the end, we'd be happy.

Everybody who saw our fuse box made 'the face' – you know the one, the face that makes it clear they're looking at a disaster of a situation! Finally, we were set up with Abed and Adasen, who came highly recommended. They'd work evenings and weekends, using high-quality equipment and parts they at a discount through their employer. Shouty Husband took the opportunity to make sure we had loads of sockets fitted all over the house, which proved a godsend over the years.

We were cash rich after selling both houses so, as we had a near-empty house to fill, we went on a spending spree.

Shouty Husband had always wanted solid wood furniture, the kind that would last our lifetime and beyond.

Our first stop was to look at dining tables at a beautiful shop that did solid oak furniture. While they had chairs, he loved none of the tables was big enough. But it turned out they had another, bigger shop fifteen miles away, so off we went. There he found a solid French oak table that would seat eight people comfortably and, after some hunting, some chairs to go with it. The two saleswomen were somewhat taken aback at the sight of Shouty Husband with money to spend in full flow.

Next, we bought an oak china cabinet and two bookcases for me, and a nest of tables. They also had modern sculptures of lovers in the window, which I couldn't resist, so they were added to the pile.

We spent £2,500, even with sale prices. I put down a sizeable deposit and the ladies agreed to hold everything back for delivery as we needed to get the house decorated and new carpets fitted after the rewiring work.

Next up was a new bed, complete with a memory foam mattress that was something new at the time, and a trip to buy bedding and a toilet brush. (Shouty Husband hated a dirty toilet, but rarely cleaned it himself – that was always my job.)!

We ended up living in the dining room for a while with my sofa and coffee table, while the kitchen just had a gas hob and a microwave. In the living room were my table and chairs, and we'd brought Shouty Husband's washing machine, dishwasher, and tumble dryer with us as they were only a year old.

We'll Bring the House Down - Slade

Next up in our United Nations of workmen were the Welsh

Shouty Husband sat in the dining room with me and got drunk while we laughed at three men making a pig's ear of trying to knock down the old shed. Eventually, he went and hit it very hard, and it came down very quickly. He always was good at brute force.

My mum offered to pay for Luke's room to be done and we wanted him to be happy, so as soon as his room was rewired and plastered the decorator – recommended by my little brother – came.

The door was always shut because he was using gloss paint, which meant Shouty husband would go blue with the fumes. So, we didn't see the room until it was finished – and it was a disaster. The paint had drips and splash marks, and you could see the joins between the lengths of wallpaper. Shouty Husband refused to pay and told the decorator he'd better not go to my mum for the money, or he'd regret it.

I rang Andy, my decorator who'd done my whole house brilliantly, and booked him to come and do the whole house when it was ready.

The next big job was getting the kitchen into a fit state to be used. Shouty Husband hated not having a decent cooking space, and the final straw came when he ended up cooking a joint of beef on the barbecue in the garden for Sunday lunch - under an umbrella in the rain. The cupboards and drawers were in a poor state of repair, but Shouty husband decided not to rip the whole lot out; instead, he bought a new upright gas cooker, a new sink and work tops.

David came to stay with us even though we were living in a bomb site, and it was great to have some company that wasn't a workman. Then it all went to hell again.

The house we were attached to was having work done on their roof, and the scaffolding had to encroach on our property a bit. That wasn't a problem, and the roofer was local – Barry, who lived just up the road – so Shouty Husband asked him to look at our roof while he was up there. The wooden batons needed replacing, and Barry quoted a good price.

Meanwhile, Shouty Husband had just fitted the new work tops. They were a shiny black and he loved them. The day the kitchen was due to be done I left lots of dust sheets out to cover the work tops and took David for a day in a nearby market town to visit a great second-hand bookshop that was there. We got home to find the work tops covered in dust and plaster.

When Shouty Husband got home and saw them, after a bad day at work, he exploded. Quietly, which made it worse. The electricians didn't know what had hit them. Shouty Husband told them they'd had plenty of time and, if they weren't finished within a week, they'd be fired and wouldn't get paid.

Give the electricians their due, they got on with it and met the deadline.

We paid the bill and asked about the certificate. That was coming from somewhere else and, in due course, the man who could sign it all off arrived. I gave him a cup of tea and he told us the certificate would cost another £200.

Shouty Husband had had enough of being mucked around. He told him in no uncertain terms that he wanted his certificate and he wanted it now, and he didn't intend to pay another penny to get it. The poor man, stuck in the corner of the kitchen with his cup of tea, caved. We got our paperwork and got it for free. Onwards and upwards. We needed to get some of the dust out of the carpets as we didn't want to throw them out until we'd redecorated.

Shouty Husband also decided my sofa needed to go into the living room, but it wouldn't fit through the door. No problem! Little John and Shouty Husband decided they could just knock out the bricks above the top of it, then replaster the damage. Alas! There was a lintel above the door, so that sofa still wasn't going through. At that point, Shouty Husband decided we needed a new sofa. We measured and measured to make absolutely sure that whatever we bought would fit through the doors and, after scouring every sofa store within a fifty-mile radius we found a lovely soft leather two-seater. We had space for two, as it goes, so Shouty Husband eventually gave in to the saleswoman's pitch and agreed to another one.

Three months later the sofas came and went to live in the garage as the house was still a mess. Before long, they were joined by the table, chairs, and bookcases.

The Fletcher Memorial Home - Pink Floyd

Norman, who'd been in our lives for ever, had a very bad chest. We popped round one Saturday afternoon just after we'd moved and realised, he really wasn't very well.

The house was still a bombsite, but the spare room was kind of ready, so we offered to take him home with us, but he declined. He'd ring if he needed us, he said.

My phone pinged at midnight with a text. I missed it but, luckily, Jordan heard it, read it, and came to wake us up. Norman needed help. Jordan was sober, thank the gods, so he drove. We bundled Norman into the car and rushed to A&E. After two hours, they said they were admitting him. I called the next day to be told Norman was in the high dependency unit and they needed to see his family. Shouty Husband took Norman's daughter, Morgan, to the hospital, where the consultant explained that, as her dad was gravely ill, they needed to discuss what would happen if he got to the point of no return. Morgan was a chip off the old block and just like her dad – she walked away and told Shouty Husband to sort it.

Norman did get better and, after a week on the high dependency unit and another on the wards, he was ready to be discharged. He wasn't well enough to be on his own, though, and Morgan wouldn't take him in, so he came to us to recuperate.

Shouty Husband had his work cut out at mealtimes, as Norman was a long-time vegetarian, and we were meat-eaters.

Norman stayed with us for two weeks then wanted to go home. We let him, but said we'd be keeping a close eye on him.

He survived five more years before he finally took the Death's hand. I wanted to go to the funeral, but he and Shouty Husband had fallen out by then, so I wasn't allowed.

For Those About to Rock (We Salute You) - AC/DC

Next on the list – getting rid of the disgusting bathroom. Abed, the electrician, said he could do it along with help from someone he knew. Enter Americo, his wife and small daughter, who were from Portugal.

We also wanted the kitchen tiling. As it turned out, Americo was a tiler by trade and wanted to start up on his own, so Shouty husband agreed to give him a chance. The tiles came from B&Q and were green, as Shouty Husband always had a green kitchen. Americo hated them; he was used to the beautiful styles and colours he saw in Portugal.

He made a beautiful job of the kitchen, though, so Shouty Husband agreed to having some expensive blue and white ones fitted in the bathroom. We went off to Ireland on holiday to escape the mess, leaving Luke behind with the animals. Americo brought along his family while he worked, which was worrying – the house wasn't safe for a small child.

When the bathroom suite was delivered, the bath had to live at the bottom of the stairs. In all, we were without a working bathroom for six weeks and I spent the end of the summer holidays trying to entertain a two-year-old with no toys in a bombsite. One day, I took Americo's wife and daughter out to a soft play barn just for a change.

Finally, it was time for Abed to fit the bathroom suite. Unfortunately, as neither he nor Americo were plumbers, it leaked. Shouty Husband threw them both out and refused to pay. After six weeks of showering at my mum's and strip-washing in the kitchen sink, he was down to his last nerve.

Americo's English wasn't very good, so one Saturday afternoon he turned up with a friend's wife who explained that as he had done the work, he should be paid. Shouty Husband pointed out they'd made £2,000 out of us and, although the tiling was great, the bathroom still needed to be plumbed in. The friend, Sofia, said her husband was a plumber, and he'd do it at a reduced price.

So along came Joe, who spoke very good English in a lovely sing-song accent. He was brilliant. He ripped out the mess left by Abed and, within two days we had our bathroom. A hot bath and shower! A toilet that flushed without using two buckets of water! It was heaven.

Life's a Gas - T Rex

The last trip was to the Republic of Ireland which was great fun. It was just after we'd moved to the new house and we wanted to escape the mess while it was ripped apart.

Jordan lent us his big, comfy Peugeot which was great on fuel, and we drove to Wales to catch the ferry across to Dublin. We got lost twice in the city's one-way system, and then we set off to Waterford.

We stopped to eat at a café on the way. It was clean and smelt ok, and Shouty Husband ordered cottage pie as he wanted a proper cooked meal.

He wasn't happy at paying the equivalent of £18 for two ready meals and two coffees. I began to worry we were going to run out of money if that was the cost of food – and bad food, at that.

We finally got to Waterford at 6pm that Saturday night to find it was shut. We did find a McDonald's and I went gratefully to the loo – after all, you never know when there'll be another clean one. Sadly, this one wasn't it – it was dirty.

When we got back to the car, Shouty Husband said Ireland was an expensive shithole, so we were going north of the border instead. Back we went along the boring roads and reached Newcastle at around 11pm. There were no lights on in any of the B&Bs, so we slept in the car next to what we thought were public toilets. I'd never done that before and I never will again – it wasn't comfy, to put it mildly.

When we woke up at 6am, we found the toilets were in fact the local sewage building. First stop, then – a fuel station with toilets. Finally, after brushing our teeth and having a wipe-down with some baby wipes, off we went.

Your Song - Elton John

Sunday in Northern Ireland. At Nutts Corner we found a car boot sale, bacon sandwiches and coffee. Shouty Husband spotted a Celtic throw in orange that he loved and said would look great on the wall. Unfortunately, two women were using it to cover their sales table, but he turned on the charm and they agreed to sell it to him.

Then we headed up to Antrim, right at the top of Northern Ireland. Sadly, it was shut, so we headed for Coleraine instead. At around 4pm I spotted a bed and breakfast with a sign indicating vacancies, and that's how we met Stan and Margaret.

They were lovely and said there was a room with an en suite or, for £20 less, a room with the bathroom opposite. Shouty Husband went for the cheap option as it was only for one night, or so we thought.

The only other resident was Michael the German, who was also there for one night. He and Shouty Husband got chatting over a beer, and we invited him to walk into Coleraine with us to find food.

Michael was on a walking holiday, travelling all over the north, and was fun to talk to. We stopped at a Wetherspoons, but Shouty Husband refused to eat when he saw Michael's food. I was hungry though, so I had a plate of chips.

Shouty Husband and Michael got stuck into some great whiskey, and a very good night was had by all.

Breakfast the next morning was huge and delicious, and Shouty Husband asked if we could stay for the week just for that.

Michael was moving on to a youth hostel in Bushmills, so we arranged to meet him later in the afternoon.

In the meantime, we decided to explore Coleraine. It was a good half-hour walk, but a nice route along the river. We found some houses of the same design as our new home and stood and watched a cormorant; it was a good day.

Coleraine proved to be a biggish market town with lots of shops. After wandering around in the sunshine, we went hunting for food. Luckily, in the daytime, there was plenty of choice.

We found the Big O café - it was full, which is always a good sign, so in we went. Shouty Husband clocked what everybody was eating, and the homemade shepherd's pie looked amazing. We ordered one each, piping hot with veg and gravy. It was delicious.

While the pie was home-cooked, though, the gravy was instant. There was celery in the gravy, which always gives Shouty Husband a bad reaction.

He had three mouthfuls and then pushed it away. The waitress rushed over, and he explained what was wrong. She took his dinner away with saying a word and returned with a dry dinner, with bread and butter. Smiling, she said there'd be no charge for the first one.

When we left, people were queuing outside to get in. – the food was that good. We wandered off, Shouty Husband feeling well fed and happy.

Goodbye My Love - The Glitter Band

Next up was a drive over to Bushmills to see the distillery. That had too many steps for Shouty Husband, so we had a walk around the town instead. Shouty husband found a bookshop and bought a small map of Ireland; this was before the world had sat navs.

We met up with Michael and went to the pub. Legally, Shouty Husband couldn't drive after even one pint, so we avoided the tourist areas and went to a small, backstreet place instead. We sat out in the sunshine so Shouty Husband and Michael could pore over the map.

Michael wanted to get the bus to the back end of nowhere to see some monolithic burial stones. Shouty Husband liked this idea and told Michael that if he fancied it, we'd go, and he could come with us for the ride.

Michael was good company, and we enjoyed the stones. Shouty Husband offered to take him to the famous Carrick-a-Rede rope bridge; not something for me, as I hate heights. I sat in the sun with my book and a glass of Coke while Shouty Husband and Michael went to play pool. The landlady came out for a cigarette and tried to speak to me in very bad German. I asked her why, as I was English; she explained she'd heard Michael's accent, that Shouty Husband was blond and they were looking at a map, so she thought we were all German.

I laughed, explained that Shouty Husband was an Irish-Welsh mix, and we had a good chat about life the universe and everything.

She's a Rainbow - The Rolling Stones

The following morning, we picked up Michael and off we went to do the coast road and the rope bridge.

We found the castle that was in the guidebook, but it had fallen into the sea; instead, there was just a notice board to say it had been there. Have to love the Irish sense of humour!

Then Shouty Husband took us to Downpatrick. We had a really good lunch in the pub we'd been to before, then off to St Patrick's Mount. This is a big hill that looks out over Strangford Lough. It's a gentle walk to the top, with lots of shrines to the Virgin Mary on the way, and a huge statue of St Patrick at the summit.

Michael loved it and took lots of pictures; he hadn't known it was there, and he was a keen – and skilled – photographer.

Another lovely day, and something else ticked off our list. The next day, we planned to go and see the monolithic burial stones.

A Day in the Life - The Beatles

The sun held out for us for yet another day. Michael sat in
the front seat with his map, as he was worried, we'd get
lost. Shouty Husband bought a disposable barbecue, and
we found a rare breed butcher who sold us burgers and
sausages. We also got some buns and Special Brew lager
for Shouty Husband, and we'd taken a flask of hot water
and the makings for a cup of tea. The monolithic burial
stones, laid for a chief, were in the middle of nowhere and
were at least 2500 years old. The view over County Down
was simply stunning.

Shouty Husband cooked for us, and we offered a cup of
tea to two old ladies who were out for a five-mile walk.
They'd come prepared with their own flask, but they
stayed to chat for a while.

Michael took some lovely photos of me and Shouty
Husband. I still have them to this day, set into coasters, on
my dining room table.

On the drive back we found all the roads were blocked off
for road bike racing, so we sat and watched the big,
powerful motorbikes speeding by.

Michael trusted Shouty Husband to find his way back, even
though he had his map. We had the radio on – which really
isn't a Shouty Husband thing! – and you've not lived until
you have done Peatbog Faeries at full blast with Shouty

Husband and Michael singing along and tapping the dashboard. (I bought the album later; it was so good.)

We dropped Michael off at the hostel and said our goodbyes. He had tickets to a show in Belfast and was moving on the next morning.

We had a fun time with you, Michael from Frankfurt, and you are remembered fondly.

The next day was sunny so, since we were chancing our luck with the weather, we decided to visit Giant's Causeway. Well worth seeing if you ever get the chance.

We got the bus down, as it's a very steep hill to walk, and had a brilliant time. Shouty Husband sat on a ledge on the side of a cliff and let me take his photo – another one that's preserved in a coaster.

An American lady dressed in what looked like a gold tin foil jacket and trousers – it was Dolce & Gabbana, I asked! – looked at Shouty Husband and said he looked like Finn McColl. According to legend, he's the giant who made the causeway. Shouty Husband took the compliment – back then, he was still in good shape and had his long, blond hair.

We went off to find a beach, armed with our trusty disposable barbecue, but halfway down the road we found picnic tables with metal trays for cooking on. So, we stopped there instead, and I read my book while Shouty Husband cooked. Everybody who passed by in their cars stopped, said hi and told us the food smelled amazing.

It tasted great as well.

We never made it to the beach, but it was a brilliant day out.

Chapel of Love - The Dixie Cups

Next day was our last in Coleraine. Shouty Husband didn't want to drive so we decided to get the train to Londonderry, or Derry as he called it.

The heavens opened on the way to the train station, but rain is soft, and skin is waterproof, so we carried on regardless.

A lady on the train told Shouty Husband all the places we should see in Derry. I do love a great church and there are three huge ones in Derry. The Catholic church was right next to a pub, so Shouty Husband went in there while I went to look round.

I walked into the wedding of Michaela and Eammon just as they were exchanging their vows. Talk about a rabbit in the headlight's moment!

I sat in a pew in the back and watched, then I looked around the beautiful church and lit a candle for those I wished to remember. I had no change for the candle box, but the priest let me off as it was a special day. I planned to escape the wedding party, but I did go to wish the bride luck and apologised for disturbing her wedding. In Ireland, though, it's considered good luck for a stranger to come to a wedding, and Michaela invited me to the reception.

However, I declined politely as I knew we had to travel back to Dublin in the morning to catch the ferry. Instead, I found Shouty Husband, and we walked around the town walls before enjoying a lovely meal. Potatoes were on every menu, which pleased him – he does love his potatoes.

The rain held off till we got back to Coleraine and then we got soaked walking back to the bed and breakfast.

Then He Kissed Me - The Crystals

Time for the journey back. We drove to County Tyrone the following day to look for crystal for me. Everything was beautiful but I didn't want to touch anything in case I broke it.

The young assistant was great, though – she said she was suffering with a hangover, but she got down everything I wanted to look at. I bought a pair of salt and pepper shakers and a key ring which still live in my china cabinet.

Since we had an afternoon to kill, we found a layby and broke out the disposable barbecue. There was a kids' Winnie the Pooh umbrella hanging in a nearby tree, which was handy as it started to rain. In between the showers, Shouty Husband built a fire with the innards of the barbecue in a broken piece of sewage pipe and cooked Irish stew from scratch. It took two hours, and it tasted wonderful.

There was a beaten-up looking farm cat keeping an eye on us from a safe distance, so when we'd finished, Shouty Husband threw over cubes of best steak for it to eat. That cat certainly ate well that day.

Then it was on to Dundalk to find a bed for the night, as our ferry left at nine the next morning. A cheap bed and breakfast, a glass of wine and a power shower later, and we were in bed.

Whiter Shade of Pale - Procol Harum

After booking ourselves in at the ferry port in Dublin, we went to the café to get a drink – coffee for me, tea for Shouty Husband. We trekked back to the car with them, and that's when Shouty Husband got angry because his tea was disgusting.

To be fair, it was – I tasted it. It tasted like dirty dishwater. (At least my coffee was good.) It had cost a lot, so back he went to complain, even though the metal stairs hurt his knees. I waited in the car.

He got his money back after a bit of an argument, and he had to board the ferry without a drink. The sea was choppy on the way back – lots of people were sick - and we were glad to disembark at the other side.

The sun was shining in Wales, so we finished off our trip by taking the scenic route home through the Brecon Beacons. It was the perfect end to a wonderful holiday that still brings a smile to my face when I remember it.

Run Run Run - Jo Jo Gunne

The time came for my decorator, Andy, to come and turn our house into a home. If we were going to do it, we were going to do it properly – and the less said about the better.

We'd already got the wallpaper for the ceilings but hadn't found any we liked for either the living room, hall, stairs, landing or dining room.

Andy told us to go and look at a shop he knew of where he could get trade prices, so off we went. Shouty Husband was like a kid in a sweet shop; he's always had good taste and picked the most expensive paper in the shop (£32 a roll!) for the dining room. The living room wasn't much lower - £28 a roll. Still, we could afford it.

Andy loved the dining room wallpaper as it went on so easily, but he did warn us the cats would love it as well – it was textured and perfect for scratching. He was right.

The last big push was the carpeting, which was done by some Polish guys – more members for our own United Nations.

We were nearly there! We made one more mad shopping trip for curtains and bits like crockery, cutlery, and saucepans...and breathe. We were done.

The last workman left the week before Christmas, after nine months of hell. But we'd made it through – hurrah!

David came for Christmas, and we could make a warm, comfortable home for Luke. Yes, we'd spent everything we had – but it was worth every penny.

This was our fresh start. A lovely home in a great area with wonderful neighbours. No mortgage, no debt, no worrying that we couldn't afford the urgent repairs that needed doing.

We could reinvent ourselves as a nice, normal family – which is what we were, as far as the neighbours were concerned. But as the saying goes – nobody knows what goes on behind closed doors…

The next visitor to the home for waifs and strays was Steve 'the Fish-Face Haddock' Craddock.

Shouty Husband was putting up a fence in the garden and Steve offered to help. Unfortunately, he's not good on his feet due to a bad motorbike accident and he fell over. He thought he'd just sprained his ankle badly, but a couple of days later he had a doctor's appointment and couldn't walk the ten minutes to the surgery, so I took him. He told the doctor about his foot and was sent to A&E, where an X-ray showed he'd got a fracture. They plastered him up and he came to stay with us, since he lived on his own and wouldn't be able to manage. My mum took him to all his fracture clinic appointments, and he stayed until he got his walking plaster on two weeks later and could go home. At least he ate meat.

Eye in the Sky - The Alan Parsons Project

Steve, the handyman who's done work for my parents over the years, came to look at our horrible windows. The patio doors were going too – Shouty Husband wanted French doors.

New windows and the doors were ordered, and everything was going well until Steve hit the French doors with a rubber mallet (which he'd meant to do) and one of them cracked. Oops. That was his profit gone.

Shouty Husband needed a room to hide in where he could play the stereo. At first it was in the dining room, but our elderly neighbour had tinnitus. One night, we didn't even have the music on loud when he knocked on the door almost in tears and said he was being deafened.

Shouty Husband invited him in and said we'd turned it down, but when the neighbour took him round to his house, he realised the noise was amplified due to how the joists ran through the living room.

Unless the neighbour was out, then – no stereo on in the dining room. Shouty Husband lived for his music, so the chill room was moved up the priority list. We decided the garage, which ran the length of the house, could be split in two – the chill room for Shouty Husband and a utility room for me. More work to be done on The House That Bodge Built, as we'd christened it.

The utility room stud wall was easy enough to put up, but the area that would be the chill room had tongue-and-groove panelling that had to come out. As Steve was ripping it down, we heard a shout – behind it, he'd discovered a mop, some super-sized slugs and a roll of asbestos. You could have knocked us all down with a feather. Asbestos! Bugger!

After some frantic phone calls to the council, we learned that if it was well wrapped and taped up, we could take it to the main recycling centre where there was a special skip. So, we all put on throwaway boiler suits, heavy duty gloves and masks, bagged and sealed the roll, and off it went. And that was the end of the asbestos, happily.

Slowly, slowly we got there. We plastered and painted and eventually all it needed was furniture.

Car boots and charity shops yielded a coffee table and a storage unit, and then Paula decided she wanted to redecorate her living and dining rooms. This included a new sofa, so she gave her old one to Shouty Husband. He loved it – it was very comfortable, and long enough for him to sleep on.

A few pictures on the walls, the stereo in and a cheap carpet down - the chill room came into being.

Love Me Two Times - The Doors

The reality of life with Shouty Husband hit home when his boss at the council, who'd kept him in work for five years, retired. The contract he worked underwent to a private company, and Shouty Husband was back on his arse and hunting for work.

The sofa from my sister-in-law had cost us £80. You'd think she'd have given it to us as we were family but no, she wanted her money. We were broke – and now Shouty Husband wasn't making any money.

When you're desperate, most of us would take whatever was going – but not Shouty Husband. He was funny who he worked for and turned down more work than he took. It meant I had to apply for tax credits, a total nightmare that caused more problems than it solved, but I did have this annoying habit of wanting to eat and Shouty Husband needed his beer, dope, fags and the heating on full blast.

The good news was this meant I could claim a grant to insulate the house. It bought rolls of loft insulation, which Jordan laid, and we got the walls filled with foam, supposedly all the way up to the roofline. The workmen gave us a twenty-five-year guarantee for that, which I assumed wasn't worth the paper it was written on; sometimes, it's good to be proved wrong.

Wherever I've lived, I've always made sure the heating was insured. It means the boiler gets serviced each year and, if something goes wrong, someone comes out to look at it the same day. If the service is due and someone's in the area, they tend to call and see if they can come round.

That's what happened on Easter Sunday, when my parents were over for lunch.

The boiler at that time was behind the fire, which was gold with curly bits. It was horrible and we rarely used it. The gasman took the fire out and gave a sharp intake of breath. I hate it when people do that – it usually means it's going to cost you.

The boiler was on its way out, apparently, and as it was so old, it wouldn't be covered by the insurance if it went wrong. I started to panic; we had no money to replace it and we still owed for the windows and the chill room.

My parents overheard what was happening, bless them, and offered to pay for it as a gift. So, two days later, with very little mess, we had a nice new combi boiler in the airing cupboard. Hot water whenever we wanted without having to use a timer.

Shouty Husband happened to be home while this was being done and mentioned to the workmen that our walls had cavity insulation. Well – the guys had to drill high up for the heating vent and discovered that it hadn't been done up to the roofline, as promised. I went to war. Armed with the guarantee, I called the company and explained what the gas men had told us. They didn't argue – within ten they arranged for a surveyor to come out. He agreed the job wasn't up to standard, so more men came and Shouty Husband watched to make sure the job was done properly. Not even a small skirmish was involved, which was a bit disappointing – but that house was insulated to within an inch of its life.

Telegraph Road - Dire Straits

The next big project Shouty Husband planned was doing something with the garden. In the one corner was a huge dirt mound with grass on top. surrounded by a wall That had to go, so Luke dug it all out for us.

Shouty Husband also got a shed, and then decided he wanted a veg patch and a lawn, which for him meant growing grass from seed.

The patio was uneven, but we were too skint to get it done properly. Instead, Shouty Husband drew what the garden would look like when we could afford it. There would be a decent patio, a rockery, a lawn and a veg patch. There'd be raised beds where the mound had been and in front of the veg patch.

As time passed, Shouty Husband talked about how he would turn it into the secret garden he'd always promised I would have one day.

My parents, bless them, gave us yet another gift and paid for us to get the garden done. Our elderly neighbour's grandson laid patios and gave us mates' rates, and my friend John built the raised beds. All the plants came from car boots, my dad and our neighbours. It came in under budget and we even had enough left to replace the back door that was falling to pieces.

I've got the secret garden I was promised now. It looks just like Shouty Husband's drawing; it's a wild haven for bees and insects, and I love it.

Too Hot to Handle - UFO

When he was in Shouty Husband's good books, Steve used to come over on Saturday afternoons and for Sunday lunch.

For his birthday once, I got him expensive vodka instead of cheap schnapps to go with his Red Bull. He drank too much and fell over, so he had to stay the night.

Shouty Husband was asleep by seven o'clock as normal and I was enjoying a bottle of wine and watching the telly. Steve was just coming round when my mobile rang; it was the police trying to find Mick's sister, as he had been run over by a car and had a badly broken ankle. We couldn't get to him as he wasn't in a local hospital, but I got in touch with his son and daughter.

On the Monday night, Shouty Husband took Mick's son, daughter, and me to visit. The doctor said Mick needed somewhere to stay; he couldn't go home as he lived in a caravan in a farmyard and couldn't put weight on his ankle after it had been pinned and plated.

So, we opened our doors again. Mick came to stay for two weeks and, as we had to work, was looked after brilliantly by Luke.

That was the end of the home for waifs and strays…but never say never!

Silver Machine - Hawkwind

As I've said before, Shouty Husband had some very well-paid jobs over the years. He was a great driver and would go the extra mile, and mostly he worked for a guy called Jeff at an agency.

If the agency work was slow, Shouty Husband would take a couple of days elsewhere as long as he knew the firm; no dodgy trucks for him. It's fair to say he vetoed far more than he accepted.

Then he was offered a couple of days that turned into two years on brilliant money.

After the first day, he came back and said the firm was looking to employ a driver, but he'd need a licence to operate a HIAB – the hydraulic grab crane on the back of some lorries. He'd always talked about doing his HIAB test – there were plenty of jobs available and he could make good money. He told me to work my magic and find out how much the course would cost.

So, magic worked. I found a test centre that offered a one-day course for £200, my mum lent us the money, and Shouty Husband was on his way. He didn't learn much – it was the kind of course where the only way to fail was if you didn't turn up – but he got the magic licence. The firm agreed to take him on for three months, and Shouty Husband promised Jeff he'd go back to him when, not if, it ended. A bit like learning to drive properly after you've passed your test, Shouty Husband then learnt how to operate the HIAB by doing it every day, delivering insulation to houses and building sites.

Jordan and his wife-to-be, Laura, had bought a house – so we had an excuse for a road trip. Shouty Husband had promised Jordan, he'd buy him a good set of saucepans and knives for his first house. He knew where to get the knives from, and he found saucepans in Asda, so he was happy.

We drove the four hours to Jordan and Laura's house, which was out in the countryside. Shouty Husband said he'd take us all out for lunch and Jordan booked a pub nearby. Once we arrived, he told us he'd invited his in-laws-to-be, as we'd never met. Shouty Husband wasn't pleased as he'd wanted it to be just us, but he gritted his teeth and put on the happy face.

. He handed over the gifts, and Jordan opened the saucepans that were supposedly brand new. The box was taped up and, though the first three saucepans were fine, the last one had clearly been used and had food burnt on it. Shouty Husband was mortified – especially as this happened in front of the in-laws-to-be.

Shouty Husband said he'd sort it out, and we all went out for lunch. The pub Jordan had picked was empty and smelled strongly of old fish. Shouty Husband immediately refused to eat there; Jordan was embarrassed, but he was adamant.

Laura's parents said there was a good pub that did decent food a few miles away, so off we went. It turned out to be an old coaching inn and the menu looked good, even if it was overpriced.

By this time, Shouty Husband was to wound up to eat so I left him to it. The rest of us ordered and the food really was wonderful. He'd offered to take us out to lunch, though, so he insisted on paying the bill and, £70 lighter, we went back to Jordan and Laura's for coffee before going home. The journey involved gnashing of on Shouty Husband's part over dirty saucepans and overpriced food.

He stormed down to Asda to return the saucepans, refusing a replacement and demanding his money back. The poor customer service assistance also offered him a £5 gift card for his trouble, and he exploded. I know he'd wanted the day to be perfect and it hadn't been, but it wasn't her fault. I mouthed a sorry to her as he walked away; one of many, many times I apologised to people on his behalf over the years.

He's never shopped in Asda since.

Proud Mary - Tina Turner

For my birthday and our wedding anniversary, Shouty Husband offered to take me to the Lake District. However, as Jordan had just got engaged, I wanted to spend some family time with my son and daughter-in-law-to-be.

For once I got my own way – though I should have listened to him. It turned out to be a complete disaster.

First off, he had toothache. The bottom tooth at the front of his mouth was loose and needed pulling, but he didn't have a dentist. Still, we enjoyed the scenic drive down...but then things went downhill.

We got to the pub we were staying in to find the photos we'd seen were nothing like the reality. The room we'd booked had looked huge – but in fact you'd struggle to swing a cat in it.

Then we went down to eat, to find the menu was full of food Shouty Husband couldn't eat – he needed something soft.

He asked if the chef could make him mashed potatoes with parsley sauce as a one-off but was told no – he could do sea bass, but not mash. So Shouty Husband proceeded to get drunk instead and I went without a meal. Next morning when breakfast came, there was undercooked bacon and cold baked beans. I'd have sent it back if I hadn't been so hungry. Shouty Husband hadn't eaten for twenty-four hours by now, so he was incredibly grumpy.

I Want to Break Free - Queen

Jordan was still unhappy with Shouty Husband's behaviour at our last visit, so he came up with an excuse when we called to arrange to see him and Laura.

Instead, we went into Norwich to have a look around and eat. We ordered sausages sandwiches to take away from a café and found somewhere to eat. The sandwiches turned out to contain one sausage that had been chopped up, so Shouty Husband went back to read them the riot act. The café staff argued but refunded him in the end, and we ended up getting bacon butties from a stall in the market.

After a wander round, we were heading back to the pub when we found a car boot to mooch round, and then we ended up in a lovely market town, Wyndham.

Wonder of wonders, we found even found a chippy that sold the elusive haddock! It would be a bit of a wait as it was fresh cooked to order, but that wasn't a problem – and it was worth it. It came with bread and fresh butter, and we sat in the sun and thoroughly enjoyed it.

As our plans with Jordan had gone astray and neither of us was happy with where we were staying, we decided to go home. Shouty Husband's loose tooth decided to drop into his lap halfway up the motorway, and he felt much better after that.

Later, Jordan called to say that he was willing to spend time with us now, so I told him we'd gone home.

The only reason we'd gone down there was to spend time with him and Laura for my birthday, so I felt very annoyed and let down. In the end I hung up on him, and I did stay cross with him for a while afterwards.

Wicked Game - Chris Isaak

The downside to Shouty Husband working for a company was that he had two bosses. One was lovely and 'got' him, but the other was so like him there was a huge clash of personalities.

Shouty Husband both loved and hated the job. There was a lot of stress, but the money made up for it. At least we were able to get lots done to the house.

As always when he's chasing money, eventually he burnt out. This manifests itself as flu-like symptoms but without the head cold, wobbly legs and a woolly head. His sleep pattern gets even worse, and he has to stay in bed for a couple of days.

Winter also knocks him sideways as he struggles to breathe in the cold. One Friday, he got home while I was still at work and texted me at my mums to say there was a real Christmas tree for us at his work and could I pick it up as it was just down the road. (You could have knocked me down with a feather at that – apart from cards, we never had anything Christmassy in the house.)

When I turned up at the yard, I went to the office and said I'd come to collect the Christmas tree. The nasty boss was there and gave me both barrels, saying Shouty Husband had let him down. I'd been at work all day and it was nothing to do with me anyway, but he still tore strips off me.

The nice boss was there too. He calmed things down and helped me get the tree into my car.

I knew Shouty Husband would be angry about his boss having a go at me – I was his property, after all, and shouldn't be disrespected. I was right – he was fuming, but he had the weekend to work out how he'd make the man suffer.

Shouty Husband started smoking tobacco when he was eight, and dope when he was thirteen. He's tried to quite numerous times, but in the end, he always goes back to the ciggies – roll-ups, Golden Virginia and Embassy No 1 are his drugs of choice.

He was never going to do it on willpower alone, so when nicotine patches came onto the market, he gave them a try. Unfortunately, he has sensitive skin, and the patches gave him a bad itchy rash. That was the end of those – he went back to smoking. Sometime later, his breathing was deteriorating, and he decided to try and quit again. This time, because he'd decided to quit, I had too as well.

We went to a smoking clinic in a small chemist's shop. Shouty Husband couldn't afford to take time off work, and this one opened in the evening. As the patches were no good, they offered Champix, a drug that helps you stop smoking by reducing cravings and helping with withdrawal. We gave it a go.

They do tell you about the potential side effects, which can be severe. The common ones are nausea, insomnia, and the urge to go to the toilet in the middle of the night. That last hit me the worst. For Shouty Husband, it was the mood swings. He's always been mercurial and his moods can change on a sixpence anyway, so a drug that altered his brain chemistry wasn't a good idea in retrospect. I wish I had known that before he started taking it.

Three months later, and he was out-of-the-ballpark aggressive – much worse than usual – with paranoia and mood swings mixed in. Add four cans of super-strength lager and dope to the mix, which he was taking every night, and you've got a truly horrendous cocktail.

I should add the upside of Champix – Shouty Husband started to hate the taste of the lager and it no longer gave him the same buzz. On one occasion we visited friends, and he asked if they had any beer in. There was a can of Banks's Bitter hiding at the back of a cupboard; piss water compared to his usual tipple, but he really enjoyed it! Then it was a case of finding a real ale that he liked – stopping drinking altogether wasn't an option. Eventually, Hobgoblin won. He was still downing four cans a night – and up to ten at the weekend – but it was 4.5% ABV now instead of 9.5%. Small mercies.

Looking back, it's frightening to think he drove a big lorry every day in this state. The standing joke was that it was a bad day when he had blood in his alcohol stream, and I don't think he'd been straight and sober for the past twenty years.

Anyway, back to Champix. It was prescription-only, which was a pain. We had to chase the doctors to issue one, send it to the smoking clinic, and then go down there each week to collect the drugs.

Shouty Husband hated going out again after he got home from work as it was; it meant he had to stay straight and sober, which put him an even worse mood than normal. Champix took that up a level to a whole new world of unbearable, especially when the mental health side effects kicked in.

Hell arrived one rainy Monday evening in June. Shouty Husband started banging doors open with the look of a man possessed. Books, photos and paperwork he'd kept for years were dragged out, along with all kinds of memorabilia and things I'd bought for his chill room – pictures, cuddly toys, interesting ornaments.

Then he built a bonfire on the patio and burnt the lot. The things he couldn't burn were covered in weed killer and put in the bin. Even things that were mine were destroyed. And neither Luke nor I dare stop him; he looked like a maniac, and we were too afraid.

His paranoia skyrocketed after that night. He'd feel I was being aggressive towards him just by being in the same room and I daren't open my mouth for fear of saying the wrong thing. I called his GP to tell him what was going on and seek help, but none was forthcoming. What could I do? Just grit my teeth and carry on.

After three weeks of Shouty Husband locking himself in his chill room as soon as he got home from work, he informed me he'd got a flat and was moving out. I really hadn't seen that coming and I was totally shocked. Daft as it sounds, I still loved him and didn't want to lose him. I knew it was the Champix talking, but I had no clue how to make him better and by now I was terrified of him and what he might do to me and Luke.

He told me what furniture he planned to take, and I agreed with all of it. He would move over the weekend –

he'd even paid the deposit and a month's rent up front. On the Saturday he was due to leave, I went to a local drop-in centre run by a mental health charity. An old friend came with me; she said I could have a chat with someone who was trained to listen. I needed to talk about my fears for Shouty Husband and what was going to happen. I didn't want my marriage to end, but I couldn't cope with him in the house as he was because I was petrified about what he might do – to me, to Luke, to our home. The listener asked how I felt about him leaving and I answered her honestly - I was glad.

Shouty Husband was still there when I got home, and he was smoking. He said he'd stopped taking the Champix, but he still intended to leave. He had a six-month contract on the flat, so I told him to go for that time, sort his head out and then, if he wanted too, he'd be more than welcome to come home. I still didn't want him to leave, but I understood why he felt he needed to.

He decided to stay with me.

Now I look back and wish he had gone; I wasn't the unreasonable one.

After a few beers and a spliff he was back to normal again, but he never tired of telling me the whole thing had been my fault.

Why - Annie Lennox

The stress of the Champix effects, his job, the bad boss and life, the universe and everything got too much for Shouty Husband. He developed chronic heartburn and had trouble swallowing and, when he finally went to the doctors after months of complaining, he was referred to an ear, nose and throat consultant.

We were sent to the hospital in Shouty Husband's hometown. They put in a tube that went up his nose and down his throat, gave him a barium drink and an X-ray, and it turned out he had a swollen uvula. That's the little fleshy hanging ball at the back of your throat.

Heavy-duty antacids and relaxation techniques were the order of the day to treat it. The consultant said if Shouty Husband continued drinking and smoking the way he did, he'd be at serious risk of a stroke, cancer and/or a heart attack.

Me and Bobby McGee - Janis Joplin

After two years, there were mutterings from head office about closing the yard and moving the whole operation to Birmingham.

For six months, Shouty Husband talked about whether or not he would commute; an hour each way, and that's if the gods were smiling. That would mean fifteen-hour days, which wouldn't help his stress levels. I knew the job was going to end, but not that this would be the start of the path that blew our world apart.

Shouty Husband had talked about getting another bike for years. We'd look at overpriced old bikes at a shop in Wolverhampton, and he'd say if he ever had the money to buy one it could live in the garage. It would mean he could do the journey to Birmingham and back more easily, he said. I thought it was just wishful thinking – silly me!

While I was out at work one day, he spent £3,500 on his first-ever brand-new bike. He financed it with a loan, organised through the bike shop, which would cost him £350 a month, and the first I knew of any of this was when the damn thing was delivered.

I was fuming. I still am. And in spite of all the things I have forgiven him for, this is the one I can't let go of. It was one of the straws that made the camel's back start to buckle. Two months later, Shouty Husband's employer did indeed close the yard and, you guessed it, he decided not to go to

Birmingham. So here we were – he was out of work, and we were broke with a huge bank loan hanging around our necks, all because he had to have a bike. My mum came to the rescue again, bless her, and offered to pay off the bike loan.

We could pay her back when he found another job. The bike was so poorly made it would have been rusty in six months if he'd kept it out the front, so it had to live in the chill room. He moaned like hell about having to share his space with the bike, so I decided to do something about it. My wonderful neighbour, Beryl, had a garage she only used for her tumble dryer. She was an old biker, and her husband also loved his bikes; he'd built a Norton Tiger motorbike in their third-floor flat in London. Beryl said they'd had great fun trying to get it down the stairs when it was finished.

I asked her very nicely if Shouty Husband could pay rent to keep his bike in her garage, and she laughed and said it would be rent-free as Shouty Husband would do little jobs for her. In the event, until Beryl died, and the house was sold, her garage became home to three of Shouty Husband's bikes.

Shouty Husband's mid-life crisis wasn't him catting around because of the seven-year-itch – it was that bloody bike and all that came after it.

Tell Laura I Love Her - Ricky Valance

One Christmas, Jordan told me he wanted to propose to Laura, his girlfriend, and asked what I thought. I said she was wonderful, and he was an idiot if he didn't, so he did. So, I would be mother of the groom, and I needed an outfit. It was easy, actually. Shouty Husband found half a dozen dresses on the House of Frazer website he thought I'd look good in, and then he took me shopping. He picked a beautiful dress – not a colour I'd have picked, it was royal blue with white splashes. But I looked good in it and anyway, any doubts I had were put to one side as Shouty Husband had spoken.

Shoes next. He picked some out that had a small heel with a peep toe. They weren't very comfortable, and I'd never have chosen them as I like my flats. (I did buy some flats too; I thought I could just wear the uncomfortable shoes for the actual wedding and the photographs.)

I wanted a hat, and I found one I loved in a charity shop. It was what Shouty Husband called 'a flying saucer hat'; it was a designer brand and would have cost a fortune new, and it was perfect for my outfit.

So, I was done, and Shouty Husband already had a suit. Now all we had to do was wait twelve months for the wedding day.

Songbird - Eva Cassidy

Shouty Husband spent the winter sitting in the house with the heating on, smoking, drinking and toking. He planned his day around the telly and playing patience and turned down any work the agency offered.

Meanwhile, I was earning 2p and a biscuit and robbing Peter to pay Paul. I applied again for tax credits and Luke, who was working, paid his board and gave me a bit extra if he'd had overtime.

Jordan and Laura's wedding was on my mind a lot. I had to find enough money for a two-night stay at the hotel and to buy a wedding present. My credit card gave me money back in the form of vouchers, so I saved them all up and my mum bought them from me. That was the hotel sorted. Now for the gift.

Jordan and Laura wanted money towards a great honeymoon, so I had a clear out and took a bunch of stuff I could live without to the pawn stop. It was a start.

Over the years, Shouty Husband had bought me jewellery I never really wore. I also had a stunning sapphire and diamond ring Mick had bought me thirty years earlier. There was a local, family-run jewellery shop that bought items to sell as preloved, rather than just for the gold weight. The ring from Mick fetched nearly as much as he'd paid for it and, with everything else, I made enough money to give Jordan and Laura a decent amount.

There were six of us going to the wedding, so Shouty Husband suggested hiring a minibus. He'd drive, and we could all travel together in comfort. My parents covered the cost and when the day arrived, off we went. It was a long journey, but the sun was shining when we arrived at Jordan's house in the late afternoon, and the forecast for the wedding was a hot one.

Jordan offered to barbecue for us in the garden; we all sat out and enjoyed the weather but Shouty Husband, who doesn't tolerate heat well, stayed in the kitchen and read his motorbike magazine.

Jordan commented that Shouty Husband wasn't being sociable, but to be honest he was always funny about joining in family events. He never felt part of the group, even though we always went the extra mile to make him comfortable.

Later we checked in at the hotel, where we had a huge room with a comfortable bed. The bath did have tiny flecks of black mould, which didn't please Shouty Husband, but it was otherwise fine.

We went into the room where the wedding would take place, and he picked out where we would sit. He was determined we'd be at the front and the Boys' Dad would sit behind us; he reasoned he'd raised the boys so deserved the best seat alongside me. Then we went exploring in the beautiful grounds so he could have a spliff and chill out.

When he wanted to be, Shouty Husband was the life and soul of the party. But this was a posh wedding with people he didn't know – it didn't bode well, and my anxiety was through the roof as I was terrified, he wouldn't get into the spirit of the day. I just wanted it to run perfectly.

We wandered into the village and Shouty Husband decided he was starving. The fish and chip was shut, so he made do with an egg sandwich from the garage. It would keep him going, along with the beer he had in the room; he'd come prepared as there was no way he'd pay hotel prices.

Truly Madly Deeply - Cascada

My day started at 4.30am because, as always, Shouty Husband was up at the crack of dawn. We planned to fill up at breakfast so we could last the day; with the wedding at 1pm followed by photographs, it would be early evening before we got to eat again.

After stuffing himself with a full English, Shouty Husband decided he wanted a pot of tea, not a cup, and kicked off at the waiter until he got his way.

By 11am, he'd started on the beer and spliffs while we waited in the sunshine for the rest of the guests. When Jordan arrived, I asked him if I would do; I never really had a reason to get dressed up, so I think he was amazed I scrubbed up so well.

When it was time for the wedding, Shouty Husband was stoned and on his way to being pissed. You'd never have known, though – he was exceptionally good at acting perfectly normal.

Shouty Husband, my parents and I sat on the front row with Luke, Amber and the Boys, Dad behind us. I don't think I've ever seen Shouty Husband so proud – he sat ramrod straight with a big grin on his face. As the happy couple exchanged vows, there wasn't a single dry eye on the front row.

Jordan had asked if I'd be a witness to the signing of the register, alongside Laura's mum, and that set me off again.

I can tell you the waterproof mascara didn't stand up to the job!

And then it was all done. We had a married son, a new daughter-in-law, and we couldn't be prouder. Now for the bun fight.

God Only Knows - The Beach Boys

The newlyweds went off for photographs and we found a shady spot on the terrace where we could wait while the photos were taken.

Shouty Husband went off to get beer from the free bar and I enjoyed a glass of Pimm's. My dad had the same, but he thought it was fruit punch. He was a bit blurred around the edges after the second glass and only then asked if it was alcoholic.

My anxiety levels were through the roof as we sat waiting for the meal. Shouty Husband had promised to be on his best behaviour, but I couldn't help being terrified he'd do something to spoil the day. I made sure he was with me the whole time, and if I went to the toilet then my mum kept an eye on him. He only interacted with one guest when I took my eye off him briefly – the girlfriend of one of Jordan's schoolfriends. Nothing untoward there that I could see; he was behaving beautifully.

The meal was fine, although Shouty Husband didn't eat. He had told Jordan he wouldn't and that it was a waste of money ordering for him, but an empty place would have looked worse. Apart from having a quiet word with the table magician for coming up quietly behind him, and sneaking out for a spliff before the speeches, he behaved himself.

I was nervous about the photos, too, as he hated having his picture taken. But again – he was fine, and we got some lovely shots. He pulled his hair band out and shook out his long, blond hair for the picture of the whole family and Laura's grandmother, who was Danish, shouted, 'Viking, Viking ' at the top of her voice. He preened as all eyes were on him.

After that, he said that as it was all over bar the shouting, he was going down to the chip shop. He was starving and said he'd fall over if he didn't eat soon. I breathed a sigh of relief as he walked away and looked forward to half an hour of peace and quiet.

We watched the cake being cut and the happy couple have their first dance, and then it was time for the barbecue and disco. We'd looked at the barbecue earlier in the day and Shouty Husband had already announced it needed a good clean and he wouldn't be eating cooked on it. We decided we'd had enough when the disco started, so I found Jordan and told him we were leaving the young ones to it and going to bed.

Breakfast the next morning was cold – my parents and I put up with it, but Shouty Husband caused a fuss and sent his back. By the time we picked up Luke and Amber, who were staying elsewhere, he was in a noticeably foul mood. The journey back was strained to say the least - but it had been a lovely wedding and he'd behaved himself. Or so we thought...

Poison - Alice Cooper

Off went Jordan and Laura on their honeymoon, leaving me to spend the summer holidays with Shouty Husband.

Then, with an email from Jordan, the proverbial shit hit the fan. It started off well enough, with tales from the honeymoon and letting me know we'd soon be able to view the wedding photos and pick which ones we wanted.

Then I got to the serpent's tooth.

Apparently, Shouty Husband had ruined the wedding with his bad behaviour, and if I wanted to see my son and daughter-in-law in future, it would have to be at my parents' house; they wouldn't come to mine as he would be there.

I was furious. How dare my child make me choose between my family and my husband?

Then came examples of this supposed bad behaviour. Apparently, Shouty Husband had upset other guests; he'd eaten his fish and chips on the terrace while complaining about the (lack of) cleanliness of the hotel's barbecue; he'd been loud and rude and totally spoiled the day.

I knew this couldn't be right. Between us, my mum and I had kept him under close watch all day. Then it dawned on me that someone had been dripping poison in Jordan's ear to make Shouty Husband look bad, and the only person who had anything to gain by doing so was the Boys' Dad.

He was jealous of the relationship between his sons and Shouty Husband, so he'd found a way to put the boot in!

Jordan got the full force of my wrath by return email. I told him it was a load of rubbish, and he should speak to his grandma for the true story.

In the event, Jordan did come to visit and he, Luke and Shouty Husband went into the chill room to sort things out. The boys explained they were unhappy about him buying a motorbike and putting us into debt, and also that he'd made no effort to find work for the past ten months. They also said they didn't like how he treated me. The conversation got very heated; Shouty Husband said he didn't have to justify himself to them or anybody else, and if he wanted to spend his money on a new bike, that was up to him.

Jordan pointed out that Shouty Husband should have talked to me first, to which he responded by doing what he did best and shouting. Jordan took the rant and then pointed out Shouty Husband's behaviour made him no better than his own stepfather. What would he have done, asked Jordan, if Shouty Husband had seen his own mother in the same position?

While Shouty Husband took that one on the chin, his relationship with the boys did suffer because of his arrogance. He did try to mend fences over the years, but I don't think Jordan ever really forgave him.

I was just glad it was kind of sorted out. I didn't want to have to choose between my boys and my husband – it was a rock or a hard place, and whichever way I jumped would have been wrong.

Rob's two daughters didn't go to school, even though they were of an age for it, due to his dislike of the system. That meant Shouty Husband had three children making noise next door all day.

They had a huge trampoline in the garden, and the noise of the girls bouncing on it drove him mad. It meant he had to have the French doors shut, which really annoyed him.

At least every morning his wife – we assumed they were married – took them to her mum's, so Shouty Husband got some quiet time. It didn't last, though.

Both Shouty Husband and Rob had booming voices. Unfortunately, Rob was a night owl and Shouty Husband never slept well, so that was a recipe for disaster.

We never did discover what Rob was doing on the phone in the middle of the night, but he did it in the wee small hours. He was also emotionally abusive towards his partner and woke us all up shouting at her. I'll give her, her due, she stood up for herself and shouted back – even if it was 3am. Then, of course, that woke the children up and bedlam ensued. Meanwhile, Luke and I were desperate for sleep as we had work in the morning.

If Shouty Husband spent any time in the garden in the afternoons or had the French doors open while he listened to music or the television, the girls were told to play on the trampoline. Then, as soon as he went inside or closed the doors, they'd go in too.

Shouty Husband bided his time. He worked out that Rob slept all day in the back bedroom so, at 10am each day – don't want to upset our other neighbours – he'd fire up his noisiest power tools. The angle grinder in particular would set my teeth on edge. He'd play with them on the patio right under the bedroom window for a least three hours – there was no way Rob would be able to sleep through that.

Dream On - Aerosmith

Rob decided to play Shouty Husband at his own game. He had a very friendly Staffie bitch called Scarlett who used to run around the garden. She wasn't a barker, which we were glad about, and his girls loved her.

One hot summer day, the whole family went out leaving Scarlett in the garden on a very short chain with no shade or water. The poor dog was never tied up usually, so she howled and cried all day.

Luke wanted to climb over the fence to give her some water, but Shouty Husband said no; Rob would have reported him to the police for trespassing. Instead, Shouty Husband sprayed the hose pipe over the fence and drenched their patio, so at least Scarlett could have a drink.

Leaving the dog outside like that totally backfired on Rob. Scarlett's howls could be heard across the estate, so people came to find out where the noise was coming from.

Shouty Husband made sure everybody was given the landlord's phone number so they could complain directly and even the RSPCA was called out.

The family got back at 7pm, by which time the neighbours were ready to lynch Rob. Soon after that, when the landlord said the neighbours were complaining, Scarlett disappeared, we never knew what happened to her.

After this, it was stalemate. The girls were still let loose on the trampoline when Shouty Husband was out, and the noise at night calmed down.

This was also when Shouty Husband decided he wanted a project to keep him going. A job, perhaps? No. A pushbike. And not just any pushbike – an expensive one.

I never should have signed him up for a credit card. He spent £150 on what was admittedly a beautiful bike to go with the expensive motorbike he never used because he couldn't afford the fuel.

It had fancy gears and a lightweight frame. Shouty Husband spent the whole summer fiddling with it to get it just right for him to ride, dragging me round bike shops to spend more money we didn't have on better tyres and parts.

Once, when he was in his usual Sunday afternoon mood after enjoying beer and dope, he decided to go out for a ride on his new pride and joy.

It was the one and only time he ever rode that bike. He hit gravel, slammed on the brakes, and fell off it, badly grazing his hands and ripping his jeans.

All that time, effort and money, and he gave the bike to Mick, who is a serious cyclist. In return, Shouty Husband got a fancy telly. We could have made around £1,000 if he'd just stripped the bike down and sold the parts separately, but instead Mick got the benefit.

Meanwhile, the war with the neighbours continued quietly and then I went back to work, so happily missed a lot of it.

Speed King - Deep Purple

Winter came – my second with Shouty Husband. I'd been panicking about the heating bill, as he liked the house to be warm, but next door must have had theirs on 24/7. Our house stayed toasty, and the bill wasn't too bad.

One Saturday morning, Luke was helping me remake the bed when we heard Rob start shouting at his missus again. He hated the area and wanted to move back to Birmingham, but the language he used to say so was very offensive. I'd reached the end of my tether and yelled through the wall, 'If you don't like it, why don't you just fuck off and move out? '

Shouty Husband heard me and thought I was shouting at Luke. When I went downstairs, I had to explain I wasn't going off on one at Luke, but at next door.

You Ain't Seen Nothin' Yet - Bachman-Turner Overdrive

Seventeen months after it seemed Shouty Husband had given up on ever working again, along came a job. His sister, Paula, was cleaning for a company that sold everything piggy to shops and butchers, from slaughter to the finished product.

She wangled him an interview and he was back in paid work. It was never going to last, though. Every Sunday night we had to do the paperwork for the following week. It was a nightmare – sometimes, there were different names for the same product, and I'm the company's systems came from the Dark Ages. Every Sunday we'd struggle to make sense of the order system for hours, but I guess at least we had money coming in for a few months and could pay off some of our debts.

The Village Green Preservation Society - The Kinks

All our immediate neighbours were elderly, and Shouty Husband used to say we lived in God's waiting room. He'd help them however he could; they liked him and would stop and chat if he was doing the front garden.

There was a standing joke that he had a fancy woman as Jane, who was of a certain age, walked her sausage dog past our house regularly and would always stop to talk – unless I came out, and then she'd quickly leave, dragging her poor dog behind her.

We got notice that the water board intended to dig up the pavements, one side at a time. It meant our drive would be blocked and there was no space on the road to park my car. This displeased Shouty Husband, who said my car would not be parked anywhere he couldn't see it; he promised me it would go on the drive.

All was normal when I went to work, but on my return, there was a huge hole in front of our drive with a mound of dirt beside it.

All our elderly male neighbours were standing out the front, gossiping about the mess. Arvan, who lived directly opposite, offered me his drive to park on. I looked at the mess, shook my head, and said Shouty Husband was not going to be happy. He could drive the car over the hole, but not with the pile of earth there. Arvan gave my shoulder a squeeze and told me it was going to be ok. I knew it wasn't.

I rang Shouty husband to warn him, then I saw a workman and asked if he could move the dirt so we could use the drive. He laughed and walked away. Our neighbour Julie's drive was also blocked so she asked him the same question – and got the same response.

While the old men talked about complaining to the local MP, I was waiting for Shouty Husband. He came round the corner with a face like thunder, got off his bike and had a word with the workman. Getting nowhere, he went in search of the supervisor.

Everybody thought he'd go off on one, but instead he rang the head office. Within ten minutes, the dirt had been moved. Julie was spitting feathers – she hated having to park in the shop car park, but she hated Shouty Husband getting his own way more.

Shouty Husband drove over the hole and onto our drive to prove it could be done. After that, we borrowed a board we'd spotted outside the nearby hotel that was due to be redeveloped. Every night, we'd cover the hole with the board so we could drive in and out easily. Every morning, we'd pull up the board and put it at the bottom of the drive out of the way.

It took a week for our side of the road to be finished, and then we gave the board to Arvan to cover the hole outside his drive. We'd planned to return the board once it was all done, but the workmen took it away with them.

Baby I Love Your Way - Big Mountain

The only time I was allowed to do something for the neighbours was the time we had to deal the pub.

It had been there for ever and the houses had been built round it. It was a quiet place that never caused any problems for the residents. And then it was sold.

If a venue wants to make any changes to its licence, the details are published in the local newspaper. The pub's new owners wanted to extend their opening hours to 2am and be permitted to play music to 1am every weekend. The neighbourhood was up in arms. Nobody wanted the noise and drunks going past our houses in the wee small hours. We had to do something. Shouty Husband told me to email the Council, to object. Then our parish councillor had leaflets printed and I went round all the houses on our estate to deliver them along with Ceris, a neighbour. I even posted on our local Facebook group to warn other areas what was going on.

The landlady took offence at our protests and got quite aggressive on Facebook. She agreed to meet some of the residents to try and find a solution, but it didn't go well.

In the end, there were ninety-seven complaints – the highest amount ever for this kind of application – and the licence changes were refused. The pub would have to operate under the existing terms, and our neighbourhood would stay as peaceful as ever.

We had won. Shouty Husband praised my efforts and made sure all the neighbours knew what I'd done; previously, they'd only known him and the things he did for them but now they knew me too. But the best bit was knowing I'd made him happy, and I basked in his admiration.

School's Out - Alice Cooper

I'd done voluntary work in a primary school, so I thought expanding my skill set by doing a teaching assistants' course and an advanced computing course was a good way to go. So back to college I went, and I loved it.

Part of the course was to look for jobs in schools and apply for a voluntary placement. A nearby secondary school was advertising for a cover supervisor, which fit the bill – it was within walking distance from my house and school hours meant it would fit around Shouty Husband.

The new headmaster was open to staff with life experience as well as paper qualifications, so I was invited in to teach a lesson under observation, followed by an interview. I didn't get that job, but the assistant head told me to reapply for an upcoming teaching assistant' role. The boys made sure I did and at 7.30pm on the day I had the interview, the head called to tell me I was in. At the time, I was dancing naked around the living room in my old house to the Rolling Stones, along with Shouty Husband. It's funny what sticks in the head.

For the next ten years I worked with students from economically and socially deprived backgrounds. It was a real eye opener, but I loved it. Yes, it was stressful and yes, the threat of violence was ever-present. I soon learnt to duck when the chairs were thrown around. Aside from that, the only real problem was in March, when we found out how many new students would be coming. If there weren't enough, there would be redundances. So, for a couple of months each year, I wouldn't know if I had a job to go back to in September.

Each time, I'd panic and really needed Shouty Husband to listen to my fears and tell me it would be ok. But that wasn't him, of course. He'd boast to anyone who would listen about my great job making a difference to teenagers' lives, but there was never any moral support when I needed it.

During my time at that school, we switched to academy status and its name changed. I worked under three different headteachers, but in the end we were told we were coming under the government's schools rebuilding scheme. To be honest, we didn't believe they would rebuild us – we thought they'd just close the school and sell the land to a developer for housing. But no – they did, and that was the year everything came to an end.

The school was a 1960s' build. It looked like a concrete cube and, depending on whereabouts you were, you either froze or boiled. The windows rattled in their frames and let the cold in, the roof leaked, and some days we couldn't use the white boards as water would run down the walls and into the plug sockets. I loved my students, but the stress, the work and Shouty Husband were pushing me to the end of my tether.

Then, at Christmas, Jordan and Laura came to visit. They handed me my present, which was a book about how to be a grandparent. It took a minute for the penny to drop, then I realised - I was going to be Grannie Annie.

I'd intended to move to the new school when it opened in September after the rebuild. Then, as it was badly in debt, it was sold to a company that bought bad schools and ran them as businesses. We were one of three they were taking on.

I went to every meeting about the changeover and did not like what I heard. There'd be no more pastoral care sessions, when I'd spend time with my students and listen to them about what was making them unhappy. Instead, we were being turned into an exam factory. Even my very low ability students would be expected to get the magic five GCSEs at grade C or above; if they didn't, my job was on the line. My permanent contract would be replaced by a twelve-month rolling agreement so that this could happen.

My students were never going to pass exams. I knew that and so did they. This was far worse than the annual March worry about redundancy. This was my career and my life. I tried to talk to Shouty Husband but, as usual, he pooh-poohed my fears and told me to just do whatever made me happy.

I found I was also expected to reapply for my job – the one I'd done well for ten years – and attend a panel interview with people who didn't know me and didn't know the needs of my students. I was burnt out from the stress, and I couldn't face any more, so I decided to take the money and run. I needed to take some time out and decide what I wanted to do for the rest of my working life. Maybe it would be something different – a change is as good as a rest, as they say.

I was going to be a grandma, and that had changed how I saw the world. So, I applied for redundancy and was accepted, along with forty other members of staff walked with me.

Oh, the freedom of no responsibilities for the next year! After the summer exams I had no students, so I helped to pack up the science rooms. I was the Queen of Bubble Wrap and had great fun helping the science technician wrap up forty years' worth of equipment.

Next was the archive room, where every student's files were kept for ten years before being destroyed. Sorting that out every year was my summer job; this time, I had to empty the filing cabinets into boxes ready for the big move. I was in my element, tucked away in a small room with plenty to organise as my iPod played in the background. I had time to think about what I'd do after the summer; I'd be paid until September, but then I needed to find a job.

A week before the gates closed for the final time, I attended my last full school assembly. All the staff who were leaving were called up and given a school badge and mug.

Then a few days later came the 'so long, it's been fun' party. It also turned out to be the day my granddaughter was born. I said goodbye to my old life and walked away with my head held high, feeling very happy about my future as Grannie Annie.

I had no idea what I was going to do next, but for now I was free.

Dirty Work - Steely Dan

My decade of blood, sweat and lots of tears resulted in a redundancy package of just over £5000. Around half of it - £2,500 – went to Shouty Husband for a new bike, and the rest was for redecorating the living room and Luke's room, as he had moved out. The side of the house needed pointing, so my money would cover that too.

After asking around, a guy called Mark came and had a look at the pointing. His quote wasn't extortionate, so we gave him the nod and Shouty Husband told him that if he did a good job, we'd ask him to do the living room too.

Mark spent a Saturday on the pointing and made a good job of it, so we booked him to remove the horrible stone fireplace and side shelves in the living room and knock out the 1970s' stone cladding under the stairs.

I ordered a skip and acted as gofer, carrying out buckets of rubble while Mark bashed away with his big hammer. He took the fire out, too, which was no loss – we never used it. The hole would be filled in and covered over.

The old owners had taken out the living room wall to make it bigger they'd had a rigid steel joist fitted across the ceiling which bolted onto another rigid steel joist by the living room door. These bars held up the ceilings, so they were important, and Mark was very careful when he started to remove the cladding. He'd got the top third off when he went white and called Shouty Husband. The joists were supposed to be bolted together to stop movement and provide a solid join. Instead, it turned out a small wedge of wood had been inserted to stop the joists moving. Yep. The whole house was being held up by a piece of wood. The House That Bodge Built just kept on giving.

Mark was very good and still pale, bolted the joists together while looking terrified. That was no surprise – after all, one false move and it would end in disaster. I felt bad as the job had ended up being far bigger than Mark had quoted for, but Shouty Husband did give him some extra money.

It took all weekend, and then it was time to strip the wallpaper. I enlisted the help of my mum – the oldest stripper in town – and we cracked on. Unfortunately, the house was built in the 1960s and the old plaster didn't like the wallpaper stripper we were using. Shouty Husband wasn't impressed, so we carried on the old-fashioned way, with a bucket of hot water and a sponge. As my mum was doing the lintel above the window in Luke's old room, a huge chunk of plaster fell down and nearly brained her. Shouty Husband went ballistic and told me it would all need to be replastered.

It took two weeks of hard work, but Mum and I stripped the wallpaper and lining paper off the living room, hall, stairs and landing, Luke's bedroom and the ceilings. I grew to hate the smell of wet wallpaper, and I was grateful to our neighbours who happily gave up their bins for me to cram in bags of the stuff.

Shouty Husband asked around at work to see if anybody knew a plasterer, and along came Ian. He was a bit strange, but we got to know each other well over the two weeks he spent making my house lovely again.

I lived without a space to call my own for nearly six weeks, Shouty Husband had his chill room, but all I had while I watched television was a hard floor and some cushions. I did have some fun before the new plaster was put on, though – I wrote all over the walls about my new granddaughter, Everly, and drew pictures.

While we were getting all this work done, Shouty Husband also had a loft ladder installed as he'd already discovered he couldn't fit through the hatch hole. Yes, he got stuck.

He decided that when the new plaster had dried properly, it would be painted white until we – and that's the royal 'we', in other words 'he' – decided what colour we wanted. (It's still white, by the way.) We had purple carpet again, and new curtains and lampshades. By the time it was all finished it did look fantastic. My money had been well spent and I was happy. I can't deny Shouty Husband had a great eye – he should have been an interior designer.

Heart of Gold - Neil Young

The only brand-new bike Shouty Husband ever owned was the Hyosung GTR250, and it was the beginning of the end for Shouty Husband and me!

As it was a sports bike, the pillion seat was very small. Not to put too fine a point on it, I have a big bum. I also struggled to get on as I am only little. I felt so vulnerable - I was high up, the riding position was uncomfortable, and so were the grab rails; my hands went numb within twenty minutes.

Shouty Husband never really wanted to take me on the back of it, and that suited me just fine. Then one of my students from school, who I'd worked with for three years, ended up in hospital and it looked like he wouldn't make it.

I got permission to visit and asked Shouty Husband if he'd take me as the hospital was in Birmingham and I couldn't face the drive. He agreed, but only if we went on the bike. I was too desperate to go to argue, so I walked onto the ward that Sunday morning in my full black leathers, looking like something out of Star Wars.

I found my student. He was ventilated and couldn't talk, but he was awake. I gave him the full twirl and he raised his eyebrows and rolled his eyes. It was so good to see him and spend time with him, and then it was time to go home on the back of that bloody bike. Shouty Husband decided to see how fast he could go down the motorway, so I hung on for grim death as he hit 94mph.

Although the Hyosung cost a fortune, it wasn't well built and eventually it died a death just like the rest. But Shouty Husband had been bitten by the bike bug, and I gave Shouty Husband a chunk out of my redundancy money to buy a new one.

He bought a Honda Deauville, which was big enough and comfortable enough for both of us to ride all the way down to see the new granddaughter.

Unfortunately, it went wrong big time and ended up back in the garage. They told Shouty Husband an expensive part needed to be replaced, so he stumped up for it – but the bike still wouldn't work. It turned out that the garage had forgotten to refit a fuse.

This bike had a back rest for me, but Shouty Husband hated me using it as he said it affected the handling. The truth was, he was struggling to hold up a heavy bike; he'd never admit that, though. Instead, he blamed the machinery and in the end, it had to go.

The Jack - AC/DC

Suddenly, it seemed every other advert on the telly was about personal protection insurance. Shouty Husband had taken out a policy with his mortgage; he knew at the time it wasn't worth the paper it was written on, but he signed up for it anyway as it meant he'd get the loan.

Now, it seemed he could make a claim for it being mis-sold. Lots of companies offered to help, but they wanted a hefty chunk of commission from any pay out, so he wouldn't use them. Instead, I 'did the Google', as my mum says, and found out all I needed to do was fill in a form and send it off.

Shouty Husband agreed, so I got on with it. There was a delay when I had to ask him for information I didn't have, and he told me he'd tell me when he was good and ready. It took six weeks before I felt he was in the right frame of mind for me to ask again.

Eventually I posted the form off. There were three follow-up phone calls asking for personal information, and I honestly thought he'd tell them to go away, but he didn't.

And then – lo and behold! A cheque arrived for nearly £3,000, and Shouty Husband was certainly happy with me then. We redecorated, got a new double-glazed kitchen door, and new carpets and curtains. He even bought me a new wardrobe.

It might have taken a while, but the house was in a much better state after we got that pay out – so it was worth all the hassle.

Well, what do you know? Just as my job was ending, Shouty Husband hit the motherlode and got a job! He'd had a call about doing a couple of days for a haulage company he'd worked for before and decided he was happy to go.

Then it transpired a couple of the drivers had been caught breaking the tachograph rules, which dictate how long they can drive without a break. Companies can be closed down if they don't follow the laws about drivers' hours, so they lost their jobs. Shouty Husband was in the right place at the right time and was offered a full-time permanent job.

He had to work three months for the agency that placed him before switching to being employed by the company, but them's the rules. So, until life and Shouty Husband's heart gave in, he had a permanent job that paid ok. Not enough – but then, for him, nothing ever would be.

Rock 'n' Roll Suicide - David Bowie

As soon as the summer holidays were over, I went job hunting. I was successful in my very first interview, and became a customer service assistant at the Co-op. That's a fancy title for a shop assistant.

Shouty Husband hated it as I had to work till 10pm at night and at weekends. He wanted me back in a school, but those roles were as rare as hens' teeth.

I applied for every teaching assistant post going. I did get four interviews but ultimately no offers, so I stayed where I was.

Then I turned fifty and decided to follow a lifelong dream.

Never Going Back Again - Fleetwood Mac

You already know that Sarah and Shouty Husband have a very distant relationship. She and Ed visited his old house once – and we weren't together at the time, so I was surprised when she called to ask me for directions – and they came to my old house for ten minutes on my wedding day. She also came to our forever home once, just to be nosy. Other than that, they only really spoke on the phone for birthdays and Christmas.

Then, for my fiftieth, I decided to have a bit of a do. I had invites made and was really looking forward to having both sides of the family together.

Sarah declined to come as she and Ed were going on holiday to see polar bears in Canada. That was a trip of a lifetime, and a great excuse not to come to my birthday.

I still sent her an invite so she wouldn't feel left out. Shouty Husband said she wouldn't have come even if they'd been here.

I had a fantastic fiftieth and looked forward to seeing the photos of Sarah's trip to Canada. And I did, and it turned out they did have an amazing time, but not until two years later.

My mum always says that, if you're going to lie, make sure you don't get caught out. Sarah and Ed hadn't been going away then at all.

Shouty Husband said it was him she was snubbing, not me, because she didn't want to see him happy with a family of his own.

I didn't care. I still took offence, and I never made the effort with her again.

Three Coins in the Fountain - Frank Sinatra

Ever since I was a little girl and my dad had talked about his holiday there, my lifelong wish had been to go to Rome. So, for my fiftieth, I went.

It would be a solo trip. Not only does Shouty Husband hate flying, but he also dislikes pasta, gets heat stroke, and doesn't do walking, culture, or history. He still managed to put a dampener on things by getting a chest infection while I was away, but luckily Luke looked after him for me. He still managed to keep control while I was away, though, insisting I only call when he wasn't watching a repeat of Star Trek or some other programme.

Still, I'd made it. There I was - a plump, middle-aged woman alone in Rome with a map. I got lost a lot and I had plenty of fun, doing all the tourist attractions and navigating the metro. There were many highlights, one of which was a trip to Pompeii, which was incredible.

I did miss having someone to talk to and share the experience with, however. On my last night, I went for an early dinner in a café not far from my hotel where the food was really good.

I was soon brought down to earth with a bump, though. Shouty Husband decided to punish me for daring to go away on my own, and I waited at the airport for two hours before he deigned to come and pick me up.

He showed no interest at all in how my trip had gone and wouldn't even look at the photos I'd taken. Never mind – I had my memories, and he couldn't spoil those.

Ain't Nothin' Goin' On But the Rent - Gwen Guthrie

The Co-op job wasn't what I wanted from life, but it wasn't too bad and at least it put food on the table.

But then my lovely lady boss got moved to another store, and replacement was what my mum calls a 'Co-op fusilier'; she was a true workaholic who lived and breathed the job, with no life outside it. Unfortunately, she expected her staff to feel the same way and I didn't.

Shortly after that, we learned our little shop was having a complete refit. That meant a month where, instead of being in the store and working thirty hours, I had to attend training sessions but only for my contracted twelve hours – so that meant a drop in income.

The new assistant manager was a tyrant and we all disliked her. The final straw came when we were restocking the shop and she told me to sweep the car park and put all the crap into a bin bag. I had a broom and a bin bag, but no gloves. I told her I wasn't happy doing that without them, as I knew we had rats; there was no way I was picking up litter with my bare hands when it could be carrying Weil's disease. She shouted at me, I shouted back, and we had a standoff. I started hunting for a new job the next day.

Shouty Husband has asthma and chronic obstructive pulmonary disease, or COPD. This has impacted our life together forever and the big, life-changing moment came four years ago when he got a chest infection.

This was a regular occurrence, but this time it was much worse than usual, and things looked grim. When Shouty Husband told me he needed a doctor, I knew it was serious. The doctor thought it might be sepsis, so an ambulance was called, and we were blue-lighted to hospital. Shouty Husband didn't even try to argue, a rarity in itself as he hates hospitals - he always comes out worse than when he went in.

As it turned out, he didn't have sepsis. He did, however, have a particularly severe chest infection that needed intravenous antibiotics and a nebuliser. That meant staying in but, as there were no free beds on the respiratory ward, he ended up on head and neck for a week.

He got all the nurses on side but really ripped into the consultant. Two men who both know they're the superior one will never end well. However, he did listen this time when he was advised to stop smoking. When he came home, he told me he'd really thought he was going to die, and we both had to quit.

I had my last cigarette at 10.20pm on Thursday, June 30th. I'd planned ahead and taken advice on using a vape, as cold turkey with Shouty Husband would never work.

After three months on antibiotics, he still wasn't getting any better and his employers were going mad about all the time off. He had no energy, so he was eating lots of high-calorie, sugary foods – that wasn't usual for him as he doesn't have a sweet tooth and he was visiting the doctor's every week.

Finally, he had his bloods done and we learned he was on the cusp of Type 2 diabetes. That really frightened him; the high-sugar foods went and, when his bloods came back normal, he was prescribed new antibiotics and medicines to help his breathing. He was also advised to get a nebuliser for home; I found one online and it really did come into its own when he was struggling to breathe.

And the fags? He only lasted three months before they crept back in.

Meanwhile, my job hunt continued. I applied for a post as a pharmacist's assistant – four hours a day, Monday to Friday, no evenings or weekends. I also applied to be a teaching assistant at a large, rural secondary school; I was sure they'd never take me on, but it had an excellent reputation and I figured nothing ventured, nothing gained.

I was offered the job at the pharmacy and accepted, and then was invited to interview for the teaching assistant role. I thought about not going, but then thought – what the hell, it's worth a try.

The interview took place on the last day of term. I was back home having a nap when the phone rang and, still dopey from sleep, I didn't realise I was being offered the job until the headmaster said my contract would be in the post. Hurrah! I was over the moon, Shouty Husband was over the moon, and sadly the pharmacy lost out on my services.

I gave my notice to the Co-op and had a couple of weeks off before resuming my career. (Three years on, I'm still there and I love it.)

Nothing Else Matters - Metallica

Shouty Husband became ill again, but this time it wasn't his chest. He kept getting stomach cramps that would have him doubled over with pain, and he said it felt like a pencil was being jammed into him just below his rib cage. The doctors sent him for ultrasounds and scans.

The pain suggested it might be gallstones, but Shouty Husband had always followed a low-fat diet due to heartburn and trouble with his stomach.

Then they sent him for a colonoscopy. You have to prep for this by drinking a vile-tasting drink that empties your gut. The second time Shouty Husband didn't get upstairs in time to go to the toilet, he decided to go to bed.

The following day I took him to the hospital for the procedure. They discovered three polyps and removed two, but the third was too big for the nurse to deal with and would need a consultant.

A few months later, he went through the prep again and was back in surgery. It went well, but he was told he had diverticulitis which meant he had to change his diet to high fibre. That, of course, didn't happen and life carried on as normal.

You Don't Own Me - Lesley Gore

The end was coming long before Shouty Husband left. Once, as I stood in a supermarket with him, I watched another man loudly and publicly berate his wife. It was like looking in a mirror.

I gave her a sympathetic look and mouthed, 'Are you ok? 'after her husband had walked away. She smiled at me, a defeated look on her face that I knew well from my own. For a moment, two strangers shared solidarity in a supermarket.

Shouty Husband hated anyone talking about illness and death, even if it affected family.

Christmas 2018 saw my mum awaiting tests for bladder cancer. Meanwhile, I had a bad cold that turned into a chest infection and knocked me over for five weeks. I could have done with some support, but I never told Shouty Husband about my fears for Mum. I couldn't deal with the mood that would follow.

I spent New Year's Eve in hospital with Mum while she had a barrage of tests, which luckily showed there was nothing amiss. She's in rude health for her age to this day.

All I wanted at that time was for Shouty Husband to hug me and tell me it was going to be all right, but I was unable to talk to him about what was going on. It was one of the worst times of my life – you'd think the person who supposedly loved me and would be there for me no matter what would give a damn.

It's hard to believe I never recognised it sooner, but life with Shouty Husband was all about control.

On a long journey, he wouldn't stop so I could use the loo until I was nearly wetting myself. Once, at a fuel station, he made me leave the queue for the ladies' because he'd decided he needed to use the gents. I developed exceptional bladder control.

If the phone rang and it was for me, I wasn't allowed to take the call in the dining room because he didn't like it. I'd have to go into the living room, and God forbid I talk for more than fifteen minutes. He'd stand in the doorway, glaring at me until I hung up, and if I ignored him and carried on, I'd get the silent treatment afterwards.

I got 'the glare' whenever I did something he thought was wrong – speaking too loudly, not fetching him his beer quickly enough, the most ridiculous things. If anybody was brave – or stupid - enough to stick up for me, I'd deflect his inevitable rage by saying it was okay, he wasn't that bad.

People ask me if I miss him, and that's a definite no, I don't. I don't miss the sinking feeling in the pit of my stomach every day, the shakes that even in the height of summer I put down to being cold. I suffered from extreme anxiety while I was with Shouty Husband, I know that now, and it took six months for it to leave. But now the pebble that lived in my throat is gone; I can go to sleep without wine helping me on my way; I've stopped taking my happy pills.

An added blessing is that I have not seen Shouty Husband since the day he left. It's been over eighteen months since I spoke to him. If I bumped into him on the street, would I be strong? Honestly, I can't say. But, right now, life isn't treating me too badly.

I know that if Shouty Husband hadn't left, I'd have stayed with him. I'd never have given up my home - too much blood, sweat and tears went into making a good life for my boys. But it took a very long time to realise I didn't have a life myself. We never had 'date night'; in fact, we rarely went out at night. I never had money in my purse, or money of my own – everything I earned became 'house money', and I had to justify needing any of it to him. His money? It was his own. After the bills were paid and he'd given me the housekeeping, the rest was his. There were months when he'd have a very healthy bank account while I had coppers in my purse.

Now he's gone, I can have my own opinions where previously I was only allowed them if they coincided with his. He'd tell me black was white and I'd agree, because it was easier that way. Sometimes I'd prove him wrong, but the fallout was never worth it.

Now, it's the little things that make me happy. Being able to eat kippers when I like, rather than on the rare occasions Shouty Husband would permit it because he hated the smell. How sad is it, that I was grateful when I was allowed kippers?

Or having an alarm clock that ticks, which I could never have because he hated a ticking clock. Moving furniture around to suit myself, buying new bedding that I love, wearing a lot of red because I know it suits me.

I've redone the garden to my taste, and I love it. I wear shea butter hand cream because I love the smell of it, and he always hated it. (I did use it while he was here, it was my little bit of defiance, but it wasn't easy.)

Now, it's my life and I'm living it my way. I am the Purple-haired Warrior with Knobs On and I AM FREE!

A Woman Left Lonely - Janis Joplin

Recently, as he'd been living in his box in my dining room for the last two years, I decided to give my friend David a final resting place.

Luke dug a big hole in the garden and Steve came round. I made a memory box that included a couple of photos of David and I, and an elephant and a turtle to represent his love of Terry Pratchett's books. Then we planted him, marking the place with rosemary and lavender bushes — rosemary for remembrance and lavender for tranquillity.

Jordan bought me a garden ornament of a wizard reading a book for my birthday, which goes perfectly on David's final resting place.

When Shouty Husband's time comes, he'll go into my garden as well. I will be the better person and follow his wishes; a bit of him will go into the river, so he can see the world; a bit will go into the canal in his hometown; the rest will have a memorial in the garden.

He'll be stuck with me forever. These days I suspect that's his idea of hell — I rather enjoy that thought.

The Great Gig in the Sky, from Dark Side of the Moon - Pink Floyd

The voluptuous lady is tuning up for her appearance. Choosing the right song for her was hard, but I settled on The Great Gig in the Sky. It's one of my favourites, although Shouty Husband hated it; he could never cope with screeching. What have I learnt in the last two years since he left?

I realised I was on an extendable lead, allowed to run full pelt or be yanked back according to the whims of the person holding it. I've learnt to manage my anxiety levels. Now, if there's a problem, I walk away and take a deep breath before returning to sort it out. I'm no longer a shaking mess who overthinks it all.

The happy pills I used to take worked well – they made me feel numb. I liked that feeling for a long time but no more.

Can You See the Light - James Brown, the Blues Brothers

The storm clouds have been blown away and the light in my life is now bright and beautiful. When I wake up, my first thoughts are no longer about Shouty Husband.

I didn't realise I was living in fear. The fear of not living in the light of his love, the fear of pissing him off, the fear that I couldn't live up to his exacting standards, the fear of not being the best wife – all of these things. He slowly chipped away at me until I was a mess of insecurities. But now...

Out of the darkness comes light.

He may have won many battles, but I won the war.

This may be the end of my story, but really, it's my new beginning.

I won.

I am free.

Today is the first day of the rest of my life, and what a life I will make it.

Epilogue

Play me - Neil Diamond

'Sometimes closure arrives two years later, on an ordinary Friday afternoon, in a way that you could have never expected or predicted. And you cry a little, and you laugh a little. And for the first time in a long time, you exhale. Because you are free.' Mandy Hale

It's funny, as my closure did come two years later. Doing my usual Saturday night. Catching up with friends on Facebook, Pink Floyd in concert on the telly, purple gin in a tin.

I decided that I needed to get a life. I did not want a relationship, but some adult conversation and company would be good. That posed the dilemma of where to start looking for a life. The last time I dated was in 1986, so dating in the 21st century was going to be interesting.

The joy of internet dating: why do men think sending a picture of their bits would work for me? How do you separate the genuine men from the scams? It was a hell of an education.

I went out on four bad dates and decided that I was never going to find my diamond in the rough. A man that would get me for me.

Then a photo caught my eye. He needed a haircut, and the glow-in-the-dark tie was just plain wrong, but his smile lit up his whole face. His profile read well, and I thought, why not just say hi? What had I got to lose?

Dave was the same age as me and divorced with a grown-up son. He was also a non-smoker, a social drinker (three pints and he has had enough), and he had a job, all good so far.

For the next two months, we texted every day, and I looked forward to our chats. I sent him a photo of me looking like me. No makeup, just a normal, this is me photo. He did the same, and I thought, why not? I liked this man, so I asked him if he fancied going out for coffee.

Our first date went very well, and I felt comfortable around him. There were no red flags, and I was looking hard. He was not in the same universe as Shouty Husband. He was kind and funny, and he made me laugh.

We have been together for nearly two years now, and it feels like we have always been together. I am so comfortable around him. He sees me, past the walls I put up after Shouty Husband left. He listens to me and encourages me to be the real me, without any strings attached. He is that rarity - a man who is not a game player, who loves me and wants the best for me.

His large, wonderful family have taken me in as one of their own. My mum, dad, and boys approve of us and see the change in me. I am happy, and it shows!

Even though Dave knows that Shouty Husband will never divorce me, and I cannot divorce him as I would lose my home, he will wait for me to be free.

We went to Cornwall, and outside Merlin's Cave at Tintagel, he nearly got down on one knee (new jeans and wet sand) and asked me if, when the time was right, would I consider marrying him?

I have found my happily ever after. I do know that there will be bumps along the way, but I know now what it is to be loved for me. So, I want at least forty years with Dave, as he is the one. It has only taken me a lifetime to find the one who I can see myself growing old with.

Never give up hope, for you never know what is around the corner. Grab life with both hands and shake all the goodness out. I did, and I am so glad that I now walk in sunshine.

I am Annie, the purple haired warrior with knobs on, and I now have the life I always wanted. It just took a lifetime to find it x

Printed in Great Britain
by Amazon

19102970R00380